Border
PINKS

Border
PINKS
Richard Bird

B.T. Batsford Ltd · London

First published 1994

© Richard Bird 1994

Typeset by Latimer Trend & Company Ltd,
Plymouth
and printed in Singapore

Published by
B.T. Batsford Ltd
4 Fitzhardinge Street
London W1H 0AH

A catalogue record for this book is available from
the British Library

ISBN 0-7134-7060-7

Contents

Illustrations

Acknowledgements

The author would like to thank all those gardeners and nursery owners to whom he has talked over the years, and around whose gardens he has been allowed to look and photograph. In particular he would like to thank Sue Farquhar, Mr Hayward of Hayward Carnations, Mr W. Rickaby of Allwood Brothers, Margaret and Michael Metianu of Church Hill Cottage Gardens, Sophie Hughes and Joan Scholfield.

Preface

One of the greatest difficulties with this book has been to define its scope. The possibility of writing a complete monograph of the genus *Dianthus* had to be discarded, partly because of the lack of space, but mainly because of the time it would involve. Little work seems to have been done in modern times on the taxonomy and nomenclature and the genus seems to be in a state of confusion that would take a lot of research both in the wild and in herbaria to sort out.

There is still a lot of disarray amongst the cultivated plants but these are generally more to hand and are of more interest to the gardener. There are possibly three separate areas within the genus that concern them, first carnations, then pinks and finally the species. Growing carnations is a specialist business, possibly an obsessive one to the exclusion of much else. Growing pinks is usually undertaken by those who are interested in them more for the decoration of their borders than because they belong to an 'enthusiast's' group, although there is an active number of people who show pinks. The species are normally grown by another band of enthusiasts, namely alpine gardeners, and are too small to be grown in the open borders, being more suited to the rock garden, raised bed or even pot culture. Since carnation and border pink growers are usually (but not always) different groups of people with different objectives, I have decided to ignore the former completely except for the occasional reference, particularly in the chapter on history. This is probably not a great loss to the readers I have in mind for this book as carnations always look stiff and out of place in the hurly-burly of the herbaceous border. They are usually grown solely for their flowers rather than the contribution they make to the whole garden. And besides there is already quite a number of books on carnations (all of which only pay lip-service to pinks!).

I have, regretfully, had to give up the idea of including species because of the reasons given above. However, I have included quite a number of varieties of pinks grown by alpine enthusiasts in the rock garden, as they can also be grown in the front of a border or in other areas where pinks are grown. My criteria for including plants in this book, therefore, has been whether a plant is likely to appeal to someone who is basically interested in growing what can be termed 'hardy plants', suitable for the herbaceous or mixed border.

Those pinks grown from seed and usually treated as annuals or biennials have also, regretfully, had to be left out as space precludes their inclusion except for a couple of odd mentions where they have similar names to those of border pinks.

Although having limited myself thus, I still have a formidable task ahead of me in that the range of heights, flower sizes and colours is relatively slight and yet there are thousands of varieties that need distinguishing. In no way could I discuss all these plants, nor would it be necessary. *The International Dianthus Register* lists over 30,000 cultivars, of which a great number are border pinks, giving a very brief description of each and this is adequate for most purposes of identification. I have limited my selection to those that are in existence or have been so in recent times. The latter group are included on the grounds that they still may be around somewhere and that there are often references to them in the literature and the reader may well want to know what they were like. I have not delved back beyond the present century except where the plants still exist or of necessity to complete the record of plants with the same name.

There can never hope to be a definitive book on the subject as many of the older varieties are no more than a name, about which, unless unknown ancient gardening books or writings come to light, we are unlikely to increase our sketchy knowledge. There are bound also to be existing ones that I have not listed or about which I have not given a full account. Any further information sent via my publishers will be most welcome.

A limited amount of botanical language will be used from time to time, but it will all be within the scope of the average gardener. Fortunately the main differences between most of the varieties are those of colour, size and shape rather than of obscure botanical deviations. Having said that, I must admit I feel more at home with the precise language of botany, however obscure, than the vague terminology of colour; distinguishing in words between two near shades of pink is not the easiest of tasks for either the writer or the reader!

Richard Bird
Rogers Rough

'Doris'

Introduction

The genus *Dianthus* has produced some wonderful garden plants over the centuries. William Robinson referred to them as 'plants of the highest garden value, containing several of our finest families of hardy plants – carnation, pink, and sweet william – besides numerous alpine and rock plants'. At an earlier time Shakespeare spoke of them in *A Winter's Tale* as

> 'The fairest flowers o' the season
> Are our Carnations and streak'd
>   Gillyflowers.'

Dianthus were some of the earliest flowering plants to be introduced into 'gardens' and are still as popular as ever.

It is not difficult to see why this popularity has continued unabated. Over the centuries they have appealed to most of the gardener's senses: their delicate shape, form and subtle colours give much for the eye to admire, many have a wonderful fragrance and, surprisingly enough, their appeal to the palate was one of the reasons for their first introduction into cultivation. It is the first two, of course, that endear them to us today.

Pinks, old fashioned ones in particular, conjure up images of cottage gardens with their flowers flopping on long stems over brick or stone paths, the strong smell, of 'Mrs Sinkins' perhaps, and the buzz of bees filling the warm summer garden, with not a drop of rain in sight. But dianthus are much more versatile and can be used in a wide variety of positions, including containers and raised beds. Even gardens of modern design that require stronger or more vibrant colours will find a large choice of plants to meet their needs. Surely there cannot be a garden that can call itself a garden that has not got at least one clump of dianthus somewhere?

The garden is not the only place where dianthus are appreciated – they make fine cut flowers for the house. Little preparation is needed and they last well in water, with their fragrance scenting the whole room.

Cut flowers are not only displayed in the house. One of the great periods in dianthus cultivation was during the last century when they were extensively bred for exhibiting. The 'florists', amateur breeders, produced many wonderful strains and this tradition has continued to this day.

The popularity of the dianthus is reflected in the number available to the gardener. In *The International Dianthus Register* and its supplements there are now listed over 30,000 cultivars. This is an amazing number and has reached well beyond the possibility of one person collecting them all in their back garden. In some ways this is sad, but in other respects there is always the excitement of coming across a plant that the enthusiast has not seen before and with 30,000 there are still a lot to see.

It is difficult to appreciate how there can be room for new cultivars to become established, but still they pour forth with subtle differences either in the colour or shape of the flower or in its habit and constitution. Most of these new plants are in the field of carnations, which need not detain us, but there are still a surprisingly large numbers of new pinks being produced.

While dianthus are a little particular

about their soil requirements, cultivation is generally not too difficult and most people can easily grow them, perhaps in containers or raised beds if their ground is too wet or acid.

The majority are not long lived, but fortunately they are easy to increase. Dianthus comes readily from both seed and vegetative methods of propagation. The latter is of course important to keep the named forms true. The ease of propagation can be appreciated by the fact that they have been in continuous cultivation for many centuries. What time there was in the past for gardening was generally given over to the life-sustaining vegetables; the flower garden was inhabited by tough plants that, in the main, were able to look after themselves (this is why many 'cottage garden' plants have such a lasting constitution or are able to self-sow). There would have been little time for difficult plants and yet pinks and carnations have come down to us from the earliest gardens indicating not only the esteem in which previous generations held the plants, but also that they must have been easy for the cottager to propagate.

Although short lived, pinks are truly hardy, able to stand a surprising amount of frost. This means they can easily be grown throughout the British Isles and most of America; indeed it is in the north of England and in Scotland where a lot of the breeding and showing has taken place over the last two centuries.

With increased travel more people have been able to see dianthus in the wild, growing in its many natural habitats throughout the northern hemisphere. In Britain the most famous pink, the Cheddar Pink (*Dianthus gratianopolitanus*), has become increasingly rare, restricted now to a few rocky ledges in the Cheddar Gorge. Neither it nor its seed should be collected under any circumstances; fortunately there is plenty of seed available from cultivated plants or from European wild stock where it is more plentiful, so that the plant can still be enjoyed in our gardens. Another relic for those with good eyes to see it is *D. caryophyllus*, which can still be seen growing on castle walls where it is reputed to have grown since its introduction in Norman times.

All these various links with the past add to the character of these plants and anyone well versed in their history can be fascinating to accompany around a garden.

The Dianthus

What is a pink? A simple question, perhaps, but not an easy one to answer. As we shall see later, most gardeners can tell the difference between a pink and a carnation or an alpine dianthus, but have great difficulty in explaining what that difference is. But first we must step back a couple of paces and look at the genus *Dianthus* as a whole.

THE FAMILY

Dianthus is a large genus of about 300 species. It is placed in the family of Caryophyllaceae, which consists mainly of herbs but also includes a few shrubby plants. *Dianthus* is responsible for the name that describes the whole family, as Caryophyllaceae is derived from the old Latin name for the clove tree, *Caryophyllus aromaticus* (now *Eugenia aromatica*), because the fragrance of many of the dianthus is spicy and reminiscent of the clove.

Other genera that make up the family with *Dianthus* include *Silene, Lychnis, Saponaria, Gypsophila, Arenaria, Cerastium, Sagina, Spergula* and many other, less familiar, names. The visual resemblance between *Dianthus* and the first three is quite clear, even to the non-botanist, and with closer examination the relationship between others can also be seen. All the genera mentioned provide species grown in both herbaceous and alpine gardens. The last two include well-known garden and agricultural weeds, but the fact that *Dianthus* is related to them should not worry anyone. All plants have wild origins and have a natural tendency to make the best use of available space; the saginas and spergulas happen to like tilled soil. *Dianthus*

itself has its own favourite niches, but it never becomes invasive.

THE PLANT

Dianthus is a distinct group within the Caryophyllaceae, which can easily be distinguished from other genera by their decorative flowers having two styles and a distinct epicalyx (see below). They are mainly herbs, although their main stems can become quite woody. There are a few shrubby species including *D. arboreus* from the Greek part of the Mediterranean and *D. fruticosus* from the Aegean. In the wild the vast majority are perennial, although in cultivation there are so-called 'annuals'. These are mainly based on *D. barbatus* and *D. chinensis*, both of which in the wild are short-lived perennials or sometimes biennial.

The leaves are usually linear (that is to say narrow and parallel-sided, like grass) and ending in a point. They are usually hairless and often with a glaucous bloom. Some have slightly fimbriate (fringed) margins. The leaves are stalkless, clasping the stems in pairs, forming a sheath round the bulbous node. Their colour varies from green to grey-blue, the latter usually induced by a glaucous bloom. Sometimes the leaves, particularly the older ones have a purple tinge or flush, especially where exposed to the sun. Not all leaves are fleshy, those of *Dianthus erinaceus*, from Turkey, for example, are bristly and very prickly, while those of *D. pinifolius*, from the Balkans, are like pine-needles.

The flowering stems have swollen nodes and are often quite brittle at this point. New stems appear from the axils of the leaves, but will only do so if the leaves are still present and healthy. New growth is very reluctant to break from old wood, below the lowest leaves; an important point to remember when propagating. They are often glaucous.

They are not herbaceous plants in that they do not retire below ground during the winter and, in spite of having woody stock, the majority are not shrubs as they do not have dormant buds that expand in the spring, but are in continuous growth from their tips. They have a suffrutescent habit, that is they have a woody stem at the base, but with herbaceous branches.

As so often with plants introduced into cultivation, the garden hybrids are usually of a much larger and more vigorous nature than their wild counterparts.

THE FLOWER

Although the hummocks of grey leaves can be attractive in some varieties, it is the flowers in which most gardeners find interest. These are surprisingly similar throughout the genus; always recognisable as dianthus. The size varies from 0.7–7.5 cm (0.25–3 in) across, the larger flowers being those found in cultivation. The number of flowers per stem is normally restricted to one or two although some varieties have one or two more. The most obvious exception to this is the sweet william, *Dianthus barbatus*, which has dense heads of many flowers. Those species that have this type of dense multiple heads also have bracts that usually stick up beyond the flowers. Again this can easily be seen in the sweet williams.

The flower itself consists of five petals, arranged in a flat plate, each with a narrow claw at right angles holding it within the calyx. The margins of the petal can be either entire, i.e. smooth, or dentate, i.e. toothed. In some cases this toothing can be deeply cut giving a fringed effect (as in *Dianthus squarrosus*). The petals are never bifid, that is deeply cut into two as in *Cerastium*, another of the Caryophyllaceae. There is often a tuft of hairs on the petal, just before it curves down into the mouth of the flower. If richly coloured, this bearding gives the flower a velvety appearance.

In the wild most flowers are single, that is they exhibit only one layer of five petals, but in cultivation there are many cultivars that are double or semi-double. This is particularly true of carnations, which all have more than their basic complement of petals; most cultivars having up to 40–60, but sometimes as high as 80, quite a contrast to the five of the single flower. Border pinks, on the other hand, vary from simple single flowers to blousy doubles with up to about 40 petals.

The colour of the flowers is one of their most variable factors, but even so this still has a relatively restricted range. Non-gardeners often believe there is a greater colour range than there actually is because of the habit in the florist trade of dipping the cut stems in dyes to increase the number available to them. The notorious green carnation worn by Oscar Wilde would have been thus treated. With one exception, the basic colours of the species are white and a range of pinks, some of which are quite dark, merging into red and purple. The exception is *Dianthus knappii*, which is yellow and has been extensively used for introducing yellow into various raised forms. This restricted palette of colours in the wild has meant a similar restriction in cultivation. This is not too much of a problem for the person growing border pinks, but is more of a disappointment for the carnation grower. Seeing as carnations are of great economic value to the cut-flower trade, no doubt genetic engineers will eventually get to work and produce blue or even the infamous green specimens.

In the cultivated pinks the range has been extended slightly to include reds so dark that they have become a deep mahogany, and the pale lilac pinks have been intensified to the point where they have produced some virulent almost, luminous colours, which fortunately have so far been mainly kept out of the borders.

But even with these increases of the range, the colours are still somewhat limited. The limitation of the range of colours is more than compensated by the way they are used on the flower. Some are selfs, that is the same colour all over: 'Inchmery', for example, is a delightful shell pink, or 'Haytor' a pure white. The colours, however, are not always pure and a pink with what appears to be one colour will, on closer examination, be seen to have a basic ground colour washed or flushed with one or more others. A closer look at 'Inchmery', for example, will show that it is far from a pure pink. Beside selfs there are also bicolors, i.e. flowers with two colours, which have a definite eye or inner ring of a distinct colour; thus 'Musgrave's Pink' has a green eye against a white background and the modern 'Doris' is an overall pink with a salmon centre. In the semi-doubles, and even more so the doubles, the central eye loses its form and simply becomes a splash of colour showing through the jumble of petals, almost like the jam in a doughnut. A further refinement is when the central eye is extended round the edge of each petal, forming a loop with the ground colour in the centre. These are the 'laced pinks'. This pattern was a favourite among breeders and there are, fortunately, still plenty of examples in cultivation, including the pink and white 'Constance Finnis' or the richer pink and white of 'London Delight'. Carnations have developed even more refinements with picotee edges and petals flecked with contrasting colours; both of these colourings also appear in some of the modern show pinks.

Most of the garden pinks have subtle colours that go with the mood they generally evoke, but one or two of the modern hybrids are a bit too brash for my taste, but are doubtless well suited to the show bench and cut-flower trade. Similarly, there are carnations with simple colouration that would suit the border, but to many gardeners their colours have been developed beyond the bounds of decency and are only really suitable for the extravagancies of showing and cutting.

REPRODUCTION

The *Dianthus* flower is a simple one with no great variation from species to species. Lurking in the centre of the flower are the sexual organs. These do not play a prominent part in the appearance of the flower as they do in, say, peonies or poppies, but they are nonetheless a vital part of the plant. In *Dianthus* there are always two styles and ten stamens. These protrude from the mouth of the tube but to no great extent. They are present in the many double flowers but are, naturally, even less conspicuous.

Some of the species are self-fertile but the majority are self-sterile (the stigma is not receptive to pollen until a week or more after the anthers shed it), which means they require pollen from another plant before they will seed. The cultivated forms of pinks and carnations are self-sterile or only partly self-sterile and to be certain to obtain seed, they must be pollinated by hand or left to the agencies of insects.

Flowers in the wild are visited by butterflies and moths, particularly hawk moths, after the nectar with their long probing tongues, and these are the insects largely responsible for fertilization.

This is not so noticeable in British gardens, mainly because the bigger insects, the butterflies, are not much in evidence at the time that the *Dianthus* is in flower.

Species are generally inter-fertile and therefore readily cross with one another. In the wild the distance between different populations tends to keep them pure, but in the garden open pollination is likely to throw up hybrids if other species or cultivars are present. Male-sterile plants occur both in the wild and in cultivation, in which case no pollen is produced, but this does not prevent the plants being fertilized with pollen from other nearby plants. There is a tendency for such plants to be smaller and more compact.

Once the seed is produced it is contained in a tubular, one-celled capsule, which opens, with four teeth, from the top. This is fortunate as the seed is not immediately scattered unless there is a wind, making the collection of seed, either in the garden or in the wild, a relatively easy task. The normal means of dispersal is by the motion of the capsule on the long flowering stalk as it is blown to and fro in the wind.

Most *Dianthus* are not long-lived plants, but this is compensated for by the fact that seed production is generally prolific and germination rates high and quite swift (they also have the advantage of being readily propagated vegetatively).

As with so many plants pollinated by moths and butterflies, the *Dianthus* has a strong, sweet scent. This must play a large part in the attraction of these insects, but experiments have shown that visual attraction also plays its part. Of course, it is not only insects that have been attracted by the scent; humans have long been captivated by this endearing aspect of the plant.

THE CALYX

The flower is held within a calyx formed by the fusion of five sepals. These can clearly be seen by the five teeth at the top of the calyx tube. While still in bud, the petals are held folded within it; once it opens it forms the base of the flower. In dianthus the calyx is always tubular or cylindrical; the variation in thickness, height and arrangement of the epicalyx is one of the determining factors between the various species.

The epicalyx is a second group of sepals tightly clasping the base of the main calyx. The calyx is quite tough and the additional strengthening of the basal area by this epicalyx could be a mechanism to help prevent the theft of nectar from the nectaries at the base of the stamens by insects puncturing the tube. A common example in gardens of such burglary can clearly be seen at the base of many bean flowers. The normal pollinators, butterflies and moths, have long proboscises capable of reaching the bottom of the flower tube from its opening at the throat in their search for nectar.

In the species the calyx is usually quite slender, but as the flower size has increased in cultivation so the calyx has swollen, sometimes looking quite gross. In some cases it becomes too small to contain the flower and it splits. The old-fashioned pink 'Mrs Sinkins' is a prime example of this. To many this is the best of all the pinks, but to others the asymmetrical head caused by the petals bursting out of one side ruins its appearance. There are a number of factors that cause splitting and carnation growers in particular go to great lengths to obviate it, including slipping supporting rings round the calyx. This is not too much of a problem to pink growers, unless they wish to exhibit, but nonetheless it will be dealt with later in the chapter on pests, diseases and other problems.

THE NAME

The distribution of dianthus centres on Greece and it seems unlikely that such a beautiful plant would have been ignored.

The plant was highly valued by the ancient Greeks and it is from their days that the name *Dianthus* is derived. It seems most likely that they named the plant 'dianthos', the flower of Zeus or the divine flower (a combination of 'dios', of Zeus and 'anthos', flower). Another explanation may be that it is derived from the word 'dianthes', flowering in succession, but, since this is not a characteristic of the dianthus, this seems less likely. Traditional translations from Theophrastus have always translated 'dianthos' as meaning gillyflower or carnation. Modern authorities have their doubts and feel that it probably referred to another plant. But in many ways this argument is irrelevant as Linnaeus, who introduced the term *Dianthus*, was under the impression that the Greeks had used the expression for the plant as he knew it, therefore there can be no doubt that the word is based on the heavenly flower of Theophrastus. Whatever the origins, Linnaeus adopted the Greek name when he drew up his famous classification in 1753.

In Britain they became known as 'gillyflowers', a wonderful name that has passed out of use. The origin of this name is obscure. In 1386 Geoffrey Chaucer referred to them in the Prologue to *The Canterbury Tales* as 'gilofre', which could well be his version of the French 'girofle' (clove). This, in turn, could have had its own origins in the Greek word 'karyophyllon', which we have already met as the original name for cloves, *Caryophyllus*, and hence the family name Caryophyllaceae.

Another possible derivation could be as a corruption of 'July flower', but Chaucer's name seems a long way from this and it was several centuries before the similarly sounding name, 'gillyflower', was used, having gone through transformations in Shakespeare's time 'gillyfors' and then on to 'gillofloures', 'gilloflowers' and 'gilliflowers'. It could be argued that pinks have no more claim to the name 'July flower' than any other that blooms during that month and indeed several other plants also bore the name 'gillyflower', including wallflowers and stocks, which has led to some confusion. (Giroflée in French can also mean stock or wallflower, which stretches the credibility of July being the origin a bit more.) Further, the current word for pink or carnation in French is 'oeillet', which, when pronounced, is not all that far removed from 'gilly'. All in all, I am inclined to dismiss the July theory and stick to the French version (which has its origins back in ancient Greece where so many, many names began) particularly when you bear in mind that those plants that went on to become pinks are generally thought to have been introduced to the UK from France.

It could naturally be assumed that pinks derived their name from their colour, but in fact it was the other way round. Pink, as the name of a colour, is a relatively new word in the English language, not coming into general use until the middle of the last century and is assumed to have been used as it is the colour of the flower pink. At first its definition was rather imprecise, covering a wide range of colour, including red. We can still see this in the use of 'pink' to describe the riding habit of a huntsman, which is in fact scarlet. To confuse matters even further, at least two centuries before the word pink became to mean the colour as we know it today, it was used to define a greenish-yellow pigment.

The term pink or pinke for the flower was first used in print by Thomas Tusser in 1573 in his *Five Hundred Points* and by Lyte a few years later. As with so many flower names, there are, again, several possible derivations. One is that it is a corruption of a Celtic word, 'pic', meaning peak and referring to the toothing on the petals (or it has even been suggested as referring to this plant reaching the peak of perfection! Strangely the Swedish word for pink or carnation 'nejlika' also implies perfection or 'no equal', as does the German 'Nelken'). A similar word occurs in 'pick' from Middle English and Old French meaning to pierce or indent, which has led to another use of pink, this time as a verb that involves either piercing or cutting a zigzag edge to a piece of cloth (as with pinking scissors). Other explanations include the German word 'Pfingsten' (Dutch 'pingster', Swedish 'pingst'), meaning Pentecost or Whitsun at which time the flowers are planted. As the fancy flies there is also the possibility of the Dutch 'pink' (English pinkie) referring to the little finger, again with reference to the toothing on the petals. All this is mere speculation and we will never know for certain and, truth to tell, I suppose it does not really matter, as it is the plant itself that is important, not the label we attach to it, but there again there is fascination in tracing back these origins.

In passing, perhaps the origin of 'carnation' will also be of interest. Again, as one would suspect with such an ancient flower, several possibilities present themselves. One is that it is derived from the word 'coronation' as they were a major constituent of floral garlands or crowns (corona) that were placed on the head in ancient Rome. Another is that the Latin word 'carnatio', meaning flesh-coloured, provides its origins. I am inclined to favour the latter explanation as many other plants would have been used in garlands, particularly as the dianthus has a relatively short flowering period. Also, the word could have come in with the Normans as it is assumed that the plant was introduced to the UK by them and the French have a similar word 'incarnat' (flesh-coloured, rosy-pink), which is obviously derived from the Latin.

So far we have been considering the Latin name and the English name for the whole group. Another aspect is the names of individual cultivars. This form of name is given in single quotes, 'Garland' for example, and since 1959 should be a name in a language other than Latin. The name can be descriptive, 'Iceberg' (a pure white flower) or named after a person 'Mrs Sinkins'. Since 1959 it should not include initials so 'E. Anderson' should be considered an invalid name whereas 'Enid Anderson' is acceptable, that is unless there has been a pink or carnation already of that name. This latter rule applies whether the original plant is still in existence or not. So if there was a seventeenth century pink called 'Pill Box' the name of which had been recorded in print but which had soon died out, then no new pink could be given that name even though the flower had not been around for a couple of centuries or more. The fact that there are over 30,000 plants listed in *The International Dianthus Register* puts a tremendous strain on the ingenuity of the introducer of a new pink. In reality few are aware of these rules and so plants with the same name invariably crop up and, although declared invalid by the *IDR*, stick with the plant. Most single names, such as 'Timothy', have been used up so a combination of names is more likely to be valid.

IN THE WILD

In a later chapter we will look at the development of the garden pink but first we must look at its wild ancestors and relations. The cultivation of any garden plant is better understood if its background is first researched and *Dianthus* is no exception.

Dianthus is mainly restricted to the northern hemisphere, although there are a few extending as far south as South Africa. Their main area of distribution is around the Mediterranean, but they push eastwards through Asia as far as Japan. However, they never crossed the northern land-bridge that spanned the Bering Sea to the Americas, but since people started introducing plants to their gardens some have become naturalised in some places on the eastern side of North America. *Dianthus armeria* is the most common of these, but *D. deltoides* and *D. barbatus*, as well as a few others, can be found.

Back in the main area of distribution, Europe and Asia, they grow in a range of climates from near the Arctic Circle to the Himalayas. However, the major centre is around the Mediterranean, where every country around and in this basin, with the exception of Malta, has at least one species growing wild. Even Egypt with its hot climate records its own endemic species, *Dianthus guessfeldtianus*. There is a particular concentration around the eastern end of the Mediterranean, especially in Greece and Turkey. They spread right across North Africa. A few re-emerge in South Africa, but they appear to be of little garden merit and will be pursued no further (although I grow *D. basuticus*, which has given me great pleasure). As they move eastwards from the Balkans and Turkey towards China and Japan, so the numbers begin to decline, Japan claiming six species and several subspecies.

The natural habitat for dianthus seems to be a free-draining, sunny position, with the majority growing in rocky places or open meadows. A few, such as *D. barbatus* and *D. deltoides*, also grow in open woodland. Many, but not all, grow on limestone formations.

Dianthus tend to hybridize as readily in the wild as they do in cultivation, however the different populations tend to be isolated from each other, but where they do meet hybrids are relatively frequently found; they are quite common in the Pyrenees, for example.

Dianthus deltoides

Cultivation

SITING

As with so many silver-leafed plants, pinks are lovers of the sun and should be sited in an open position where they can soak up their fill. Sometimes they are seen growing in partly shady conditions, under trees for example, but here the plant becomes very etiolated and the long flowering stems all lean forward into the light, usually becoming top-heavy and flopping in a mess.

As well as providing sufficient light, open conditions also allow the air to circulate around the plant preventing it from lying in a damp position in a moist atmosphere. While pinks must have moisture for growth, they dislike damp conditions and many of the deaths of pinks, especially during winter, can be laid at the door of this kind of position. On the other hand, they should not be so open that they are prey to the buffeting of every wind that blows. Avoid wind tunnels created by air funnelling between two buildings or trees.

Since pinks are amongst the shorter plants that we grow in our gardens it is a good idea to grow them near the front of the border. This not only prevents them being swamped by their more rampant neighbours but also allows them to be more easily seen. It is also an advantage to have them close by so that their perfume can be appreciated. The old cottage garden habit was to grow them alongside paths, over which they often flopped. This practice still has much to recommend it.

The smaller varieties should definitely be grown close to a path or even in it. These are best suited to rock gardens but many have a place in a general garden as long as they are not swamped. They are ideal for growing in or on top of walls, or in small gaps left between stones on a terrace or patio. They also make good subjects for permanent plantings in containers such as troughs and sinks.

SOIL

Dianthus are generally plants of alkaline soils, although most can be successfully grown in neutral ones. Acid conditions do present a problem for many, but the addition of garden lime at a rate of between 60 and 120 g/m^2 (2–4 oz/yd^2) will normally prove sufficient to allow most to be grown satisfactorily.

The stress on alkaline soils can be overdone. I have a neutral soil that, if anything, tends to lean towards acid. I can grow rhododendrons quite happily and bracken grows on the margins of an adjacent field and, although I have not limed the soil, pinks grow vigorously and have done so for many years. I do not recall ever losing a pink yet to lime deficiency. This is not to say that you can wander far over into acid conditions. Acid soils are often wet and this is the real killer of pinks.

It has already been stated that pinks do not like wet conditions, but equally they do not like a soil that is permanently dry; they must have adequate moisture to keep them alive. This means that the soil should be free draining but moisture retentive, a condition that does not frequently occur naturally in most gardens. If the soil is heavy, its drainage can be improved by adding grit or gravel. The moisture-retentiveness can be increased by adding humus or organic material. This can be in the form of leaf-mould, peat, garden compost or well-rotted manure. The ideal will be reached when all excess moisture drains away but there is sufficient held in the humus to supply the roots of the pink with the water it needs for growth.

This is, of course, the ideal situation. In practice pinks can be grown under a wide variety of conditions and I can well remember at my parents' home 'Mrs Sinkins' being grown on heavy wealden clay for many, many years.

Although the soil may need humus, especially on lighter soils to help retain moisture, it should not be too richly fed with nitrogen-rich compost or manure. While pinks do not like a sterile soil, they do not want overfeeding. Some well-rotted manure or a general fertilizer, preferably a slow release one, can be added when the bed is prepared but the plants should not be surrounded by heaps of rotting manure as one often sees around rose bushes, for example. A good material to mix into the soil is well-rotted mushroom compost as this contains a certain amount of lime. More about feeding will be mentioned under the section on maintenance.

OBTAINING PLANTS

Since we are dealing with cultivars rather than species, pinks should be acquired as plants and not as seed. It is possible to use seed for some of the strains offered by seed merchants, but these are usually for annual bedding and will have a natural variation in their form and colour. Sometimes seed merchants offer seed of named cultivars. 'Mrs Sinkins' for example has recently been offered. These will not produce plants true to that name and should be avoided.

If you are adventurous and wish to raise some of your own cultivars, then it is worth trying seed, but be prepared to throw away any resulting plants of inferior quality and, to be honest, the majority will be just that.

Most pinks, then, will be obtained as plants or as cuttings. Plants can be purchased from a wide range of outlets from garden centres to specialist nurseries. The range at the former is extremely limited and the naming can often be very suspect. Nurseries are a much better bet, especially those that specialise in them. Even here the naming can sometimes go awry (after all, one pink out of flower can look very much like another and nurseries, like the rest of us, are not infallible and pots or labels do occasionally get mixed up) but if you do get one that is wrongly labelled, the majority of nurseries will willingly rectify their mistake.

The range of pinks at nurseries is much greater and you will often be spoilt for choice. Garden centres tend to have modern pinks rather than the old-fashioned ones as the former look more substantial in pots when young.

The Plant Finder lists all those varieties generally available from nurseries in the UK and is an invaluable way of tracking down wanted plants. However, the editor is unable to check to see if the plants listed in catalogues are actually what they purport to be and quite a number of plants listed are under the wrong name, so it is best to see the plants in flower, if it is at all possible, before you buy them.

As pinks are relatively easy to propagate they are often seen on sale tables at garden openings and plant sales.

Another way of acquiring plants is to obtain cuttings from friends or other people's plants. Never do this without permission as the owners of gardens quite rightly get annoyed when plants are stripped. Most, however, will quite readily agree as pinks produce a mass of cutting material and the loss of one or two pieces does no harm to the plant. They should be put straight into a polythene bag to keep them fresh. This method of propagation will be dealt with in detail in the next chapter.

PLANTING

Having acquired your plants either by purchase or growing them yourself, they should be planted out, preferably in the autumn. This date is not sacrosanct, but if planted out then they will be at a good flowering size by the following year. In practice I often plant them out when I get them, as long as the ground is not too waterlogged or too dry. It is best to avoid times of drought and strong sunshine unless the plant is kept watered and shaded until it has become established. It is also best to avoid frozen ground, but then I would not advise planting in winter any way.

Having prepared the soil as mentioned in an earlier section, dig a hole and plant out the young plant at the same depth that it is in the pot. The distance apart depends on the plants. Those with a compact bushy habit should be planted closer than those with a mat-forming tendency. If possible, water the plant in its pot the previous day so that it has drunk its fill and is not limp and flagging. Try not to disturb the roots unless they have become pot-bound, in which case they should be gently teased out of their spiral. Once the plant is in the ground, backfill the hole and gently firm down. Water immediately.

MAINTENANCE

Once planted pinks need little attention apart from general border maintenance such as weeding and deadheading. Being low, the plants can quickly become swamped by weeds so these should be removed as soon as they are seen. A special eye should be kept for tufts of grass appearing in the middle of the plant. The grass is often similar to the leaves of the pink and can go

unnoticed until it has taken over the plant.

In autumn make certain that fallen leaves do not accumulate in or under the plant. If left they will help keep the plant wet during the winter, which will probably cause it to rot and die.

On the whole there is no need to stake pinks, indeed nothing looks worse than stems forced upwards and throttled by a hoop of wire. It is virtually impossible to stake pinks in a way that looks natural. Let them flop. Having said that, if you grow pinks for show or specifically for cutting, then you will have to stake. Those with the long stems and large heads, such as the show pinks or the imperials, are the ones that will need particular attention. For perfect blooms, stake individually; for general cutting, a hoop can be used.

In the early spring top dress the beds with a little general balanced fertilizer at the rate of about 60 g/m² (2 oz/yd²). An alternative is to work in a little well-rotted, friable farmyard manure or compost (well-rotted mushroom compost is a good material to use for this as it contains a certain amount of lime). Do not use too much or the plants will become overblown and also run the risk of rotting off if bulky manures allow the soil to hold too much moisture. Farmyard manures can also adjust the pH values unfavourably, so a light application of lime may be needed on neutral or lightly acid soils. It is useful, especially for the perpetual-flowering, modern varieties, to also top dress with fertilizer once or twice during the growing season.

As the summer progresses, deadhead any spent flowers. This will encourage a longer season of flowering and prevent the flowers from becoming smaller as the season proceeds. Any plant that becomes straggly or unattractive, and some decidedly do, can be cut back after flowering, but remember that many pinks are reluctant to throw up new growth from bare woody stems. Often the most unattractive plants are the older ones and these are best replaced that autumn with new plants raised from cuttings. Sometimes they can be reprieved by top dressing with a soil-based compost so that the prostrate stems are just covered. Keep this just moist until new growth is seen. In effect this is layering the plant and new plants are formed round the perimeter of the old. This will be dealt with in more detail in a later chapter.

PESTS AND DISEASES

Fortunately pinks are reasonably trouble free and for the majority of people growing them are unlikely to cause any problems. The two most likely causes of death are wet conditions (allowing fungal diseases to get hold and rot the plant) and old age. The former can be prevented by selecting an open, sunny, position and providing a well-drained soil. The latter can be avoided by regularly renewing the plants by taking cuttings. This is particularly important with the mule pinks, which have a tendency to flower themselves to death.

The commonest pest is probably aphids or green fly. These not only cause distortion in the leaves and stems but can introduce virus diseases. They can easily be dispatched by using a chemical insecticide if you do not mind using them or by squeezing them between your finger and thumb (fine pointed tweezers are necessary to get those right down in the leaf axils).

Slugs are the next most troublesome pest. These love to live under the cool shelter of the pink and if you lift up the skirts of the plant you are liable to see them. Again fingers are the most easy method of removal. They can either be collected as just described or by going out at night with a torch when they will be seen in amazing numbers. Put them in a jar of water containing a little washing-up liquid or rehouse them well away from the garden if you do not wish to kill them. There are various forms of slug bait including 'safe' ones that you can use if you do not like handling them.

Ants can be a nuisance if they build their nest amongst the roots of the pink; unfortunately they like the same conditions. A proprietary ant killer is the only sure way of removing them.

There are also occasional problems with other pests but very rarely enough to worry about unless you are proposing to show your pinks. The biggest of these problems to some is the fact that the calyces split, allowing all the petals to flop out ('Mrs Sinkins' is a good example of this). To the majority of us this does not matter at all but if you are a flower arranger and need a 'perfect flower' it is possible to buy or make calyx rings that can be placed around the calyx like a truss to hold everything in place. There are various theories as to why pinks and carnations split their calyces and there are cultivation methods that are advocated for the avoidance of this nuisance. This, however, really only applies to carnations and if anyone is desperately worried about it, I recommend they get a book or books on carnations.

Good hygiene and a well-prepared, open site, with an eye kept out for aphids and slugs, will normally be the only precautions that need to be taken to keep your pinks healthy.

Propagation

Although some individual plants will go on seemingly for ever, the majority benefit from renewal every few years. Some (particularly the mule pinks) have a tendency to flower themselves to death and it is essential that these are propagated every year against this event. Although perfectly hardy, most losses occur in mild, wet winters when plants rot off. For all these reasons it is essential that you should have a planned annual campaign of taking cuttings, particularly of your most cherished pinks.

Fortunately the propagation of pinks is not difficult, does not take up too much time or space and can be undertaken over quite a large part of the year whenever time is available.

Because we are concerned with named cultivars rather than species or strains of annuals, propagation must be achieved by vegetative means. A plant grown from seed will not be identical to its parents. Unfortunately, some named pinks have been sold as seed, which has muddied the water as regards to the 'true' plant. As if it were not already confused enough, 'Mrs Sinkins' has recently been made available from seed by one of the major seed merchants.

Seed is obviously necessary if new varieties are being considered as it is the only way other than sports that they can be raised and the only way that existing plants can be 'improved'. For those who wish to pursue this path seed will be dealt with in more detail later.

CUTTINGS

The vegetative methods mainly used for the increase of pinks is from cuttings or by layering of which the former is by far the more important.

Cuttings are best taken between July and August, but this can be easily extended from June to September or even any month, except in the dead of winter, if you have means of providing bottom heat.

The easiest, but also the crudest, method is to remove part of the plant and stick it in the ground. This has been cottage garden practice for many generations and was used successfully by my mother for all her pinks. It works best in a light soil, although the cuttings must be kept just moist. It is a rather hit-or-miss method and not one to be really recommended, but it does work with a large number of varieties and has been responsible for the continuance of many of our older cultivars.

It is, however, better to take more trouble and care over your cuttings. The reason that the above crude method works is that pinks are very easy to strike from cuttings and even a beginner can have a high success rate.

The cutting compost can be a mixture of equal parts by volume of sharp sand and peat. If you have not got the ingredients to hand, it does not matter as pinks are accommodating enough to root in virtually any medium and any soil-based potting compost will do.

The plants from which cuttings are taken should be fresh and not flagging. If it is during a dry period and the plants look a bit weary, give them a good soaking with water the day before cuttings are taken. Remove lengths of stems for cuttings and put straight into a polythene bag. If you are taking cuttings from more than one variety label each one as it is very easy to get the cuttings mixed up (the cause of much of the current misnaming). The cuttings should be of non-flowering stems and should be longer than will eventually be required. They should be of half-ripe stems, that is the stem should be pliable but not too flexible. Experience will soon tell you what is just right.

Keep the cuttings in the bag, out of sunlight, until you are ready to deal with them. Take the cuttings out of the bag one at a time and trim them to length, about four to five joints from the top, cutting cleanly across the stem just below a node (the swollen joint where the pairs of leaves join the stems). Cut away all the lower leaves leaving just a few pairs at the top of the stem.

Dip the cut end of the cutting in a rooting compound and insert it into the compost. Pinks generally do not need any aid with rooting, but the compound is useful in that it contains a fungicide that helps prevent the cuttings rotting off.

Unless you are going into commercial production, enough cuttings can be accommodated in a 9 cm (3.5 in) pot. This should be filled just to the rim with compost and then tapped smartly on the bench to settle it. It can be gently firmed with the bottom of another pot but it should not be compacted. The final level of the compost will be just about level with the inner rim of the pot.

Make a hole in the compost using something like a pencil and place the cutting in it so that it is buried almost up to the first leaves. Firm the compost around the stems so that no large air spaces have been left. Avoid pushing the cutting straight into the compost as this action causes the sand to make abrasions on the stem through which infection can enter. It also removes most of the hormone powder. Place the cuttings round the edge of the pot. When

finished, stand the pot in a tray or bowl of water that comes half-way up the pot until the surface of the compost changes colour to indicate that it is wet throughout. Remove and leave to drain.

Place in a cool, well-lit but sun-free place. There is no need to put the pot in a polythene bag as is practised for many other cuttings as this will produce too close an atmosphere (most grey-leaved plants dislike this kind of condition). Keep the compost moist.

The appearance of new growth on the cuttings indicates that they have acquired roots and are ready for potting up (do not delay doing this for too long as the cutting compost contains no nutrients with which to sustain life for long).

Pot up individually in 9 cm (3.5 in) pots in a soil-based compost, replanting the cutting at the same depth. Water the pot from below (or above if you prefer) and put in a cool place out of the sun until it has established itself.

Once the new plant is growing away it may be necessary to 'stop' it, i.e. pinching out the top 2.5 cm (1 in) or so of the stem to make it bush out. This is not usually necessary for the old-fashioned pinks, indeed it may delay flowering if it is done, but it is important to do it with the modern pinks, which will grow up into a single stem if left as they are. Do not plant out a plant that has just been stopped, allow it first to recover with signs of new growth appearing.

Some pinks, in particular the mule pinks, offer very little cutting material as nearly every stem is a flower stem. Here it might become necessary to grow an extra plant that is regularly sheared over in an attempt to produce a few stems for propagation rather than for flowering. For the most part, however, there is usually sufficient cutting material available on each plant.

Having started off this part of the chapter with a somewhat crude method,

I cannot help but record an even cruder way mentioned in an article in the 1945–6 *Carnation Year Book* in which Mr G.J. Miller of Bayham Abbey Gardens advocated gathering up a bunch of long flower stems from a straggly and untidy plant and tying them into a knot. Plant this in the ground to just below the level of the old flower heads. By the next year roots will have formed along the old stems and there will be a generous display of blooms. Apparently this technique can be carried out at anytime between flowering and September. I have not tried out the method but I offer it to you for whatever it is worth.

A traditional method of preparing pink cuttings is by the use of pipings. Instead of cutting the stem below a node, it is gently but firmly pulled so that the stem parts at a node rather like pulling it from a socket. I can see no advantage of this over cutting the stem.

LAYERING

Another traditional way of increasing pinks is by layering them. Again, there does not seem to be any real advantage in this as most pinks come very readily from cuttings (although it can be useful for the one or two that are not so easy by the method). Generally it is a technique of more use to carnation growers.

The idea is quite simple. You bend over a shoot and pin it to the ground until it puts down roots, a bit in the manner of a strawberry runner. Once established it can be severed from the parent and treated as a new plant. The formation of roots is accelerated if that part of the stem in contact with the soil is split for a short distance. The layer can be kept in place by a weight, such as a stone, or more usually by some form of peg. Keep the compost moist in the area of the layer.

SEED

Seed is only used as a method of propagation for species or for raising new cultivars. The seed can be sown either when fresh, in the autumn, or in the spring.

There is never much point in sowing vast quantities of seed otherwise you will be swamped with seedlings, so for most purposes a 9 cm (3.5 in) pot will suffice. Fill the pots with a soil-based sowing compost and tap it smartly on the bench to settle and level it. It can be lightly flatted with the base of another pot if so required, but under no circumstances should it be rammed down tight. Sow the seed thinly and evenly across the surface of the compost and cover with a layer of grit about 0.7 cm (0.25 in) deep. Stand the pot in a tray of water until the surface grit changes colour indicating the pot is thoroughly soaked and then stand in a shady spot until the seed germinates.

There are varying grades of grit, but the most useful for top dressing pots of seed is that sold by agricultural merchants and larger pet shops as 'chick grit'. It does not matter where the pots are stood as long as they do not dry out or become too waterlogged. They will come to no harm if they get frosted. Germination can be speeded up by giving the pots a little heat, but this is far from necessary and I usually leave mine in open frames in a shady position.

Dianthus germination is usually very generous and the seed pot can become very overcrowded if sowing was not thinly undertaken. Pot up the individual seedlings as soon as they are large enough to handle, using a soil-based potting compost. In any pot of seedlings there is usually at least one or two that, even at this stage, look different from the rest. It is always worth potting these up as they may produce something interesting.

RAISING NEW CULTIVARS

New pinks can be raised in either one of two ways, vegetatively as sports or by crossing two pinks to produce a new form using seed.

Every so often a plant can be seen that has thrown up a flower that is not the same as the rest on the plant. This is known as a sport. It may be a different colour or striped or just smaller or bigger (in plants other than dianthus it is most commonly seen as variegations). If it is worth keeping, then the stems on which it is growing can be removed and treated as an ordinary cutting. Being a vegetative means of reproduction the cutting will produce a plant that carries identical flowers to the sport. Once established, cuttings can be taken from this plant producing more plants and so on until a stock has been built up. If you do produce a good sport, multiply it up as soon as you can because if your first and only plant dies it is lost to cultivation.

The other and most common method of producing new plants is by hybridisation. This can be left to chance or carried out deliberately. Dianthus are quite promiscuous with insects carrying pollen from one plant to another without discrimination and so any seed produced in a garden where there are more than one type of pink is likely to produce offspring different from either parent. Many commercial pink growers capitalise on this and collect all the seed from their plants at the end of the season and sow it in one large bed. When the resulting seedlings first come into flower they select those that they think are suitable and throw away the rest. They generally have no idea as to what the parents were.

A more controlled method can be carried out by choosing the parents and transferring the pollen yourself, keeping detailed records of what you have done. Pinks are generally not self-pollinating as the pollen ripens at least a week before the stigmas on the same plant are ready to receive it. When ripe the pollen is a grey or creamy coloured powder. The stigma of the flower of the other parent is ripe when it curls back and is glistenly sticky. The pollen can be easily transferred using a soft brush or a cotton bud on a dry day when no rain is forecast. Mark the stems that carry the pollinated flowers with a label or a piece of coloured wool. The petals will soon collapse if the pollination has been successful and the seed capsule will swell. When it turns brown it is ready for collection. The seed can be sown in the usual way.

History

ORIGINS

One of the saddest sentences ever penned in gardening history was written by John Gerard when writing about carnations and pinks in 1597: 'A great and large volume would not suffice to write of every one at large in particular, considering how infinite they are, and how every year, every clymate and countrey bringeth forth new sortes, ans such as have not heretofore bin written of.' Oh if only he had written that 'great and large volume' we would know so much more about the history of pinks and carnations!

The history of these flowers goes way back into the mists of time; they must be amongst the earliest of our cultivated flowers and yet Gerard's statement is one of the first references to the subject. What a difference to our knowledge of the early pinks there would have been if the book suggested had been written. As it is we know of quite a number of early varieties from around Elizabethan times onwards. With a few exceptions these tend to be mainly singles with serrated edges that are not too far removed from the wild *Dianthus plumarius* that was their ancestor.

Before the sixteenth century things are decidedly sketchy. Dianthus of one sort or another had been grown in gardens; they were not used medicinally but were used for flavouring wine (they were much cheaper than imported cloves but imparted the same qualities) and for their smell, particularly in posies. These were mainly derived from *Dianthus caryophyllus* from which carnations developed, but also from *D. plumarius*, which, probably hybridised with *D. ca-*
ryophyllus, was the main constituent of the pink.

The story still persists that the original plants of both of these species were brought over to England, probably as seed, on the stones that the Normans imported from France to build their fortresses. *Dianthus caryophyllus* can still be seen on the walls of Rochester Castle in Kent. This hypothesis is as good as any other but the plants may equally have been deliberately imported at some time.

By the time John Rea was writing (1676) the carnation had definitely become established and he was able to list 360 by name. Pinks were a different matter. He lists only a few of these and then only by categories of pinks (such as 'Painted Lady' and 'Pheasant's Eye') whose names cover a number of pinks of the same type. He belittles them as 'being of little esteem, they only serve to set the sides of borders in spacious gardens, and some of them for posies'; the very reason that I love them!

LACED PINKS

Interest in pinks only really got going after James Major had successfully introduced fully laced pinks with his 'Lady of Ancaster' from which he raised 'Lady Stoverdale' and several other varieties of the same type. This left the way open for further refinement (reducing the number of petals in the doubles, for example, so that they appeared flatter and more even) and the rise of the pink as a show plant.

Florist societies were already flourishing for other plants and from 1780 onwards pinks were also adopted for showing and competition*. Their heyday was probably across the middle years of the nineteenth century. During this period a great number of varieties were bred by amateur growers and nurseries just for competition. One of the most famous areas for growing these pinks was in the Paisley region of Scotland. In spite of their fame none of the names of their pinks has come down to us and even though some plants have been found in gardens of the area, we cannot be certain that these are some of the original plants, although they are clearly related. In the absence of names those that have managed to survive have had to be given new names, hence names such as 'Paisley Gem' and 'Dad's Favourite', which are twentieth century appendages to what are generally assumed to be older plants.

Up to the middle of the nineteenth century the stimulus for growing pinks came mainly from competition, but around this period they came to be more seriously regarded as plants for the border and many new plants started to appear that were introduced for this purpose. Probably the most classic of all pinks, 'Mrs Sinkins', was introduced by Charles Turner of the Royal Nurseries Slough in 1868. Turner introduced many famous pinks, quite a number of which survived well into the twentieth century and appear in the main section of this book. As so often happens nowadays, many of these plants were raised by private individuals, in the case of 'Mrs Sinkins' it was John Sinkins, and then taken up and introduced by a commercial nursery.

One development of the border pinks that came about during the middle of the century was the introduction of mule pinks. These were a cross between the

sweet william, *Dianthus barbatus*, and the pink, *D. plumarius*. The resulting plants were a cross between the two with multiple heads of fragrant double flowers that appear over a long season and with green foliage. Many were raised and introduced in France by André Paré of which 'Emile Paré' and 'Napoleon III' are probably the most famous. They are called mules as they are unable to produce seed. The one drawback is that they are inclined to flower themselves to death and so need constant propagation to ensure their survival, but in spite of this a surprising number are still in cultivation and will be found listed in the main section of this book.

TWENTIETH CENTURY

A number of nurseries were selling pinks for the border by the end of the century but it was at the beginning of the twentieth century that really serious breeding began when Montagu Allwood started to take an interest in pinks. Allwood had been primarily interested in carnations when he set up his nursery, with his brothers, in 1910. By the end of the decade he had crossed his perpetual-flowering carnations with the 'Old Fringed White' pink and produced a new race of border pinks that was to revolutionize the concept of border pinks. As well as introducing pinks with an interesting range of colour, Allwood managed to breed the perpetual element of his carnations into them and so, for the first time, it was possible to have plants that flowered for the whole of the summer and often on into the early days of winter, instead of the limited period of just a few weeks in early summer when the old-fashioned pinks bloomed.

This race was dubbed *Dianthus* x *allwoodii* by the Scientific Committee of the Royal Horticultural Society. Although Allwood's introductions had an impact that is still very much felt today, he was not, in fact, the first to have

Florists, prior to our century, referred to people who bred and grew flowering plants for exhibition.

introduced perpetual-flowering pinks. E.T. Cook was already able to report in 1905 (before the Allwood brothers had set up their nursery) that Ladhams of Shirley Nurseries, near Southampton, had already produced them from a breeding programme that seemed to have involved a large number of species, mule pinks and 'Mrs Sinkins'. Curiously, not only did Ladhams produce these perpetual-flowering pinks but they also gave them personal names such as 'Florence', 'Marion', 'Ethel' and so on, which also predates the Allwood practice of similarly naming their pinks. What these pinks were like is difficult to say as none seem to have survived and little was written about them, but one can assume, I think, that because of the lack of contemporary enthusiasm they were reasonably unimpressive and to all intents and purposes the Allwood plants were the first real perpetual-flowering pinks.

Allwood have continued to produce a constant stream of new *allwoodii* pinks to the present day, although many, through fashion or perhaps lack of vigour, have fallen by the wayside. This, however, was not the brothers' only claim to fame. Using the *allwoodii* as a basis they created two other major lines. The first has, sadly, almost vanished. In the period between the two world wars Allwood crossed their modern perpetual-flowering pinks with various alpine species and produced a dwarf race of *allwoodii alpinus* plants for the rock garden, most of which were single flowered. Many of these were given names derived from gods and fairies and so there were 'Apollo', 'Blossom', 'Echo', 'Goblin', 'Jupiter' and so on. Alpine pinks are fiddly and time-consuming things to propagate and many of these were lost, not only at Allwood, but also in many gardens, as during the Second World War there was little staff or time to attend to them. Of those that still exist 'Mars' is the most famous.

The other Allwood area of development has mainly been since the Second World War, with the introduction of their 'Show' and 'Laced' series of pinks, such as 'Show Achievement' or 'Laced Monarch'. Here the initial plants were created by crossing nineteenth century laced show pinks with their own *allwoodii* pink.

Allwood have not been, by any means, the only nursery specializing in pinks, but over the years they have been one of the most important and nearly all other breeders have used either directly or indirectly *allwoodii* blood in their plants.

Many other pink nurseries and growers have risen to importance only to have faded away. Two that have had a lasting influence have been C.H. Herbert of Acocks Green, near Birmingham and C.H. Fielder of the Lindabruce Nurseries at Lancing. The Herbert pinks started to appear around the First World War, being based on seedlings of an old variety called 'Progress', which has long since disappeared. In spite of their need to be continually propagated a number are still in existence. They were mainly used as show pinks but are nonetheless also good as border plants. One of the most famous, and considered by many to be one of the best pinks ever raised, was 'Bridesmaid', which became the parent of many later pinks.

Fielder introduced a range of what he termed imperial pinks. These were initially created by crossing *allwoodii* with Herbert pinks, in particular 'Bridesmaid'. Many of these are still in existence (although the firm has now vanished) with Hayward Carnations, in particular stocking quite a number.

Another firm that had a long history before it petered out was Douglas of Great Bookham. This produced a steady stream of pinks from the last century right through to the mid 1960s. After the Second World War they concentrated on a large series of pinks to which they gave bird names, some, such as 'Nightjar', being rather outlandish for pinks. It is curious but none of these seem to exist today and one cannot but think that they just produced a nonstop line of seedlings all of which (at least from existing descriptions) having not much variance from each other. They cannot have been very garden-worthy if none at all have survived. Mansfield claimed that they were distinguished by their clear-cut shape. If anybody has, or knows the whereabouts of, any of their vast output I would be interested to hear about them.

Another large series of pinks, mainly dwarf ones for the rock garden was developed between the First and Second World Wars with names prefaced with 'Highland'. These were introduced by P.S. Hayward of Treasure Holt Nurseries at Clacton-upon-Sea. These were very variable plants as they were sold as seed as well as plants. The most famous, and one that is still in cultivation, is 'Highland Fraser', but because it was often raised from seed there is great variability in existing plants. 'Highland Queen' is another extant plant but, again, with great variability. Hayward also introduced another large series, this time with names beginning with 'Clan' (e.g. 'Clan Fraser') but these seem to have all vanished without trace.

Often in the literature of pinks there occurs the description 'Winteri-type'. This refers to large single pinks, often highly coloured and with a bright central zone. The original series of plants was raised by Sidney Morris and were distributed by Gordon Winter (hence the name) and then by J.L. Gibson.

Since the Second World War the pinks scene has been dominated by individual growers of which F.R. McQuown and his famous series of 'London' pinks ('London Girl', 'London Glow' and so on). In the main these growers have been mainly concerned with producing show pinks, although many of them make first rate garden plants. Perhaps one of the most influential was Oliver Wyatt of Colehayes, Bovey Tracey, who raised many plants that form the backbone of commercial pink production, such as 'Haytor White', 'Cranmere Pool', 'Houndspool Ruby' and the various ones with Wyatt in the name, 'Valda Wyatt' for example.

There has not been a great deal of development of cultivars for the rock garden since the Second World War when so many disappeared. One person who has been raising new forms since the early 1950s is Joan Scholfield of Whatfield, after which she has named her series. The original plants that started her series were derived from 'Echo' and seed of the *allwoodii alpinus*, both from Allwood Brothers. Many of these plants can be seen on the raised beds at Wisley and are commercially available, including the most striking 'Whatfield Magenta'.

CURRENT PLANTS

I think one has to admit that there are very few pinks that we can say with any certainty have come down to us unchanged from before the beginning of the present century. Indeed I would be surprised if there were very many that have survived since the Second World War. Most of those that we think of as being very old are more likely, in fact, to be more recent plants that are very close or identical to originals but that are, in all probability, seedlings, possibly one or more generations on from the original plant.

Another problem is accurate identification. It is very difficult, even with a precise definition, including colour chart coding, to be able to identify a current plant. To be able to positively ascertain a plant from some of the vague descriptions of the past is nigh on impossible, yet many of the old plants currently around have been named on this basis. We can all identify 'Mrs Sinkins' from 1868, as it is still commonly available, but can we be so certain? When you look at several from different sources you will notice that they are often likely to have differences, sometimes quite markedly, and none of them have the red markings mentioned by Catherine Sinkins and her son. Another factor is that 'Mrs Sinkins' is still vigorous and it is well known that a plant of that age, which can only be increased by vegetative means, should have lost a lot of this vigour. So which, if any, of the versions currently grown under this name is the true plant?

But does any of this really matter? I love the 'Mrs Sinkins' that I grow and I do not really care whether it is over 100 years old or not. The palette of colours and the range of patterns and forms of pinks is sufficiently limited to make me believe that we currently have near identical plants with nearly all those of the past and any that we have not are likely to crop up again some time in the future. We certainly have more than enough for our gardening needs of the moment. New ones are constantly appearing and some old ones disappear, but the general pool from which we draw our stock remains roughly the same. There are currently several hundred different plants available commercially and many more available between friends, and yet very few gardeners will want to grow above 20 varities.

It is interesting to note that even plants considered first class by some people are totally ignored by others. The Royal Horticultural Society has had a committee of one form or another for over a century to judge pinks, but only a very small percentage of the plants to which they have given awards are still in existence. Even plants awarded top hon-

ours as recently as the 1980s have disappeared without trace through lack of interest. Perhaps some of these will linger on in odd gardens only to be rediscovered later, giving somebody the horrendous task of identifying them.

There is a fascination and romanticism about plants with a history, but this should not blind us to a plant's beauty. I would happily discard a miffy 100 year old plant for a beautiful vigorous seedling with no history.

Having said this, I am a bit concerned about some modern commercial trends with pinks. They seem to be pushing the pink beyond its traditional bounds almost into the field of the carnation, both in colour and size. I am not hidebound enough to like only old-fashioned type pinks, although I have a predilection in that direction, but will give space to many of the modern pinks. However I do consider that many of the sports, often unstable ones, introduced in recent years do not make very good plants under any circumstances. Their colours do not fit happily into the borders (indeed, the colour sometimes does not even fit happily on the flower!), the plants are often top-heavy, drooping their cabbage-like heads in the mud, and they lack scent. Fortunately there are still a number of individuals and nurseries that are producing first-rate plants and have not been caught up with gimmicky colourings and names just for the sake of a few extra sales to an undiscerning public.

Seedlings can be an embarrassment to those who are asked to identify pinks. I would almost go so far as to say that there are more seedlings than named plants in existence, many of them singles with a coloured eye. I have often stopped the car beside a country or urban garden as a pink has caught my eye only to discover that it is yet another seedling. In reality this does not really matter as many of them are extremely attractive and are worth the garden space they occupy (on the other hand many are not). I am very reluctant to suggest that if you have any of these that you should name them, but I would urge you not to throw away good plants just because they have not got names or a past.

Pinks are to be enjoyed, history or not, names or not.

'Charity', 'Patchwork', 'Highland Fraser'
'Penny Red', 'Casser's Pink', 'Old Square Eyes'

'Thomas', 'Laced Romeo', 'Sam Barlow'
'Enid Anderson', 'Pink Mrs Sinkins', 'Laced Joy'

'Valda Wyatt', 'Gwendoline Read', 'Swanlake'
'Freckles', 'Ballerina', 'Petticoat Lace'

'Whatfield Polly Anne', 'Whatfield Fuchsia', 'Whatfield Mini'
'Whatfield Peach', 'Whatfield Dorothy Mann', 'Whatfield White'

'Hollycroft Fragrance', 'Messines Pink', 'Glebe Cottage White'
'Mars', 'Whatfield Cyclops', 'Inshriach Dazzler'

'Christopher', 'Show Glory', 'Haytor Rock'
'Picture', 'Cranmere Pool', 'Jenny Wyatt'

'Oakington', 'Paddington', 'Anna Wyatt'
'Old Dutch Pink', 'London Delight', 'Ruby Doris'

'Garnet', 'Casser's Pink', 'Hope'
'Nellie Clark', 'Brympton Red', 'Sweetheart Abbey'

'Binsey Red'. 'Valerie', 'London Brocade'
'Squeeks', 'Show Beauty', 'Paisley Gem'

'Allspice'. 'Coste Budde', 'Old Irish'
'Herbert's Pink', 'Damask Superb', 'Fair Folly'

'Whatfield Misty Morn', 'Whatfield Hart's Delight', 'Whatfield Nine Star'
'Whatfield Cherry Brandy', 'Whatfield Crushed Strawberry', 'Whatfield Beauty'

'Earl of Essex', 'Laced Joy', 'Laced Monarch'
'Whatfield Pretty Lady', 'Frances Isabel', 'Whatfield Blue Bird'

'Madonna', 'Albatross', 'Mrs Sinkins'
'Sally's Mauve', 'Bridal Veil', 'John Gray'

'Mandy', 'Rose de Mai', 'Widecombe Fair'
'Doris Supreme', 'Doris', 'Valerie'

'Musgrave's Pink', 'Fragrantissima', 'Crossways'
'Old Fringed White', 'Spencer Bickham', 'Betty Buckle'

'Irish Pink', 'Saint Nicholas', 'Horton'
'Allspice', 'Frank's Frilly', 'Houston House'

'Patchwork', 'Inglestone', 'Inchmery'
'Highland Fraser', 'Penny Red', 'Camilla'

'Raeden's Pink', 'Rose de Mai', 'Lawley's Red'
'Pink Mrs Sinkins', 'Valerie', 'Terry Sutcliffe'

'Susannah', 'London Glow', 'Susan'
'Clare', 'White and Crimson', 'Alice'

'Oakington', 'Gran's Favourite', 'Sops in Wine'
'Charity', 'Dusky', 'London Brocade'

'Indian', 'Lady Granville', 'Beauty of Healey'
'Sweetheart Abbey', 'Lady Wharncliffe', 'Laced Hero'

'Priory Pink', 'Freda', 'Fortuna'
'Helen', 'Oliver', 'Purple Jenny'

'Bobby', 'Christopher', 'Ian'
'Laura', 'Charles', 'David'

'Queen of Sheba', 'Painted Beauty', 'Sir David Scott'
'Farnham Rose', 'Cockenzie', 'Old Dutch Pink'

'Waithman's Beauty', 'Unique', 'Fanal'
'Old Dutch Pink', 'Gloriosa', 'Audrey's Frilly'

'Laced Hero', 'Hope', 'Lady Wharncliffe'
'Old Velvet', 'Paddington', 'Dartington Laced'

'Lady Salisbury', 'Fountains Abbey', 'Black and White'
'London Lovely', 'Old Fringed', 'Argus'

'Laced Joy', 'London Poppet', 'Saint Winifred'
'Gran's Favourite', 'Camelford', 'Bat's Double Red'

'Jane Austen'. All six blooms were taken from the same plant, demonstrating how the flower changes as it ages.

'La Bourboule'

'Red Denim'

'Becky Robinson'

'Saramanda'

'Ursula Le Grove'

A–Z of Border Pinks

INTRODUCTION

Availability

Many of the plants in the following list are either no longer commercially available or not in cultivation. I have tried to include all pinks now being grown, but I have not considered availability as being an over-important criterion as plants come and go in the market place and what might not be available this year, might be next. Another important factor is that plants not commercially available often move very readily between gardeners either as gifts or swaps, and they are often bought and sold at the many plant sales around the country. As to those not in cultivation, my excuse for including them is that one is never certain whether they are or are not available. I am convinced that quite a number I have branded as extinct are still lurking somewhere and it is hoped that this guide may act as a stimulus for gardeners to resurrect some of the older forms they may have kept going. Surely someone still has some of the Allwood alpinus rock garden pinks that were so popular, for example, or what happened to all those plants that Douglas introduced with names of birds? It would be nice to think that the next edition of this book would include a lot more that are 'still in cultivation'.

Another important factor for including plants no longer around is that they still occur in gardening literature and a passing reference in a book of, say, 20 years ago of a plant that was then a familiar one may not give the present-day reader sufficient information to appreciate the plant in that context. Descriptions, then, of most plants that have been in cultivation for the last 40 or 50 years since the Second World War have been included, as well as many of importance prior to that. Where there have been plants in the past with the same name as the main one I wish to describe, I have included details of them, no matter how obscure, to ensure that no confusion can arise should the plant surface or should it appear in literature. On the whole, however, obscure plants of the past have been omitted.

Awards

The Royal Horticultural Society regularly makes awards to pinks it thinks make worthy plants for the border, rock garden or for exhibition. They are, in ascending order of merit: PC (Certificate of Preliminary Commendation), C (Commended), HC (Highly Commended), AM (Award of Merit), FCC (First Class Certificate) and AGM (Award of Garden Merit). The system was slightly changed in 1992 but all plants listed were judged before then.

Breeders Rights

Some plants have a breeders' copyright applied to them, which gives the copyright owner the protected right to be the only person or firm to distribute the plant. It is therefore illegal to sell cuttings or plants, or to propagate the plant to be sold by anyone else.

Colour

I defy anybody to be dogmatic about the colour of pinks. There are a number of problems, not the least of which is that all the colours are a variation of pink (except the white, of course). Different eyes see these variations in different ways. When it comes to describing the different shades of pink, the terms available are rather vague and we are all likely to have different interpretation of them (for example, does salmon pink refer to the fish's colour when it is fresh, tinned, boiled or smoked?). One colour can also vary depending on its context. I have noticed that the same colour on a colour chart can look like purple, varying shades of dark red, brown or black depending on the surface of the petal, the surrounding colours, as well as the lighting conditions.

Another problem is that one plant will have flowers that vary considerably in their colour depending on their age. The light and the surrounding colours can also make a considerable difference. To add to the cataloguer's miseries, plants grown in different areas on different soils with differing amounts of feed and water, as well as those grown under glass, as opposed to the open ground, can all vary in colour. The colours as given are therefore to be taken as a guide and not a definitive statement.

I have tried to see as many plants as I possibly could and have compiled my colour descriptions as a consensus after comparing plants in different places. In the hope of bringing some sense out of the chaos, I have tried to give as many of the colours as possible the value allotted to them in the Royal Horticultural Society's colour charts. This in itself is fraught with difficulties, not the least being that only a small percentage of my readers will possess a copy. The other main problem is in using the charts. It is interesting that *The International Dianthus Register*, the RHS *Proceedings* and myself have often all come up with differing numbers. On checking them all out one realises that they are as valid as each other, each

being nearly right but not quite as the actual colour is not present on the chart. This is particularly true of the rich crimsons and maroons that so many pinks have in their eye, as these colours do not exist in the charts. Another problem is that few pinks have a single colour on their petals but are usually made up of a paler colour suffused with a darker one, which when seen from a distance looks like a distinct colour but when checked close to with a colour swatch, breaks down into its components in such a way that it is very difficult to work out either what each is or what the general effect is. Unfortunately there have been times when I have been able to write a description of a pink but unable to give it a colour reference as I either did not have my charts with me (they are jolly heavy) or I could not get close enough to the plant without wreaking havoc to a border or display stand.

There are many other problems with colour (the time of day and the quality of the daylight for example can change things drastically) but enough is enough as I think I have apologised sufficiently for producing colours with which you are bound to disagree. I hope that at least I have been as consistent as I possibly can and therefore, on a comparative basis, the colours as listed should have some validity and should be useful in identifying the different cultivars.

Unfortunately I have had to rely on other definitions for plants I have not been able to see, in particular those that are no longer in existence, and here the complications get worse. Quite naturally a nursery does not want to list all its pinks as the same colour, even when they are, but usually waxes lyrical that one is pale pink, while another is shell pink and yet another soft pink, while a fourth is blush pink or light rose pink, when in reality they are all the same and should really simply be called pink. These definitions have been taken over into other publications, including the *IDR*. It is not uncommon to find colours wildly out simply because the nursery has been using its artistic licence in the middle of the winter, as it compiles its catalogue, months after last seeing the plant in flower. It is not really surprising that the finer nuances of the range of pinks become distorted. These colour aberrations have all been faithfully taken over into the *IDR* which, because of its vast size, was restricted to written sources and could not examine all the plants it lists. For those for which I have had to rely on written word, I have tried to check them out in as many different sources as possible and have taken the consensus of their opinion.

Definite articles in names

In keeping with convention, where a name begins with the definite article 'the' it is ignored in the filing order thus 'The Bride' can be found under 'Bride'. The same applies to articles in foreign languages ('Le', 'La', 'Die', 'Der', etc.)

Flowering Time

It is impossible to give accurate details of when a pink will flower. It varies according to the part of the country in which it is grown and the type of season that is prevailing. As an average most pinks start to flower in early June, but in milder areas and in early seasons they will be well under way in May.

The main flush of flowers is usually over in July and although some go on flowering until the autumn, they are often only sporadic. This is particularly true of the alpinus group for the rock garden. The modern pinks generally continue to flower quite well into the autumn, but even these are not so prolific as in their first flush. Flowering can be prolonged by regular dead-heading.

Height

The height of the same cultivar will vary considerably depending on the position of planting, soil and so on. I have seen plants on the same nursery that have been 10 cm (4 in) in a raised bed with good drainage and light and 23–25 cm (9–10 in) in a better fed and slightly shaded border. Plants grown in pots seem to be more drawn than those grown in the open garden but even this is not always true. The heights given here are those given for plants growing in their 'normal' habitat, i.e. rock garden plants in a rock garden or raised bed and border pinks in a border. But even so they can only be taken as a guide.

Present existence

It is impossible to tell whether many of the plants listed here are still in existence or not. I have looked at as many gardens and collections as possible and hope I have mentioned most that are still around. However there must be some, many I hope, that are lurking in odd corners, either still known by their original name or simply appreciated without any knowledge of their name or origin. Increasingly it is going to become impossible to identify the latter as so many definitions of disappeared pinks consist of a description little more than 'rose pink ground with a darker centre', often not even stating whether it is single or double.

The Plant Finder lists most of those that are currently commercially available in the UK. Serious collectors should also obtain the catalogues of all those nurseries that specialize in pinks as these often contain detailed descriptions as well as other information.

Raiser's location

The raiser's locale is given in the vain hope that perhaps lingering nearby are some of the plants that may have disappeared from general cultivation.

Scent
Where known that a plant is fragrant, the information is given. However, scent can be illusive, especially in cool weather, and in some cases plants ascribed as having a 'slight scent' may be stronger in more favourable conditions than those that prevailed when I managed to get my nose into the flower.

Synonyms
In some instances more than one pink bear the same name. Descriptions of all the important ones have been given and just a note is made of any others. Similarly there are often carnations with the same name. Where these are listed in *The International Dianthus Register*, the number is given for each type so that the reader will be aware that confusion can arise and that a reference to that particular name in a magazine, book or catalogue might not refer to the pink.

'Allspice'

'ABBOTSFORDIANA'   This hybrid is mentioned by Will Ingwersen in 1949 but seems to have disappeared from cultivation. He describes it as a pretty semi-double with pink flowers and very silver leaves. The flowers are grown on 15–23 cm (6–9 in) stems and appear from mid-summer onwards.

'ABBOTSWOOD'   *see 'Caesar's Mantle'*

'ADONIS'   A form of *Dianthus alpinus* found by Reginald Farrer on the Schneeberg. It has fine broad petals with a salmon pink colouration that fades to a pearly pink. By the 1960s, although the colour was still the same, the petals had become much narrower, and it has now seemed to have gone completely from cultivation, although I would not be surprised if there was not a plant or two lurking somewhere. There are four other pinks with this name, three from the last century and of no significance. The fourth was introduced early in this century and had a rosy red ground and a darker centre. There were also nine border carnations and five perpetual-flowering carnations with this name.

'ADORÉE'   A clear rose-pink, single flower with overlapping petals that have a buff reverse, possibly indicating that it is a *D. pavonius* hybrid. The flowers are up to 5 cm (2 in) across and born on 10 cm (4 in) stems. It is a long flowering form that had the reputation of a second flush of flowers if cut over after the first. It was probably a pre-Second World War plant that seems to have disappeared in recent times.

'A.E. AMOS'   This is one of the many introductions by C.H. Herbert of Acocks Green. The flowers have a white ground with a crimson central zone and appear on 30 cm (12 in) stems in June and July. It is reputed to have had a good scent. It was introduced in 1930 but seems to be no longer in cultivation.

'AGATHA'   This is a double-flowered pink with a deep rose ground with a carmine eye. It is old fashioned in appearance but was still in existence in the 1960s. Two other pinks have been given the same name. One was a pink double, probably introduced before the Second World War. The other, recorded in the *IDR* as being introduced by H. Lang in 1965, was also a double, this time a light purple ground with a red-purple eye. The colours are sufficiently close to the first-mentioned

plant to think that they are perhaps the same plant and that Lang was registering an older plant.

'A.J. MacSELF'   *see 'Dad's Favourite'*

'AKBAR'   This is one of the many pinks introduced by the Douglas family. It has a bright red flower with a maroon eye produced on 30 cm (12 in) stems. The flowers are fragrant and have a long flowering period. The plant was still in existence after the Second World War but seems to have disappeared since, unless it is lingering somewhere. Douglas also produces a border carnation of the same name.

'ALAN TITCHMARSH'   A pure white, flat double or semi-double with a trace of a mauvy pink (78A) central band inside of which is a zone of yellow (3D), which disappears down the throat. It is slightly perfumed and has a long flowering period. It is a short, compact plant with 5.8 cm (2.25 in) flowers. It was introduced by Steven Bailey of Sway, Hampshire, who holds Breeder's Rights on the plant. It is still in cultivation.

'ALBATROSS'   This pink has a double flower that is nearly a white self but there is a hint of pink in the eye. The petals are delicately fringed. In general appearance it is a bit similar to 'Mrs Sinkins' but it is slightly smaller and not quite so blowsy, in spite of frequently splitting its chubby calyx. The flower is 3.8 cm (1.5 in) across and is strongly scented. The plant is mat-forming with silver foliage and a good upright growth. The flowering stems are 25–30 cm (10–12 in) in length. The *IDR* also registers three border carnations and one perpetual-flowering carnation with the same name. It is currently commercially available.

'ALBUS PLENUS'   This is semi-double frequently found in Holland. It is white with a slight touch of green in the throat. Very occasionally there is a small fleck of purple on some of the older flowers. In diameter it is 3.2 cm (1.25 in) across but often appears larger when it splits its calyx. It is fragrant. The petals are quite deeply fringed giving it a frilly appearance. It is a floriferous plant and, again, not dissimilar from 'Mrs Sinkins' although it is not quite so double. The plant is mat-forming with blue-green foliage. There is no record of the plant in Britain, although, curiously enough, Moreton describes a 'Plenus Albus'. He gives this as a tufted plant for the rock garden, with pure white flowers that are finely fringed and sweetly scented. He calls it an old pink but it seems now to have disappeared.

'ALDER HOUSE'   This is a clear pink self first recorded in the Holden Clough Nurseries catalogue in 1953. They still stock the plant as do a number of other nurseries. Confusion could arise as other plants have recently appeared mistakenly under this name. These have single, fringed flowers with a rich reddish pink (63A) ground (slightly striped on underlying paler colour) and a well-defined maroon (redder 59A) inner zone. They are good long-flowering plants that require a name.

'ALDERSEY HOUSE'   A pink with double flowers that are clear rose pink selfs carried on 15 cm (6 in) stems. It has a neat upright habit and a long flowering season. It was introduced by and named after Aldersey Gardens, near Chester, in the early 1960s. It is still commercially available.

'ALICE'   This is one of Allwood's famous 'name' series of modern pinks. This has a semi-double flower with a white ground and a large splash of raspberry (59B) in the eye covering more than half the petal and occasional maroon lacing to the petals. The reverse is white tinged with purple. The petals are noticeably fringed. The flowers are fragrant and appear over a very long season on 30–38 cm (12–15 in) stems. The diameter is 4.5–5 cm (1.75–2 in). The foliage has the coarseness of a modern pink but forms a good fresh-looking plant, although the brashness of the colour might make it difficult to assimilate into a border. The leaves are blue-green. It was introduced in 1930 and is still available. After garden trials as a border plant it was awarded a HC in 1933, AM in 1950 and FCC in 1969. It was one of the parents of 'Saint Oswald', 'St Asaph' and 'St Neot'. Several border carnations have also been named 'Alice' and there is one earlier pink, recorded as being pre-1854 of a purple form introduced by a C. Turner and Son.

'ALICIA'   A semi-double shell pink dianthus, which Mansfield (1951) claims is 'similar in colour and habits to 'Inchmery''. However, although it is also scented, it has taller flowering stems of up to 38 cm (15 in). It flowers in June and July. It does not appear to be currently in cultivation.

'ALLEN'S BALLERINA'   This is a modern pink with fully double flowers 5 cm (2 in) in diameter. They are a pure white, although they appear creamy when the petals are still bunched up towards the centre. It is fragrant. The petals have slightly serrated margins, but much less so than 'Haytor', giving the flower a more solid appearance while still appearing frilly. 'Ballerina' is a good description as it looks like a ballerina's full skirt. It was raised by Donald Thomas of Allensmore and introduced in 1984. It is currently available. It is one of the parents of 'Fair Tina'.

'ALLEN'S HUNTSMAN'   This double pink is a bright scarlet (43B) self, paling towards the centre. The flowers are 5 cm (2 in) across and have a very strong scent. The foliage is grey-green. It has a long flowering period from June well into autumn. This was raised by Donald Thomas of Allensmore and introduced in 1986 and is still available. It is one of the parents of 'Fair John' and of 'Fair Louise'.

'ALLEN'S MARIA'   This is a double of a deep rose (bright 60A) ground flushed from a large central zone of crushed strawberry (62B), bearing a resemblance to Allwood's 'Mandy'. It is quite noticeably fringed with the fringing taking on the strawberry colour giving it quite a frilly appearance. The flowers are about 5–5.8 cm (2–2.25 in) across. It is slightly scented and has a very compact growth. It was raised by Donald Thomas of Allensmore and introduced in 1986. It is quite widely available. It is also seen under the name 'Maria'.

'ALLOWAY STAR'   A single pink with a reddish purple (66B) centre that flushes out onto a pale pink ground in the form of a star. A plant from the 1950s or 1960s that is still in cultivation.

'ALLSPICE'   This is a much-loved old-fashioned pink from the seventeenth century. It has single flowers with overlapping petals and a slightly ruffled look. They are a mottled purple (74A), which fades with age. The petal margins have a thin edging of white and each has two white spots that becomes suffused with a lilacy-pink as the flowers fade. The reverse is white suffused with the purple showing through. The petals have a medium fringing, which is accentuated by the thin white margins. The flowers are 3.8 cm (1.5 in) across and are carried on 30 cm (12 in) stems. The foliage is blue-green in colour. It is a very floriferous plant when suited. It is still frequently grown and widely available.

'ALYSON'   This is one of Allwood's modern pinks. The flowers are double and cerise (57C)

'Allspice'

flushed purple (63A) in colour, a pale duller colour on the reverse. They are slightly smaller than others in the series, about 3.8–5 cm (1.5–2 in) across, and held on 30–38 cm (12–15 in) stems. They are fragrant with a clove-like scent. The petals are fringed. The foliage is a grey-green and has the typical coarseness of a modern pink. It has a bushy but spreading habit. The plant was introduced in the 1960s and is still in cultivation. In 1968 it was awarded an AM as a border plant in RHS garden trials.

'AMARINTH'   This is a single dianthus with flowers of a deep pink ground and a dark maroon centre ring. There is a flush of white in the throat. They are fragrant and held on 30 cm (12 in) stems. The petals are fringed. It was raised as a chance seedling by T.J. Wood of of Southcombe Gardens, Devon. Although this plant was commercially available in relatively recent times, it seems to have now disappeared.

'AMY'   Although this is an Allwood, it is different from most of the others in the 'name' series in that it is a single flower. It is a deep rose (57C) pink with a crimson (59B) central zone. Like most of the Allwood plants it is very free-flowering and

very fragrant. The 5 cm (2 in) flowers appear from summer into autumn on 30 cm (12 in) stems. It was introduced in about 1931. After garden trials as a border plant the RHS awarded it the AM in 1933 and HC in 1948. It does not appear to be in cultivation.

'ANDREW'   One of the Allwood 'name' series, this time it is a double cerise (61B) self that looks darker towards the centre when the petals are still folded. The flower gets paler and flatter as it ages. The petals are fringed. Occasionally 'Andrew' double-buds with a new bud pushing up through the flower, splitting the calyx. This gives the impression of a cuckoo in a nest with the fresh new growth sitting on top of the paler petals of the old flower. It was raised as a sport from 'Timothy'. It is still commercially available.

'ANNA WYATT'   A modern pink with a carmine-pink (48D) flower lighter towards the edges and darkening slightly (50B) towards the centre. It is a double with fringed petals and a slight clove scent. The flowers are about 5 cm (2 in) in diameter and are carried on stems 45 cm (18 in) long. It is a vigorous upright plant. This dianthus was introduced by Cecil Wyatt of Colehayes, Bovey

Tracey, in about 1978. It was awarded an AM as an exhibition plant in 1980 and another AM as a border plant in 1982 after garden trials. It is currently commercially available.

'ANNABELLE'   A double dianthus of a light rose-pink (a darker 73C) colour, fading to a lighter pink giving it a slightly washed-out appearance. There is a slight trace of a dark rose flecking in the eye and the petals are fringed. It is fragrant. The whole flower is somewhat reminiscent of 'Pike's Pink' but without the eye. The flower is about 3.8 cm (1.5 in) across and carried on 15–20 cm (6–8 in) stems over blue-green leaves. It flowers in June and July. The plant was raised and introduced by Thomas Carlile in about 1957. The RHS, after garden trials, awarded it HC in 1958, AM in 1960 and FCC in 1971, all as a plant for the rock garden. The name is sometimes seen spelt 'Annabel'. There is also another plant being mistakenly sold under this name. This is a large single flower coloured pink with a narrow reddish pink zone and with a deep fringing around the margins. A desirous plant that needs identifying or naming. A further confusion lies in the fact that there is also a plant called 'Ramparts Annabel' (*qv*).

'ANNE'   Another of characteristically named Allwood's modern pinks. The double flowers have a salmon (49A flushed slightly darker) ground with a darker, more reddy (43B) central zone. The flowers are up to 5 cm (2 in) across and are carried on 30–36 cm (12–14 in) stems. They have a very strong fragrance and the usual Allwood long-flowering season from summer until late autumn. The broad petals are fringed. The plant was introduced in about 1948. After garden trials the RHS have awarded it a C in 1950, HC in 1956 and an AM in 1957, all as a border plant. The *IDR* also lists one perpetual-flowering carnation with the same name. It does not appear to be currently commercially available.

'ANNE BOLEYN'   A pink that has long disappeared but which is of some historical importance. It was one of the first laced pinks to have a pink ground. The plant was in cultivation in the 1830s and was still about nearly a century later when it was one of the few pinks actually mentioned by name in Montagu Allwood's famous book. He put down its longevity to its 'beauty as a flower and for its pleasant perfume'.

'ANNIE MACGREGOR'   A pink from about 1780 discovered in a cottage garden at Hidcote. It has large flowers with a pure cerise-pink ground and a ruby central zone. The foliage is very blue. The plant was still around in the 1950s but has since seemed to have disappeared. It was also known as 'Hidcote Pink'.

'ANNIVERSARY'   A modern pink that many would consider a carnation. It has very large (up to 7.5 cm (3 in) across) floppy flowers of a pale pink (36C) colour with a slight trace of a reddish band, inside of which is a zone of a buff colour, which disappears down the throat. This inner zone looks like a washed-out or faded blood stain. The flower fades to a very pale creamy pink. It is fragrant. This is probably better as a cut flower than as a border pink. It was introduced by Steven Bailey, who has Breeder's Rights on the plant. There is also one perpetual-flowering carnation with this name, which probably invalidates the name for this plant as it is a recent introduction.

'ANN'S CHOICE'   A modern show pink. It is double with a white ground and a lilacy-purple (186A) central zone, which occasionally bleeds out as streaking onto the rest of the petal. The flowers are 3.8 cm (1.5 in) across and are fragrant. The plant was raised by J.W. Radcliffe of Romford in the mid 1970s. The RHS awarded the plant an AM as an exhibition plant in 1977.

'ANONA'   *see 'Whatfield Anona'*

'APOLLO'   One of the Allwood alpinus group, this has a double flower with a magenta (71C) ground and slight maroon markings in the eye. The flowers are 3.2 cm (1.25 in) across and carried on 15–20 cm (6–8 in) stems. They are strongly scented. The broad petals are deeply serrated. The plant has a compact bushy habit with erect stems. As a rock garden plant it was awarded an HC in 1959 and an AM in 1961 by the RHS after garden trials, although it was first exhibited in 1938 without success. It does not appear to be currently available. This is a popular name and there have been another three pinks, 12 border carnations and two perpetual-flowering carnations all so called. None of the pinks have been described. When it was put up for award in 1946 it was named erroneously 'Appollo'.

'AR DAWN'   A name that will make many gardeners cringe and may put them off the plant.

Indeed, the colouration of the flower is amongst my least favourite for pinks: a pink with bright mauve flecks and broad stripes, giving it a garish appearance that makes it difficult to place in the border. The flowers are about 5 cm (2 in) across. The petals are very fringed. It is not noticeably fragrant. This flower is very similar to 'Candy' except that its mauve is brighter and the stripes are not so broad. It is still in cultivation.

'ARABELLA' A dwarf pink for the rock garden or front of border. The flowers are double with a mauvy-pink ground (72C) and a slight purple (58A) central zone, which fades away down into the centre of the flower. They are up to 2.5 cm (1 in) across. The petals are noticeably fringed. It is in cultivation but is not particularly outstanding.

'ARGUS' This is an old single pink that would have great distinction if it were not for its floppy habit. The flower has a pure white petals with a very striking velvety dark maroon (187A) eye and a white throat. The flower is rather large for a single being 3.8 cm (1.5 in) across. The petals are fringed and curve up slightly so that the flower's shape is held in spite of its width. The flower stems rise 30–38 cm (12–15 in) above the blue-green (greener than many others) foliage. It mainly flowers in June and July, although Margery Fish claims it is always in flower. It is sometimes seen misnamed 'Argos'. There is a similar flower, 'Black and White', which is superficially similar, except that the latter has less fringing and the central zone distinctly curves upwards towards the edge of the petals. *IDR* lists one other pink (a rosy red pre-1910 plant) and four border carnations. It is still available.

'ARIEL' (1) This is one of the hybrid species of the so-called Winteri Pinks. It was raised by Sidney Morris of Thetford in the 1920s. It is a single with a magenta ground and a deep maroon centre and appeared to be very floriferous, flowering from summer until autumn.

(2) One of the Allwood alpinus group was also given this name. This is a single-flowered plant with a mauve ground with a crimson eye. It was introduced by Allwood in about 1929.

(3) A third pink under this name was introduced by E. Ladhams of Godalming in about 1937. This is a semi-double coloured a bright rose pink. The flowers are up to 4.5 cm (1.75 in) across and are borne on 38 cm (15 in) stems. After garden trials it was awarded an HC in 1939 as a border plant by the RHS. It does not seem to be around.

(4) According to the *IDR* there are two other pinks (one laced (1793) and the other purple (1853)) and five border carnations with the same name.

(5) 'Ariel is also a synonym for 'Crossways' (*qv*).

'ARTHUR' One of Allwood's modern pinks. It is a double with a dark red ground and a darker centre. It was raised in about 1920 but no longer appears to be around. It also went under the synonym 'Red Riding Hood'. *IDR* lists three border carnations with the same name.

'ATKINSONII' This is one of the old mule pinks, which is possibly a cross between *D. chinensis* and *D. barbatus*. The influence of the latter could be seen in the broad green leaves and the habit. It is a single flower of intense blood red, borne on stems up to 30 cm (12 in) high. It is very floriferous, blooming from summer into autumn, and nearly always has a tendency to flower itself to death, a characteristic of these mules. It is necessary to reserve one plant for propagation and shear off all flowering stems to produce sufficient cutting material to keep them going. Like all mules it is sterile. To add to the problem of keeping it going, it seems that it suffers badly from smut. As with a number of the mules it does best in a humus-rich soil, possibly in partial shade rather than full sun. It was still going in the 1950s, but Will Ingwersen said of it in 1949 that it was 'of poor constitution and seldom seen now'. This seems to have been a very attractive plant but difficult to keep going, possibly because of its age (it was introduced in 1844 by Atkinson of Bacton, Norfolk). It does not seem to be around any more.

'AUDREY PRICHARD' This is a double pink with deep rose pink flowers. They are clove scented and carried on stems up to 23 cm (9 in) tall over a long season from summer well into autumn. It is probably a pre-Second World War plant. It was sometimes called 'Aubrey Prichard'.

'AUDREY'S FRILLY' A pert semi-double flower with a clear-cut central zone and lacing. The ground is pure white and the markings are a rich crimson (187C). The flower is only about 2.5–3.8 cm (1–1.5 in) across. The petals are slightly indented, with the central tending to stand up when the flower first opens. It is still in cultivation.

'AVALON' *see 'Musgrave's Pink'*

'AVOCA PURPLE'   An old semi-double pink from Ireland. The flower has a pale purple ground streaked with a darker purple and with an even darker purple central zone. It is still to be seen.

'BABY TREASURE'   A double pink with the pale pink (nearest 56D) ground and light red (46D) central zone. The flowers are 4.5 cm (1.75 in) across and are carried on 23–25 cm (9–10 in) stems. They are fragrant. The plant has a bush habit. It was introduced by Mrs Desmond Underwood of Ramparts Nursery in the early 1960s. The RHS awarded the plant a HC in 1962 and an AM in 1963, both as a border plant.

'BADENIA'   A low-growing dianthus (flower stems only 5–7.5 cm (2–3 in) high) with bright red (61B) flowers with slight trace of a darker central zone. The petals are fringed and are a duller red on the reverse. It is slightly fragrant. The flowers are single and about 2.5 cm (1 in) in diameter appearing in June and July. The foliage is a blue-green and forms loose hummocks. A low growing plant for the rock garden or raised bed. The earliest reference is in 1985, so its introduction must pre-date this.

'BALLERINA'   (1) A pink introduced in 1957 by Mrs Desmond Underwood of Ramparts Nursery, Colchester. A white ground with a mauve centre. It does not appear to be in cultivation.

(2) A double pure white self that is very fragrant. It is a compact plant. It was introduced by Steven Bailey of Sway and has Breeder's Rights attached to it. Still in cultivation but its name appears to be invalid.

(3) There are also two border carnations and three perpetual-flowering carnations with the same name.

'BARBARA'   (1) This is another of Allwood's modern pinks. This one is a flat double or semi-double with dark crimson flowers. The flowers are about 5 cm (2 in) across and are quite coarsely fringed. It is typical of the series in that it is floriferous, fragrant and of an upright habit. It was introduced in about 1920 but its present status seems in doubt.

(2) There is also one of the Winteri group with the same name. This is single-flowered with a white ground and deep crimson eye and lacing. It was introduced by G. Winter of Wramplingham in about 1929 but does not seem to be still in cultivation.

'BARKERS BEAUTY'   A modern semi-double pink with a pink ground and pale mauve stripes. The flowers are up to 5 cm (2 in) across and carried on 30 cm (12 in) stems. They are scented. The plant was raised from 'Doris' by Barkers at Whipley Nurseries and introduced in 1985.

'BARLEYFIELD ROSE'   A dwarf pink with tight hummocks of dark green foliage and supporting bright red flowers with white markings. First listed by Hartside Nursery in 1984, although it was raised as a chance seedling, possibly with *Dianthus deltoides* blood in it, in a garden in Norfolk. Barleyfield was the name of the house.

'BAT'S DOUBLE RED'   A famous pink introduced by Thomas Bat in the late seventeenth century and rediscovered growing in the Oxford University Botanic Garden. In spite of its name, this has semi-double flowers, the colour of which is that of a red wine stain (64A) with a slightly darker (59A) eye. They are about 3.2 cm (1.25 in) in diameter and carried on 25–30 cm (10–12 in) stems. The petals are coarsely fringed. It flowers in June and has a fitful repeat flowering in the autumn. The leaves are a blue-green and quite wide, a bit in the manner of modern pinks. It is now safely in cultivation and is readily obtainable. When discovered at Oxford it was under the name 'Double Ruby Pink'. It was also reputed to have been sold by Ernest Ladhams of Godalming in the 1930s as 'Emperor'.

'BEAUTIFUL'   The flowers are a rich velvety shade of rose pink (51A) with a crimson (187C) central zone. The flowers are 5 cm (2 in) wide and carried on 25 cm (10 in) stems. The petals are broad and deeply fringed. It was raised by S.J. Rudge of Radlett and was awarded a C by RHS in 1953 and an AM in 1955, both as a border plant, but has subsequently disappeared.

'BEAUTY OF HEALEY'   A late nineteenth century pink named after the village of Healey, Rochdale, where the raiser, W. Grindrod, lived. The flower is a semi-double with some petals standing up in the centre giving the impression of a full double. It has a white ground and a rich maroon (61A) eye giving way to a more purple (74A) narrow lacing with glistening white 'eyes' in the centre of each petal. The reverse is white. The white area takes up at least half of each petal. The flowers are 3.8 cm (1.5 in) across and are carried on 20 cm (8 in) stems. The petals are very slightly fringed but are almost smooth. The plant is a bit straggly with floppy flower stems. Propagation can be a bit difficult. It is still commercially available.

'BEAUTY OF LYONNAISE' *see 'Glory of Lyonnaise'*

'BECKA FALLS' A popular vigorous and free-flowering modern pink raised by Cecil Wyatt of Colehayes, Bovey Tracey, in about 1977. It has a double flower of a bright scarlet red (43A). As with so many of the brighter colour, they are prone to white spots, caused by damp weather, which tends to mar the blooms. The flowers are about 5 cm (2 in) across and are borne on 30–38 cm (10–15 in) stems above a grey-green foliage. The petals are quite broad and minutely fringed. It has a clove scent. The RHS awarded it an AM in 1984 and after garden trials, an AM as a border plant in 1982. It is widely sold.

'BECKY ROBINSON' This is a very pretty double modern pink that comes quite close to some of the old prints of laced pinks. The flowers have a rose-pink (55B) ground (very slightly flushed or striped a darker pink) and a crimson (59A) zone, with slightly paler (61A) lacing, which is a bit irregular. It is white down in the throat. The body colour grows darker as the flower ages and gains an almost luminous appearance. The reverse is pink. The lacing is somewhat jagged giving the petals a fringed appearance when in fact they are smooth edged. The flowers are about 3.8 cm (1.5 in) across and are carried on 30–40 cm (12–16 in) stems. They have a strong clove fragrance. The plant is vigorous with foliage that has the typical modern pink coarseness about it. It is a blue-green with a paler margin that gives the plant a fresh look. The plant was raised by J. Galbally of Eastbourne in 1984 with 'London Brocade' being one of the parents. It is currently commercially available. The RHS awarded it an AM in 1986 and a FCC in 1988, all as a border plant. At least one nursery lists it as 'white with maroon lacing' which, if a true description of its plants, means that there are plants not true to type in circulation.

'BEDALES' *see 'Esther'*

'BELINDA' A modern pink of the Allwood type. It has a double flower that is coloured a strawberry pink with a maroon central zone. It is scented. It has a compact habit with flowers produced on 30 cm (12 in) stems over a long flowering period, from summer through to the late autumn. It was introduced by F.R. McQuown pre-1944. He unsuccessfully put it up for award in 1946. It does not seem to be currently in cultivation.

'BELLA' A dwarf pink for the rock garden. It is a semi-double with pink flowers carried on 5 cm (2 in) stems over a blue-grey foliage. There are two perpetual-flowering carnations of the same name.

'BELLS' A plant of the Winteri group. This is a single with bright red flowers and a large crimson eye produced on 30 cm (12 in) stems. It is well scented. The flowering season is long, from summer until late autumn. As with most of this group it can be grown from seed. It was introduced by S. Morris of Thetford.

'BENJAMIN BARKER' A modern double pink with a carmine-rose ground and deep purple stripes. The flowers are fragrant. It was raised from 'Joy' by Barkers at Whipley Nurseries and introduced in 1985.

'BERTHA WHITAKER' A semi-double pink that is white with the base of the petals being a yellowish green as they enter the throat. The flowers are 3.8 cm (1.5 in) across and are carried on 30 cm (12 in) stems. They are strongly fragrant. The broad petals are fringed. The plant was raised by F. Osborne of Orpington in the early 1970s. The RHS awarded the plant a HC as a border plant in 1976.

'BERTIE' A modern single pink with a rose red (50C) ground flushed slightly darker. The flowers are 5 cm (2 in) across and are carried on 36 cm (14 in) stems. They are slightly fragrant. The plants have a bushy habit. It was raised by H.G. Cooke of East Molesey in the early 1960s. The RHS awarded it a C in 1965 as a plant for the border.

'BESARION' A single pink with velvety dark red-purple flowers with a lighter edge and two spots on each fringed petal carried on 20 cm (8 in) stems. This was raised as a chance seedling by T.J. Wood, Southcombe Gardens, Devon, in about 1985.

'BETTY' This is one of the original Allwood modern pinks. It is a double flower that opens flat giving it a semi-double appearance. Its flowers are very fragrant and of a pure white with a reddish purple (darker 57B) eye. They are about 4.5 cm (1.75 in) across and are carried on stems up to

30 cm (12 in) long. As with all the series it has a long flowering period and makes a good cut flower. The plant is bushy in habit. It was first introduced by Allwood in 1918 and was awarded a HC in 1949 as a border plant by the RHS after garden trials. There are two border carnations and one perpetual-flowering carnation that share the same name.

'BETTY BUCKLE'   This is a wonderful plant with a fine 'clean' look to it. The flowers are single and coloured a bright pink (67A) with a crimson (darker 57A) zone and lacing. Both colours are slightly darker when the flower first opens. The lacing generally forms two 'eyes' on each petal, but as the flower ages these merge to form a horseshoe. The reverse is a pale pink. They are about 3.2 cm (1.25 in) in diameter. It is a good mat-forming plant with a good blue-green foliage. This is a fine plant but very similar to 'Highland Fraser' and may have been derived from it although it is a larger plant with slightly bigger flowers. The colours are also deeper and the lacing narrower. 'Highland Fraser' has been sold as seed and this could possibly be a seedling, but I have no idea of its true origin. It is commercially available.

'BETTY NORTON'   This is a popular pink that was first produced in the 1920s by G. Winter of Wramplington, Norfolk. The single flower is a deep pink with a maroon eye. The petals fade to white around the edges as the flower fades. The reverse is pink. They are about 3.2 cm (1.25 in) across and borne on stems up to 30 cm (12 in) long. The petals are fringed and the whole flower is fragrant. It has a long flowering season from summer well into autumn. This is an old pink still reasonably widely available and well worth growing. *IDR* has it listed under 'Betty Morton' and there are other references to it as 'Cherry Norton'. In appearance it is very similar to 'Ipswich Mulberry'. Just to confuse the issue further, it is also called 'Gwendoline'.

'BETTY WEBBER'   A modern double pink with a pale pink (49D) ground flushed with a deeper pink (49A) that pales towards the margins. These are overlaid with purple (64A) stripes and flecks. Sometimes the flowers can become quite blotchy with odd patches of crimson as the colour does not seem completely stable. It can also revert to its parent, 'Sandra', from which it was raised as a sport. The flowers are from 5–5.8 cm (2–2.25 in) wide, with fringed margins. The flowering period is a long one and there is a slight fragrance. It was

introduced by S. Bailey Ltd of Sway, Hampshire in about 1982, who have Breeder's Rights on the plant.

'BEVERLEY PINK'   An old pink from the eighteenth century. It has a dark red ground and is flaked with creamy white and yellow. In 1946 George William (in his 86th year) claimed that it had been grown in his garden near Beverley since his great grandfather's time, giving it a continuance of 150 years. Unfortunately I have been unable to find evidence that it is still around.

'BINSEY RED'   This is a semi-double pink with a rich purple-pink (61A) ground, paler in places, and with white margins and occasional white specks or blotches giving it a stippled effect. The flower opens wide so that the white throat is exposed. The reverse is white suffused with pink and often shows as the petals often curl upwards at the margins. The flowers are 3.2 cm (1.25 in) in diameter and borne on 30 cm (12 in) stems. The foliage is finer than most modern pinks and with a better blue-green colour, but it does get straggly as it ages. It is currently available.

'BLACK AND WHITE'   A striking single, similar in many respects to 'Argus'. It is a pure white flower with a large, very dark, almost black, maroon (187A) centre. Unlike 'Argus' the top edge of this blotch at the base of each petal is U-shaped, curving upwards at the margins. This makes the white part of the petal seem almost circular. The petals are slightly fringed, but nowhere as much as on 'Argus'. The flowers are up to 5 cm (2 in) across but the petals do not flop. It is an old cultivar of unknown origin that, fortunately, is still in cultivation. The *IDR* gives this as a semi-double but all the flowers that I have seen have been single. This semi-double was mentioned in Moreton as having been found in gardens around Chetwode in Buckinghamshire.

'BLACK CAP'   A double pink with a pure white ground and a crimson central zone. The flower is fragrant. It was raised by Douglas of Great Bookham. It does not appear to be in cultivation.

'BLACK CURRANT PINK'   A plant with an intriguing name evidently given to it because of the dark blur in the centre. It was of eighteenth century origin but was still around in the 1950s, although it now seems to have disappeared.

'BLACK PRINCE' (1) A pink that until the 1950s was grown in Ireland. It is a large double with a white ground and a very dark black-purple eye. Its current status is unknown but it has probably disappeared.

(2) This name has also been popular for border carnations with seven bearing it. There is also one perpetual-flowering carnation with the same name. Probably the best-known plant with this name is the annual *Dianthus chinensis* 'Black Prince', which is used as a bedding plant.

'BLAIRSIDE CRIMSON' This is a single pink with very large flowers, sometimes up to 6.4 cm ($2\frac{1}{2}$ in) across, but it has strong stems that give it a strong upright habit. The main colour is dark pink and it is centred in deep crimson. The flowers are fragrant and are borne on 15 cm (6 in) stems. It flowers from May until July. The origin is unknown but is probably pre-Second World War. It is not certain whether it is still in cultivation.

'BLANCHE' (1) As its name suggests, this is an Allwood modern pink. It is a double with a pure white ground and a touch of green in the eye. The broad petals are coarsely fringed, but not enough to make it look frilly. The flowers are up to 5 cm (2 in) across and carried on 36 cm (14 in) stems. They are very fragrant with a clove scent. As with all this species, it has a long flowering season. It was introduced by Allwood in about 1939. The RHS awarded it an AM as a border plant in 1957 after garden trials. It is not currently available.

(2) There is another pink, introduced by Vilmourin-Andrieux of Paris in about 1963. This has a white ground and a purple eye. It is uncertain whether it is still around.

(3) There are also six border carnations and two perpetual-flowering carnations with the same name.

'BLISLAND' A modern double pink with a deep pink (48C) ground flushed with a deeper, salmon pink (43C). It pales towards the centre. The flowers are 5 cm (2 in) across and are borne on 30 cm (12 in) stems. They are fragrant. The plant has a bushy habit. It was raised by Geoffrey Dunworth of Blisland in the 1960s. The RHS awarded the plant a HC as being suitable for the border.

'BLOODIE PINK'   *see 'Caesar's Mantle'*

'BLOODSTONE'   *see 'Whatfield Bloodstone'*

'BLOSSOM' This is an Alwoodii alpinus type for the rock garden, with single flowers of a lilac pink and a deep chocolate eye. It is fragrant. It has a neat habit with 15 cm (6 in) flowering stems. It is free-flowering with a long flowering season from early summer until late summer. It was introduced by Allwood in about 1932 and as with so many in this series, seems to have disappeared.

'BLUE BIRD'   *see 'Whatfield Blue Bird'*

'BLUE HILLS' A very floriferous, neat dianthus for the rock garden. It has single flowers of a rich crimson. They are carried on 7.5 cm (3 in) stems above neat blue-green foliage. The origin is unknown but it was introduced sometime before 1966. It is still currently available.

'BOBBY' Another of the Allwood name series of modern pinks. As with most of them, this is between a flat double and a semi-double. It has intense, luminous scarlet red (45B) flowers that are almost impossible to look straight in the eye. There is a dusky flush to the petals, which pale slightly towards the centre. As with so many of these bright-coloured pinks, it is prone to white flecking caused by damp weather. This is particularly noticeable with the ageing flowers and the plant can look rather messy, so regular deadheading is essential. The reverse is a paler red. The petals are slightly fringed, but as they curl up at the margins they give the impression of a deeper indentation. The flowers are 5 cm (2 in) in diameter and are carried on 25–30 cm (10–12 in) stems about a typical coarse modern-pink foliage, which is blue-green in colour. It was introduced by Allwood in 1980 and is still available. The RHS awarded it a PC as a plant for the garden and exhibition in 1984, and a HC in 1985 and an AM in 1986, both as a plant for the border.

'BOMBARDIER' This is a pink akin to the Allwoodii alpinus type. It has a double flower of a bright scarlet-crimson. The flowers are 2.5 cm (1 in) across and carried on 10 cm (4 in) stems. It is a very floriferous form. 'Bombardier' is very similar to 'Mars' except that it has larger flowers and is a deeper red. It was introduced by S.T. Byatt of Chippenham in about 1963. The plant is still widely available, although some of the plants on offer under this name are imposters. There is also one border carnation with the same name.

'La Bourboule'

'LA BOURBOULE' A very popular floriferous pink for the rock garden. The single flowers are pink with a slight veining of a darker colour. The flower is only 1.25 cm (0.5 in) across and the petals are serrated. It is fragrant. The plant forms a compact plant of silver grey leaves and flowering stems only 5 cm (2 in) high. It is possibly a hybrid of *D. gratianopolitanus*. In June the plant becomes a mass of flowers. Details of its introduction are not known but it was certainly around in Britain before 1952 and probably before the Second World War. The spelling of the name causes confusion and it is often seen spelt 'La Bourbrille' (in spite of the *IDR*'s preference for 'La Bourboule', this is the most popular spelling), 'La Bourbille', 'La Bourboulle', 'La Bouboulle' or 'La Boulville'. There is a plant being sold incorrectly under this name that has flowers of pale pink fading into a distinct white eye. This form is noticeable fringed.

'LA BOURBOULE ALBA' A white form of the above, which, except for colour, it resembles in other respects, including the misspellings of its name. It is widely available.

'LA BOURBRILLE' *see 'La Bourboule'*

'BOVEY BELLE' A modern pink in the Allwood style but produced by Cecil Wyatt of Colehayes, Bovey Tracey. It has double flowers that are a bright, almost luminous, purple (74A) in colour, paling slightly towards the centre. Being a strong colour it is often marred by white spots caused by moisture. The flowers are fragrant, are about 5 cm (2 in) across and borne on 45 cm (18 in) stems. The petals are serrated. The calyx splits allowing the petals to flop out untidily. It was introduced in about 1973 and is still widely available. The RHS awarded it a HC in 1983 and an AM in 1984, both as a border plant after garden trials. It has produced the sports 'Hound Tor', 'Jane Bowen' and 'Laurie Belle'.

'BOYDII' This is a very good, single pink for the rock garden. It has a lilac pink ground with a narrow, darker central zone that quickly fades into the paler throat. The margins of the petals are quite deeply cut and are slightly turned up, giving the flower head a saucer-shaped appearance. It seems quite likely that it has *Dianthus callizonus* in it. Its height is about 10 cm (4 in) and its flowers appear in June and July. It was introduced by W.B. Boyd of Upper Faldonside, Abbotsford, Scotland, somewhere around 1918. Fortunately it is still available.

'BRAMBLING' One of the pinks introduced by the Douglas family of Great Bookham in their series named after birds. This one is a double with a rich pink ground and a crimson eye. It is fragrant, flowering in June and July on 30 cm (12 in) stems. It was introduced in about 1949 but does not seem to be available now.

'BRANSGORE' A dwarf pink introduced by D. Lowndes of Macpenny Nurseries, Bransgore, after which the plant takes its name. The flowers are crimson, flecked with pink. They are carried on 30 cm (12 in) stems. It has a short flowering season confined to June. At least one nursery still stocks this plant.

'BRENDAN ELLIS' A semi-double with a pink (67D) and a crimson (185B) zone. The flowers are 5 cm (2 in) across and carried on rigid 30 cm (12 in) stems. It was raised by Messrs A.V. Ellis of Warmsworth. The RHS awarded it an AM in 1951 as a border plant. It does not seem to be still in cultivation.

'BRIAN' Yet another of the Allwood modern pinks given people's forenames. Like most of the others, this is a double with a long flowering period from July into October. The fragrant flowers have a red ground, flushed and flecked with a light maroon. It has a compact habit, only 23 cm (9 in), with much shorter flowering than most others in the series. It was introduced in about 1948 but does not seem to be currently in circulation. There is also a border carnation that bears the same name.

'BRIDAL VEIL' A very old and popular pink from the late seventeenth century. This is a double with deeply fringed, frilly petals. The flowers are white with a mauve eye (78A), which is quite a narrow band, and flush of green showing down the throat when the calyx splits open revealing the claws of the petals. The reverse is white. They are up to 5 cm (2 in) across (even bigger when the calyx splits) and are carried on 25–30 cm (10–12 in), or even longer, stems. They are very fragrant with a heady scent. It is one of the earliest pinks of the season to flower. The mats of foliage are grey-green and individual leaves are quite narrow. It can become a bit straggly in habit and the heavy heads can become floppy. In spite of its age it still seems vigorous and is still widely available. It has been distributed by at least one nursery under the name 'Frilly'. There is a similar plant with the name 'Madonna', but 'Bridal Veil' is bigger, has

slightly coarser fringing and much paler markings. The two are often confused. There is also another plant being sold with this name that has markings that are very broken and only just visible; they are also paler. This is possibly a seedling from 'Bridal Veil'.

'THE BRIDE' This is a pure white double pink introduced by C.H. Herbert of Acocks Green at the beginning of this century. It is a highly scented flower on long 30 cm (12 in) stems and has a long blooming period from June well into autumn. In 1951 Mansfield reported that 'the strain is now by no means as strong as when it first originated and may be that unless suitable repropagation takes place it will disappear from our gardens'. It appears that it might have done just that. There was another plant with the same name that originated at about the same time. This has a purplish rose ground and a darker centre. There were also five border carnations and three perpetual-flowering carnations, all with the same name. There is also an annual pink *D. chinensis* 'The Bride'.

'BRIDESMAID' As one would imagine, this name has been applied to a number of pinks.

(1) C.H. Herbert of Acocks Green introduced one in the early 1920s. Both Mansfield and Genders claim it to be one of the finest pinks ever raised. It has a double flower, which is pale salmon pink in colour with a deeper, almost red, central area. (Mansfield (1951) claimed that it is flecked with scarlet.) It is floriferous, very fragrant and has a long flowering period from June well into autumn. The margins of the petals are smooth. The flowers are carried on 30 cm (12 in) stems. The RHS awarded it an AM in 1922. It sets seed well and has become a popular pink amongst breeders giving rise to several offspring including 'Carlotta', 'Crimson Glory', 'Gaiety', 'Model' and 'Othello'. It is still in cultivation.

(2) A flat double with a flesh-pink (38C) ground and a narrow carmine (52B) central zone. The flowers are up to 6.4 cm (2.5 in) in diameter and carried on 36 cm (14 in) stems. The petals are broad and their margins are slightly serrated. It is a vigorous, bushy plant. It was introduced by Allwood and was awarded an HC as a border plant in 1952 by the RHS. It does not seem to be in cultivation.

(3) C. Turner of the Royal Nurseries, Slough, produced one of the 1860s that was laced crimson purple and was awarded the FCC by the RHS in 1862.

(4) There was one of unknown origin that was a white self.

(5) Finally there was a blush pink self introduced by the Douglas family of Great Bookham in 1965.

(6) For the record, three border carnations and three perpetual-flowering carnations also have this name.

'BRIDGET'   One of the famous Allwood modern pinks. This is a semi-double, verging on double, with a salmon-pink colouration. The petals are fringed and the flowers very fragrant. The flowers are up to 5 cm (2 in) across and are carried on stems up to 25 cm (10 in) high. It had a long flowering season, from June well into autumn. It was introduced by Allwood round about the beginning of the 1930s but seems to have now disappeared. It was awarded an AM in 1938 as a border plant by the RHS after garden trials.

'BRIGADIER'   Another of the dwarf plants introduced by S.T.Byatt of Chippenham that he named after military ranks. This one has a semi-double flower with reddish purple (61C) petals. It was introduced around 1965. After garden trials the RHS awarded it a HC in 1965 and an AM in the following year, both as a plant for the rock garden. It can appear under the synonym 'Mars'.

'BRILLIANT'   *see 'Whatfield Brillaint'*

'BRYMPTON RED'   This is a marvellous pink. It has large, single flowers with rounded, overlapping petals. The colours are rich with the ground being a pink purple (61C) and the wide zone and lacing a chestnut brown-red (53A), darkening (185B) towards the edges. The ground only really shows as the large horseshoe in the centre of the petals and just briefly at the extreme margins. The central zone also fades to a pink purple as it descends into the throat. The reverse colour is the same as the ground colour. The petals are only slightly indented. The flowers are fragrant. They are 4.5 cm (1.75 in) across and are borne on 30 cm (12 in) stems. As with so many plants the origins are obscure, with cuttings being generously passed from one person to another. This plant was spotted by Lady Lilian Digby of Lewcombe growing in a workhouse garden (a source of many good plants) in Beaminster. She took cuttings and passed the plant on to Mrs Clive of Brympton D'Evercy. It was she who gave it to Margery Fish, who named the plant. This is one plant that does not seem to have become confused as all nurseries and gardens seem to have the same plant under the same name. However, there is a slight mystery in that Mrs Fish describes the plant as 'handsome bright crimson

'Brympton Red'

with *white* markings'. This description hardly fits the plant at all. Several possibilities arise. First is that she became confused and wrote down the wrong details, second that somehow the name has become attached to the wrong plant (but it has done so with remarkable consistency), or third, she may have been referring to the odd, un-characteristic, irregular white flecks that oc-casionally occur on the flowers, caused by spots of moisture (or even thrips). Having looked at hundreds of 'Brympton Reds', I would never have said white was present until I was looking closely at one of my transparencies and saw a white moisture spot. Whatever the reason, it does not really matter as this is a wonderful flower and, at least, it is consistently named, even if there has been a hiccup in its past. Fortunately it is well established and widely available.

'BUCKFAST ABBEY'   A modern pink with double flowers of a reddish purple darkening to-wards the centre. They are fragrant and borne on long 45 cm (18 in) stems. It is a cross between 'Valda Wyatt' and 'Kestor' raised by R. Hubbard of Hill House Nursery, Devon in about 1984. It is commercially available.

'BULLFINCH'   The Douglas family produced two pinks of this name, or at least the *IDR* lists two. The first, with which Mansfield concurs, is a cyclamen purple with a carmine centre. The sec-ond, this time with which Genders agrees, is an apple blossom self. Genders muddies the waters by going on to say that it has a carmine zone. This could be a printer's error as it is a repetition of the previous entry in his book or it could be that he is right and in fact the two plants are the same with slight misinterpretation of the ground colour by one or both authors. All this is probably ir-relevant as neither plant seems to be in cultivation.

'BUNGAY CASTLE'   A show pink with a pale pink ground, evenly laced with a velvety crimson. The inner edge of the lacing is crisp and the outer fades into the pale pink margins of the petals. These margins are very slightly fringed. The flowers are about 4.5 cm (1.75 in) across and are fragrant. The petals overlap in an attractive manner. It is still in cultivation.

'BUNGAY SEEDLING'   A double show pink with a white ground flushed with the velvet crim-son (59D) of the eye and lacing. The flowers are about 4.5 cm (1.75 in) across. It is in cultivation.

'BUNTING'   Another of the Douglas bird series. This has double flowers with a crushed strawberry ground and a central zone and lacing of blood red. They are fragrant. It was introduced by the Douglas family in about 1954.

'CAESAR'S MANTLE'   This is a very old plant from the sixteenth century. It is a large single with good upright growth. It has a deep crimson (53C) ground flushed with a dusky red and zoned with a darker, maroon (187A) centre that pales as it goes down the throat. It is blessed with a strong scent. The 5 cm (2 in) wide flowers appear on 25 cm (10 in) stems over a blue-green foliage. The petals are deeply but coarsely fringed. The plant is a bit straggly and its age has taken its toll as it is now not very easy to propagate, but fortunately it is still in cultivation and commercially available. It also goes under the names 'Abbotswood' and 'Bloddie Pink'.

'CAMELFORD'   A semi-double flower with a white ground and deep crimson (187A) eye and purple (brighter 61A) lacing. The flowers are about 3.8 cm (1.5 in) across and are carried on 40 cm (16 in) stems above a blue-green foliage. The flowers are fringed and the lacing is irregular, emphasising the fringing. It was named after the village where it was found. It is one of the parents of 'Saint Teilo'. It is currently available.

'CAMELFORD A'   *see 'Lady Wharncliffe'*

'CAMILLA'   This double flowered dianthus has a wonderful chestnut (187B) colour with very nar-row margins in white, tinged with purple. This colour also appears on the reverse, which is very prominent in this flower as the petals curl up revealing the back, giving the flower a very frilly look. The colours do not seem to deteriorate with age. It is very floriferous with flowers about 3.2 cm (1.25 in) across and carried on 38–45 cm (15–18 in) stems. Unfortunately these stems are very floppy and need support. There are often a lot of dead leaves in the centre of plants and old plants often have no foliage left even while in full flower, so that they look very untidy. A mixed pink then, with rather fine flowers on a scruffy plant.

'CANARY'   This is an unusual border pink as it is a single yellow self. It is a compact plant supposedly of a *D. alwoodii* and *D. knappii* cross, the latter giving it the yellow colouration and also the multiple flower-heads. It was introduced by

'Casser's Pink'

Allwood in the early 1950s. It does not seem to be in cultivation (possibly because of something else it inherited from *D. knappii*, which is a short-lived species). There are two border carnations and one perpetual-flowering with the same name.

'CANDY' The plant recently introduced under this name has been renamed 'Sway Candy' (*qv*).

'CARINA' This is a dwarf pink with semi-double flowers of a carmine red. It was introduced by E. Knecht in about 1985. It is currently available.

'CARLOTTA' This is one of the imperial pinks raised by C.H. Fielder of the Lindabruce Nurseries, Lancing. The flowers are large, double and of a claret red colouration. They are very fragrant and appear on 30 cm (12 in) stems. The petals have a slight indentation. It was raised in 1946 and was obtained by crossing 'Bridesmaid' with one of the Allwoodii pinks. Plants can still be obtained. There is also one perpetual-flowering carnation of the same name.

'CAROL' An Allwood modern double pink with deep pink (55A) petals, deepening even more

towards the centre. The flowers are 5.8 cm (2.25 in) in diameter and are carried on 51 cm (20 in) stems. The broad petals are serrated. The flowers are slightly fragrant. The plant has a bushy, erect habit. It was introduced in the mid 1950s but seems to have now disappeared. The RHS awarded it a C in 1955 and a HC in 1960, both as a plant for the border.

'CASSER'S PINK' There are not a great number of mule pinks around today but this is one of them. It is double with a vivid crimson (60B) colour, paling to a more purply (67A) colour towards the centre. The reverse of the petals is a paler wine red. The flowers are about 3.8 cm (1.5 in) across and are borne on 30 cm (12 in) stems. They prolifically appear in June and July, and are perfumed. The petals are slightly fringed. It is an upright-growing plant with little basal foliage. What there is, is green, often blackening at the tips in the manner of a sweet william. It is a plant that needs constant attention as it is likely to flower itself to death. Cuttings must be taken each year and it may be necessary to put one plant aside to be sheared over to provide cutting material. Even this does not always work as it still persists in throwing up flowering stems. After garden trials the RHS gave it an AM in 1952 and a FCC in 1955 as a border plant.

'CASTLEROYAL' A whole series of 16 show pinks by John Douglas of Wokingham, most of which are about 5 cm (2 in) semi-double to double flowers with a white ground laced with red, the exceptions being 'Castleroyal Milady' (white ground with purple red lacing), 'Castleroyal Princess' (sugary-pink (pale 73B) ground with raspberry red (bright 61A) red zone and lacing and a pale pink, fading to white margin beyond the lacing; still in cultivation) and 'Castleroyal Fancy' (a fancy pink with small spots and occasional flecks of purple-red which give it its dominant colour; the spots are particularly intense towards the margins; still in cultivation). The others are 'Castleroyal Balletgirl', 'Castleroyal Chieftain', 'Castleroyal Coronet', 'Castleroyal Emblem', 'Castleroyal Emperor' (white ground, flushed pink when first opened, with a velvet crimson central zone and a narrow band of lacing quite close to the margin of the petal; a very clean-looking flower still in cultivation), 'Castleroyal Gaylord', 'Castleroyal Monarch', 'Castleroyal Pageboy', 'Castleroyal Prince', 'Castleroyal Sceptre' (still in cultivation), 'Castleroyal Sovereign' (white ground, crimson (59B) zoning and lacing; flowers up to 4.5 cm (1.75 in) across, awarded an AM as an exhibition plant in 1970), 'Castleroyal Sparkler', 'Castleroyal Warrior'. They were raised between 1967 and 1975.

'CATHERINE LOWE' A show pink with a flat-double or semi-double flower. It has a white ground with a purply-pink lacing and a crimson central zone. The lacing has jagged edges giving the flower a frilly look although the margins of the petals are only slightly fringed. The flowers are about 3.2 cm (1.25 in) across. It is still in cultivation.

'CATHERINE WHEEL' Large flowers of crimson and pink. They are fragrant and appear on 23 cm (9 in) stems. It seems to be still grown but is not currently available.

'CATHERINE'S CHOICE' A flat double, show pink with flat rounded petals. They are bright red with a dark, dusky bloom towards the margins and pale towards the centre as they age. The flowers are about 4.5 cm (1.75 in) across and are only slightly fringed so as to appear almost smooth. It is in cultivation.

'CATHIE'S CHOICE' A modern double pink with a purply-pink (54A) ground and a red (53A) central zone. The flowers are 5 cm (2 in) wide and borne on 30–36 cm (12–14 in) stems. The broad petals are slightly fringed. The flowers have a slight fragrance. The plant was raised by J.W. Radcliffe of Romford in the early 1970s. The RHS awarded the pink a C in 1975 and an AM in 1976 as a plant for the border.

'CAVALIER' According to Roy Genders this was a new hybrid in 1962 for the rock garden, but it seems to have disappeared without trace, unless it has changed its name. It was single flowered, with a pink ground and a chocolate central zone. The petals are fringed. The flowers appeared on 12.5 cm (5 in) stems.

'CEDRIC'S OLDEST' An old pink discovered by Cedric Morris in a cottage garden near Manningtree in Essex. It is a double with a white ground splashed with a mixture of colours including cream and purple. It sometimes splits its calyx and the petals spill out. Its age seems to be showing as it is not long lived and quite difficult to propagate. Sue Farqhuarson recommends propagating it late in the season. There is a problem, as with so many pinks, with the name of this plant. It is also called 'Sir Cedric Morris' and 'Manningtree Pink'. The form used here is that of the *IDR*. It is still commercially available.

'CERES' The flowers of this pink are semi-double and coloured a strawberry pink with a maroon eye. The flowers are 4.5 cm (1.75 in) across and are carried on 30 cm (12 in) stems. It was introduced by E. Ladhams of Goldalming around 1937 but seems to have disappeared. The RHS awarded it a HC in 1939 as a border plant.

'CHAFFINCH' There seem to be two pinks of this name both introduced by the Douglas family. Neither appear to be currently available.
(1) Introduced in 1955, this one has flowers of a pure white with a beetroot red centre.
(2) This has salmon pink flowers with a crimson central zone. It was introduced in 1949.

'CHARITY' (1) A low clump-forming plant with grey foliage and semi-double flowers that are white with slight pink stripes. The reverse is white. The petals are fringed and incurve slightly. The whole flower is fragrant. The flower is only 1.25 cm (0.5 in) across and appears on 15 cm (6 in stems).

It flowers in June and July. It is still extant.

(2) This name was also given to an Allwood modern pink. It had a double flower with pure white petals, with a central zone and lacing of crimson. It was introduced by Allwood around 1954. This one seems to have disappeared.

'CHARLES'   Another Allwood modern pink in the same series. This is a double with rich velvety red (53A) flower, duskier towards the edges of the petals. It is quite purplish when it first opens, but pales as the flower goes over, especially towards the margins. The reverse is quite pale compared to the front, particularly where it enters the calyx. The flowers are up to 4.5–5 cm (1.75–2 in) in diameter and are carried on 30 cm (12 in) stems above typically coarse modern foliage. The petals have a slight indentation and the whole flower is scented. The calyx has a tendency to split. The flower does not go over gracefully, leaving the plant looking straggly. It is best to deadhead at an early stage. It was introduced by Allwood and is still available. The RHS gave it an AM as an exhibition bloom in 1972, an HC in 1973 and an AM in 1975, both the last two as a border plant.

'CHARLES MUSGRAVE'   *see 'Musgrave's Pink'*

'CHARLIE'S ACHIEVEMENT'   This is a double fancy show pink with rose pink (54B) ground with occasional distinct purple (59A) stripes and flecks. The flower is about 3.8 cm (1.5 in) across and the petals are slightly fringed. It has a slight clove scent. The flowers are carried on 25 cm (10 in) stems. It was raised by C.A. Sands of London in about 1986 as a sport from 'Show Achievement'.

'CHARLOTTE PIPER'   A modern pink with double flowers of a white ground and a crimson (59A) central zone and stripes. The flowers are about 5 cm (2 in) across and carried on 38 cm (15 in) stems. The broad petals are deeply serrated. The plant is bushy with an erect habit. It was raised and introduced by F. Piper of Barking in the 1950s. The RHS awarded it a C in 1954 as a border plant.

'CHARM'   (1) This is one of the imperial pinks introduced by C.H. Fielder of Lindabruce Nurseries, Lancing. The large flowers are double and of a reddish salmon pink. It has a long flowering period from June until the end of autumn. It was introduced somewhere around 1948 and is still in cultivation.

(2) C.H. Herbert of Acocks Green introduced a double with rich crimson petals. This one was clove scented. It was introduced about 1932.

(3) E. Ladhams of Godalming chose this name for semi-double rose pink self he introduced before 1940.

(4) There are also four border carnations and one perpetual-flowering carnation bearing this name.

'CHARMING'   (1) An Allwoodii alpinus pink for the rock garden, the single flower has a blush-pink ground and a crimson central zone. The plant was introduced in about 1931. It was trialled at Wisley in that year. It no longer seems to be around.

(2) Allwood also introduced another rock plant with the same name in the 1960s. This was a single white. It also has disappeared.

(3) There are two border carnations and two perpetual-flowering carnations with the same name.

'CHASTITY'   (1) An older form that has a white semi-double flower with a yellowish (4C) tinge to the centre. The flower has a nice simplicity to it (it is perhaps well-named) as it opens flat with the tips of the petals curving upwards in rather an attractive manner. The margins of the petals are slightly indented but the concurving of the petals make them appear smooth. The flowers are up to 3. 2 cm (1.25 in) across and emerge from long slender calyces. They are borne on 10 cm (4 in) stems, which makes the plant suitable for the rock garden. The flowers have a fine fragrance. The fine-leaved foliage is a pale green. It is a wonderful plant, one of my favourites and, I am glad to say, still in cultivation.

(2) I have seen several examples of this plant from different sources and they all agree with the above description. However, the *IDR* lists it as single (which it could seem to be if only given a quick glance) and one catalogue declares that it is double. It is quite likely that these both refer to the above plant.

(3) Some of the plants offered by nurseries have reddish-purple markings around the centre. Whether these are wrong plants or whether this colouration has anything to do with the weather I am not certain (several pure white flowers seemed to have abnormal reddish-purple markings in the hot summer of 1991).

'CHELSEA PINK'   This old plant, possibly first raised around 1760, is a semi-double, verging double, of a crimson colour and white lacing. The flowers are borne on 20 cm (8 in) stems. It has a long flowering period from summer into autumn. The name is assumed to come from the fact that the plant was widely cultivated in the Chelsea area in the eighteenth century. It is not a very easy plant and its age is making it difficult to propagate. It is also called 'Little Old Lady'. It is in cultivation and available from nurseries.

'CHERRY BRANDY' *see 'Whatfield Cherry Brandy'*

'CHERRY NORTON' *see 'Betty Norton'*

'CHERRYRIPE' (1) This is a plant introduced by C.H. Herbert of Acocks Greens with large double flowers of a cherry-red ground with a crimson zone. The flower is fragrant.

(2) The second plant under this name is one of the imperials introduced by C.H. Fielder of Lindabruce Nurseries, Lancing. This is a flat double and, as the name would suggest, cherry red (46B), although there are extant plants under this name that are more of a reddish pink (46D) paling towards the centre. The flowers are up to 5 cm (2 in) wide and are borne on 38 cm (15 in) stems. They occasionally split their calyces, particularly as they go over. There does not appear to be any scent. It has a long flowering season. It was introduced in about 1959 and is still in circulation. The RHS awarded it a C in 1962, an AM in 1963 and a FCC in 1964, all as a border plant.

'CHERYL' *see 'Houndspool Cheryl'*

'CHETWYN DORIS' This is one of the very many sports from 'Doris'. It is a double with a pink (56C flushed darker) ground and a red (43A) eye fading towards the inner edge, flecked and striped mauvy purple (68A). The flower is about 4.5 cm (1.75 in) across and is carried on 36 cm (14 in) stems. The petals are slightly fringed. The flowers are slightly fragrant. The plant has a tendency to die out a bit in the centre and the flower stems are a bit floppy. It was raised by F.T. Gillies of Bolton in 1986. It is currently available. The RHS awarded it a PC in 1990.

'CHIFFCHAFF' The Douglas bird series became quite extensive although very few, if any, of them are still around. This one is a pure white with a dark red central zone and lacing. The flower is double and scented. It was introduced in about 1957.

'CHRISTOPHER' Another of the Allwood series. The flowers are between double and semi-double and of a reddish pink (46C) that pales quite noticeably toward the centre. The reverse is slightly paler in colour. They are large flowers, up to 6.4 cm (2.5 in) across and carried on 38 cm (15 in) stems. They have a clove scent. It was introduced by Allwood in about 1966. The RHS awarded it an HC in 1970 and an AM in 1977 as a border plant. It is still widely available. It is one of the parents of 'Fair Beccy', 'Fair John' and 'Fair Louise'.

'CILLA' An Allwood modern pink. The double flowers are pure white with a red (47B) central zone. The flowers are 4.5 cm (1.75 in) across and carried on 36–38 cm (14–15 in) stems. They are scented. The petals are very slightly serrated at the margins. The plant was introduced in the early 1970s. The RHS awarded it a PC in 1972, an HC in 1973 and a FCC in 1985, all as a border plant.

'CINDY' This has salmon pink flowers with a red central zone. They are carried on 30 cm (12 in) stems. It was introduced some time before 1988. The *IDR* does not accept the name as there is already a perpetual-flowering carnation so called. It is still available under this name.

'CIRCULAR SAW' This is a large flowered single. The flowers are milk white with a purple eye and a white throat. The margins are very deeply toothed, hence the name. The flowers are borne on relatively short stems, about 15 cm (6 in), which emphasise even more the size of the flower, which is 5 cm (2 in) across. The petals have difficulty in keeping themselves horizontal and are slightly recurved. It was introduced by Michael Williams of West Hoathly, but was raised at Ingwersens from a random batch of seed.

'CLAN PINKS' A whole range of pinks raised in the 1930s by P.S. Hayward of Treasure Holt Nursery at Clacton-on-Sea. They were doubles and semi-doubles in a wide range of colours including many fancies and picotees. They went under such names as 'Clan Fraser' and 'Clan Gordon'. None seem to survive.

'CLARE' One of the Allwood modern pinks between a semi-double and a double. The flowers are a lavender pink (66D) with an irregular wine-red (53A) eye fading to pink down the throat. The reverse is a paler version of the same colours. They are about 5 cm (2 in) in diameter and are carried on

30–38 cm (12–15 in) stems. There is a clove–scent to the flower. The petals are quite broad and coarsely toothed, which gives the flower a frilly appearance. The blue-green leaves are the typical coarse foliage of most of the modern pinks, but it does make a good vigorous plant, and the flowers are held upright. It was introduced in about 1974. It is still available and quite widely grown. The RHS awarded it a PC in 1975 and a C in 1978, both as border plants.

'CLARET JOY'   A modern pink raised by Donald Thomas. The flowers are double and bright scarlet (44A) in colour, paling slightly towards the centre. The flowers retain their colour well even when they age. They are fragrant and 5 cm (2 in) in diameter. The margins of the flower are not really fringed but just occasionally indented giving it an almost ragged appearance. The calyx sometimes splits. It was raised as a sport from 'Joy'. It is currently available.

'CLEA WYATT'   A semi-double or double introduced by Cecil Wyatt of Colehayes, Bovey Tracey. The large flowers are a pink (63B–63C) paling towards the base. They are about 5.7 cm (2.25 in) in diameter and are carried on 30 cm (12 in) stems. The broad petals have almost smooth margins. The flowers have a slight clove scent. The plant has a slightly spreading habit. It was introduced in about 1981. The RHS awarded it a HC as a border plant in 1984.

'COBWEB'   One of the Allwood alpines. This is a single with fringed cyclamen-pink flowers. It is moderately fragrant and has a long flowering period. The flowers are borne on 15 cm (6 in) stems. It was introduced in 1932. Like so many of these forms for the rock garden, it seems to have disappeared.

'COCKENZIE PINK'   This is a famous pink originating from about 1720 from Montrose House in Scotland. It was rediscovered in the village of Cockenzie, hence the name. The flower is a semi-double to double with a dark pink (73C) ground and an even darker pink (59A) eye. The ground colour is not pure, but diffused with that of the eye, giving it a slightly striped effect. The reverse is a lighter pink. The flower is not very large, being only about 2.5 cm (1 in) across and fragrant. The petals are fringed. It is a clump-forming plant with blue green foliage and flowering stems that reach about 25 cm (10 in) high. It has quite a long flower-

ing season and is one of the first to flower. It is also called 'Montrose Pink' after its original home. It is safely in cultivation.

'COLE TIT'   Another of the Douglas bird series. This is a fringed double with a blush rose ground and a central area of bright purple. It flowers in June and July on 30 cm (12 in) stems. It was introduced by the Douglas family in about 1950. There is no evidence that it is still cultivated.

'COLEHAYES CRIMSON'   This double, modern pink was raised by Cecil Wyatt of Colehayes, Bovey Tracey, hence part of the name. The other part comes from the crimson colour of the petals.

'COLETON FISHACRE'   A single pink with reddish-brown flowers. It is of unknown origin, but is named after the National Trust Garden. It is still in cultivation.

'CONSTANCE'   One of Allwood's modern pinks. This is a semi-double with reddish pink (50B) zoning, which bleeds with flushes and stripes into the white or pale pink (56D) ground on each petal. The reverse is mainly the reddish pink of the central zone. The petals are only slightly fringed. The flowers are about 5 cm (2 in) across and are slightly fragrant. It has good strong growth with grey-green and 40 cm (16 in) stems. It was introduced by Allwood in about 1955 and is still available. The RHS awarded it an HC in 1955, an AM in 1963 and a FCC in 1977, all as a border plant. The *IDR* lists two other pinks with this name, both of which have probably long since disappeared. One is dark red laced and introduced by McLean of Colchester sometime before 1867, and the other is just given as laced and was introduced by Fellowes of Shottisham Rectory around 1908. There are also eight border carnations and one perpetual-flowering carnation with the same name.

'CONSTANCE FINNIS'   This is a delightful pink very much in the old style. It is quite a large single flower of about 3.8–4.5 cm (1.5–1.75 in) diameter. The ground colour is white and has bright reddish pink (59C) markings as a central zone, and lacing that meets down the centre of each petal creating two white 'eyes'. The colour is not uniform but has a rather delicate stippled effect. It is at its brightest down the centre of the petal and, although the colour fades and varies slightly in its pattern as the flower fades, this stripe remains the strongest. The flowers are fragrant and carried on 30 cm (12 in) stems. It was introduced by Mrs C.S. Finnis of Reigate. The RHS awarded it a HC in 1969 as a border plant. It is quite widely available but some plants of 'Hidcote' have been offered for sale as this plant, so there may be some confusion ahead.

'CORAL QUEEN'　One of C.H. Fielder's imperial pinks created as a cross between Allwoodii pinks and Herbert pinks. This one has a double flower of a coral pink colour. It has a long flowering season from June until late autumn on compact plants. It was introduced in about 1947, but does not seem to be around.

'CORNISH SNOW'　This is a dwarf plant suitable for the rock garden. It has white flowers. It is currently available.

'COSTE BUDDE'　This is one of Valerie Finnis' introductions that has a wonderful fresh-looking flower when it first opens. It is a single pink with a white ground and reddish purple (bright 61A) central zone and lacing, which meet down the centre creating two distinct white 'eyes'. The edge of lacing is irregular, emphasising the fringing. The flowers are fragrant. They are 2.5–3.8 cm (1–1.5 in) in diameter, depending on age, and are carried on 36 cm (14 in) stems. It was introduced in 1978 and is still available.

'COTTAGE LOVELINESS'　This is a single flowered plant with broad, extremely fringed petals. The flower is coloured rose purple (darker 73C) and has a clove scent. They are 3.8 cm (1.5 in) in diameter and carried on 38 cm (15 in) stems. The plant has a compact, upright growth and is vigorous. It was introduced by R.E. Gardiner of Far Oakridge, Gloucestershire, but does not still appear to about. It was awarded a HC as a border plant by the RHS in 1952.

'COTTAGE MAID'　Mention is made by Will Ingwersen (1951) of this plant, but no other reference can be found so it must be assumed that it has disappeared. It is a double flower, coloured soft pink with a carmine centre and a strong, heavy scent. He describes it as 'nice but not exceptional'.

'CRADDOCK PINK'　A dwarf dianthus with small double flowers coloured pink. It was raised as a seedling of 'Highland Fraser' by Nellie Britton of Washfield Nursery, when it was at Tiverton. It no longer appears to be about.

'CRAKE'　A strange name for a pink but it is one of the Douglas bird series. This one is a double-flowered form, the main colour being a deep ruby-rose with a blood red central zone. It is fragrant. It was introduced by Douglas of Great Bookham in 1960.

'CRANMERE POOL'　This has very pale pink flowers, almost white, flushed darker towards the centre, which consists of a slight, irregular bright red (53A) zone. I have examined many examples of this plant in different parts of the country and they all have the same very pale pink, which, although it tends towards white, in no way can be considered the 'ice white' of the IDR and many nursery catalogues. I suspect these have all been written up from the original distributor's catalogue rather than from an examination of the plant. On some plants the occasional crimson spots appear on the pale ground. The slightly fragrant flower is double and fairly large, at about 5 cm (2 in) or more in diameter. They appear on 25 cm (10 in) stems that tend to flop a bit. The petals are serrated and can occasionally flop out as the calyx sometimes splits, which gives the plant an untidy look, especially when going over. At this stage the plant often appears untidy even if the calyx has not split. It was raised by Cecil Wyatt of Colehayes, Bovey Tracey in about 1971. It is still quite widely available. The RHS awarded it a C in 1985, an AM in 1986 and a FCC in 1987, all as a border plant. Some growers consider this plant to be of doubtful hardiness, although I have personally not come across this as a problem. Make certain that it is planted in a well-drained position and take cuttings, overwintering the resulting plants under glass, if you have any doubt.

'CRIMSON ACE'　This is either a flat double or semi-double crimson (53A) self with a slight flush of a darker red (60A) on the petals, especially towards the margins. Some flowers have a touch of a pinker colour (57A) at the base of some petals as they enter the throat. The flowers are about 4.5 cm (1.75 in) across and have fringed petals. It is mainly grown as an exhibition plant but may be grown in the border. Introduced by Lindabruce Nurseries before 1967 it is still in cultivation. The RHS awarded it an AM for exhibition blooms in 1967 and a HC in 1968, an AM in 1970 and a FCC in 1975, all as a border plant.

'CRIMSON CLOVE'   Here we are dealing not with one plant but a whole collection of cultivars that have been given this name over the years. The original plant (if there ever was a single plant) goes back to at least Elizabethan times. It is reputed to have probably disappeared from cultivation in Britain and was reintroduced from Dutch stock. There are many claimants to this old name, but it is unlikely that any of them are the original plant even if, indeed, there was one. Like 'Sops-in-Wine', it probably was used for a number of slightly different plants in various parts of the country and at different times. The characteristics that they all claim is that it is a double crimson self with a strong clove scent. (See also 'Old Crimson Clove'.)

'CRIMSON GLORY'   This is one of C.H. Fielder's imperial pinks. The double flowers have a deep red (46A) ground, shaded with a brighter red (45A). They are carried on 30 cm (12 in) stems and are fragrant. The broad petals are finely serrated. It has a long flowering season, from June into the autumn. One of its parents was the Herbert 'Bridesmaid'. The RHS awarded it an AM as an exhibition bloom in 1948 and followed this with an AM in 1950 and a FCC in 1955, both as a border plant. In spite of its previous popularity, it is no longer available. There is also one border carnation with the same name.

'CRIMSON GLOW'   Another of the imperial pinks. This one is similar to 'Crimson Glory'. It is a double with crimson flowers but without the shading. It is a floriferous plant producing many fragrant flowers from June right through to the end of autumn. As with all this group, it was introduced by C.H. Fielder of Lindabruce Nurseries sometime before 1955. The RHS awarded it an AM as an exhibition bloom in 1955 and a HC as a border plant in 1956. It does not appear to be about now. One border carnation and two perpetual-flowering carnations also bear the same name.

'CROCK OF GOLD'   A modern pink with semi-double flowers. They are, unusually, coloured yellow. The plant is not very robust. It was introduced by R. Hubbard of Landscove in about 1987 and is still in cultivation.

'CROSSBILL'   One of the Douglas bird series. This has a double flower of apple-blossom pink and a deep crimson central zone. They flower in June and July, and are borne on 30 cm (12 in) stems.

The flowers are fragrant. It was introduced in about 1950 but does not appear to be extant.

'CROSSWAYS'   A single pink for the rock garden or front of border with mats of grey-green foliage. The flowers are a cerise red (between 66A and 74A) with a very narrow central band of deep maroon (187A), turning to metallic grey as it goes over. The flowers are about 2.5 cm (1 in) across and are noticeably fringed, the petals turning slightly upwards at their tips. They have quite a long flowering period from June into autumn. It can be so floriferous as to flower itself to death. The stems are 10–15 cm (4–6 in) high. Some growers prefer to grow it in a leafy soil. It is probably a hybrid involving *D. gratianopolitanus*. This plant has also been known as 'Ariel'. Whichever has the priority of naming the plant, it is probably best to stick to 'Crossways' as there are already several other pinks called 'Ariel'. It is still available.

'CRUSHED STRAWBERRY'   *see 'Whatfield Crushed Strawberry'*

'C.T. MUSGRAVE'   *see 'Musgrave's Pink'*

'CURLEW'   Another of Douglas' bird series. As with all of them this is also double. The ground colour is lilac rose with a dark crimson centre. The flowers are fragrant. It was introduced in about 1958, but seems to have disappeared. There is also a border carnation with the same name.

'CYCLOPS'   The existing plant that is sometimes seen with this name is in fact 'Whatfield Cyclops' (*qv*) but there are three other pinks listed in *IDR* (one introduced by M. Fenwick sometime before 1952, one by Ladhams of Godalming in 1937, and the third by J. Stormont of Kilbride in about 1928). They all have descriptions similar to 'Whatfield Cyclops' in that they have a rosy pink or rosy crimson ground and a deep crimson eye. A fourth (not listed in the *IDR*) was also in existence at the beginning of the century when Miss Willmott used it as the seed parent of her 'Warley'. None of the four appear to be in cultivation. There are also two border carnations with the same name.

'DABCHICK'   One of Douglas' bird series of pinks. This is a double with a peach-blossom pink ground with a bright carmine ground. The petals are fringed. The flowers are fragrant and borne on 30 cm (12 in) stems during June and July. They do not seem to be around.

'DAD'S CHOICE'   This is a new pink named, possibly, in the hope that it becomes as popular as 'Dad's Favourite'. It is a double with creamy white ground and an orangy-red (39A) eye that just appears in the middle of the petals and fades as it disappears down the throat. The reverse is white. The petals are slightly indented. The flowers are about 4.5 cm (1.75 in) across and are carried on 30 cm (12 in) stems. They have a slight fragrance. The flowering period is quite long. It was raised and introduced by Stephen Bailey of Sway. Breeder's Rights have been put on the plant. The RHS awarded the plant a PC in 1990.

'DAD'S FAVOURITE'   An old but still very popular pink that is widely grown. It is a semi-double or a flat double. The ground colour is white with a velvety maroon (59A) zone and narrow lacing, the latter fading to purple (71A). The white is quite extensive and extends beyond the coloured lacing. The reverse is white tinged with purple. The petals are slightly fringed. The flowers are about 3.8 cm (1.5 in), but sometimes up to 5 cm (2 in), across and borne on 25–30 cm (10–12 in) stems above a mat-forming foliage of a good grey-green colour. It has a short flowering period from June until July. It was discovered by A.J. MacSelf in a garden in Northumberland and could have been raised in Scotland in the eighteenth century. Whether we still have the same plant in cultivation now is open to debate. Certainly there are different versions of the plant about. One of them is undoubtedly 'Paisley Gem' (*qv*) to which it is very similar. This plant has finer flowers than 'Dad's Favourite', the lacing is more uniform and of a darker, almost black colour. The RHS awarded it an AM in 1949 as a border plant. It is sometimes seen under the synonym 'A.J. MacSelf'. Some plants of 'Hope' have been on sale under this name. It is one of the parents of 'Fair Lace' and 'Saint Petroc'.

'DAILY MAIL'   A new double pink with a pure white ground with an orangy-red (42B) eye diffusing into an off-white in the throat. It is also flushed slightly into the white ground colour. The bunched petals have a slight apricot flush to them as they open. It has a slight fragrance. The petals are quite broad and have only a slight indentation. The flowers are up to 5 cm (2 in) in diameter and are borne over a long period. It was introduced by Stephen Bailey of Sway. This plant has Breeder's Rights attached to it.

'DAINTINESS'   One of C.H. Fielder's imperial pinks. This one is double with salmon pink petals. It has a long flowering period from June until late autumn. It was introduced by Fielder's Lindabruce Nurseries of Lancing in 1947. It does not appear to be extant.

'DAINTY DAME'   A dwarf pink for the rock garden. The flowers have a white ground with a maroon eye. It was raised by Mr Fox and introduced by Michael Williams through Ingwersens in the 1980s. Its parents are unknown. It is currently in cultivation.

'DAINTY MAID'   A low-growing pink for the rock garden with interesting colouring. It is a single flower with a purple (74A) ground with a crimson eye and white margins. The flowers are about 2.5 cm (1 in) in diameter. They are carried on 10 cm (4 in) stems. It was introduced by S.T. Byatt in the early 1950s. The RHS awarded it a PC in 1953, a HC in 1955, an AM in 1957 and a FCC in 1959, the last two as a plant for the rock garden. If this plant could be found it would be one worthy of reintroduction.

'DAMASK SUPERB'   This is a lovely old single cultivar fortunately still well-established in cultivation. The flowers have a rich velvet wine (187D) colour with shading off down the throat to a whitish rose pink and to a deeper chestnutty (187A) colour towards the margins. The ground colour is not pure but slightly spotty and uneven. When the flower first opens the colour is really wonderful. The reverse is white diffused with purplish pink. The flowers are 3.2 cm (1.25 in) in diameter and are borne on 15 cm (6 in) stems over grey-green foliage. The petals are fringed and somewhat recurved under their weight. As the flower ages, gaps appear between the petals. It is fragrant.

'DANUM BEAUTY'   A modern double pink with pale pink (paler 50D) ground flushed with white and a red (duller 46B) central zone. The flowers are 5 cm (2 in) across and carried on 25 cm (10 in) stems. The petals are quite broad and slightly fringed. The flowers are slightly fragrant. The plant was raised and introduced by Mrs E. Hudson of Hatfield, Doncaster in 1982. The RHS awarded it an AM as an exhibition plant in 1983 and a HC in 1984 as a border plant.

'DANUM CANDY'   A fancy double pink with a white ground, just touched with pale pink, and marked with flecks and stripes of deep salmon pink (47C). The flowers are up to 5 cm (2 in) across and are carried on 45 cm (18 in) stems. The broad petals are slightly fringed. The flowers are slightly fragrant. The plant was raised and introduced by Mrs E. Hudson of Hatfield, Doncaster in 1983 and is still in cultivation. The RHS awarded it a HC in 1985 and an AM in 1986, both as a border plant.

'DANUM LADY'   A modern semi-double pink with a pink (63C) and a crimson (60B) central zone and lacing. The flowers are up to 3.8 cm (1.5 in) across and are carried on 30 cm (12 in) stems. They are fragrant. The petals are quite narrow and very slightly fringed. The plant was raised and introduced by Mrs E. Hudson of Hatfield, Doncaster in 1983 and is still in cultivation. The RHS awarded it an AM as an exhibition plant in 1985.

'DAPHNE'   One of Allwood's name series of modern pinks. This has a very large flower that looks very positive with its dark eye and simple pink surround. It is a single with a pink (64C) ground that is slightly uneven, striped and blotched with a paler colour, and a maroon (59A) eye, changing to very pale pink or white as it enters the throat. The flowers are 6.35 cm (2.5 in) in diameter and borne on 30–45 cm (12–18 in) stems above a blue-green foliage typical of modern pinks. They are strongly scented. It was introduced by Allwood sometime around 1934 and is still available. It was awarded an AM by the RHS in 1935 as a border plant. There are several border carnations sharing the same name.

'DARTINGTON DOUBLE'   A dwarf compact pink with small 2.5 cm (1 in) semi-double flowers borne on 20 cm (8 in) stems over grey-green foliage. The flowers are light purple (74D) paling towards the throat after the slightest of traces of a slightly darker band. They are fragrant. It was raised at Dartington Hall in the 1980s. It is still available.

'DARTINGTON LACED'   This is a full, but not frilly, double with a pink ground somewhat tinged by the rich ruby (187A) zoning and lacing that diffuse into it and that often only shows as irregular blotches. The flowers are 3.8 cm (1.5 in) in diameter and are fragrant. The petals are just very slightly fringed and have a very fine line of white running round them. It is still extant.

'DARTMOOR FOREST'   A rather sprawling, straggly plant somewhat redeemed by its wonderful deep crimson (53A or 46A) flowers, which are slightly dusky towards the edges and a bit prone to occasional white flecking. They are fully double and clove scented. The flowers are large, 6.4 cm (2.5 in) in diameter, and are carried on 25–30 cm (10–12 in) stems above blue-green, typical modern pink foliage. The heads are a bit heavy and they have the tendency to flop. The petals are fringed. The calyx is a bit weak and occasionally splits. It was introduced by Cecil Wyatt of Colehayes, Bovey Tracey in 1978 and is still available. It was awarded an AM as an exhibition plant in 1981 by the RHS and then another AM as a border plant in the following year.

'DAVID'   One of Allwood's modern pinks in the name series. This is a double, coloured a glowing scarlet (45A). Some flowers are slightly streaked with a darker colour and there is the occasional white fleck. The reverse is a dull scarlet. The flowers are 5 cm (2 in) across and are carried on 30–38 cm (12–15 in) erect stems above a blue-green foliage. The flowers are slightly fragrant. It arose as a sport from 'Ian' and is currently still available. The RHS awarded it an AM in 1971 and a FCC in 1979, both as a border plant.

'DAWN'   *see 'Whatfield Dawn'*

'DAYDAWN'   *see 'Prince of Carrick'*

'DEBUTANTE'   (1) A modern pink with double orangy pink (33C) flowers. The reverse is a paler version of the main colour. There is no scent. The flowers are 3.2–5 cm (1.25–2 in) across and are borne on 20–25 cm (8–10 in) stems. The flower is contained in a dumpty calyx that has the tendency to split. It was introduced by Allwood in 1966 but does not now seem to be available. The RHS awarded it a HC as a border plant in 1967. Although Allwood originally thought of this as a border pink, they subsequently decided (according to later catalogues) that it was more like an alpine pink.
(2) The *IDR* lists another pink with the same name: a single with a pink ground and a dark eye. It was introduced before 1952.
(3) There are also two perpetual-flowering carnations with the same name.

'DELICATA'   (1) This is a single-flowered pink with a pink (70D) colour that pales to a white in the throat. It also fades to almost white as it goes over. The petals have gaps between, are curled up along the margins and are deeply fringed. The flowers are 2.5 cm (1 in) across and carried on 20 cm (8 in) stems held well above the grey-green foliage. The flowers have a clove scent and appear in June and July. It is extant but not currently available commercially. Sometimes it is seen labelled as 'Delicatus'.

(2) The *IDR* lists three other pinks with this name. The first, introduced by C. Turner of Slough sometime around 1861, was a lilac pink and was awarded a FCC. This might be the same plant as several of his introductions, most notably 'Mrs Sinkins', have lasted the course.

(3) The other two were one with a white ground tinged red and possibly introduced by R. Dean of Ealing in about 1894, and a later one in 1907 by P. Schwarze of Nossen, Germany, which was a double pale rose self.

(4) There are also six border carnations, one perpetual-flowering carnation and one malmaison carnation, all with the same name.

'DELIGHT' An annual strain of pinks raised by Allwood by crossing 'Sweet Wivelsfield' and 'Roysii'.

'DELMONDEN FAIRY' This is a double pink with a shrimp pink ground and a narrow band of scarlet near the centre. It is a very upright plant. The leaves are close-jointed and upright. It was probably raised in the mid-eighteenth century and was discovered in the garden at Delmonden, near Hawkhurst. Will Ingwersen misspelt the name as 'Delmondham Fairy', which may have caused some uncorrected labels. It does not seem to be extant in spite of Moreton's enthusiasm for it in the 1950s. He claims that the flowers are similar to 'Bridesmaid' (2) except that they are smaller.

'DENIS' An Allwood modern pink in their name series. This is a double flowered form that is a rich cerise (brighter 53A) self. Unfortunately it is not very attractive when it goes over and regular dead-heading is required. The flowers vary in size, but some are large, up to 5.8 cm (2.25 in) in diameter. They are carried on stems up to 38 cm (15 in) above a light blue-green foliage that is almost silver in some lights. The petals are coarsely toothed. The smaller flowers are almost flat and the larger ones have some petals that stand up in the centre. The calyx is not very strong and does occasionally split. The flowers have a slight fragrance. It was introduced by Allwood in about 1959. The plant is still reasonably available. The RHS awarded it a C in 1961, a HC in the same year and an AM in 1963, all as border plants. The name is sometimes seen as 'Dennis'.

'DENNY' Another Allwood modern pink and one that could be confused with the previous plant, but only in name, as it is a single with a rose pink (65B) ground and a crimson (185B) central zone. The flowers are large (5.8 cm (2.25 in) across) and fragrant. The petals are very broad and fringed. This is a very floriferous, compact plant with a strong upright habit. It was introduced by Allwood in about 1946 and awarded an AM that year as a border plant. It is not currently offered commercially.

'DEREK' By choosing Christian names Allwood seem to have an endless supply of names for their modern pinks. This one is a double with a crimson (59B) ground, flushed rose red (redder 57A). The flowers are 5 cm (2 in) across and carried on 28 cm (11 in) stems. It is fragrant and flowers from June until the late autumn on compact, very free-flowering plants. The broad petals are finely serrated. It was introduced by Allwood in 1948. The RHS awarded the plant an AM as an exhibition bloom in 1948 and followed that with a C in 1952 and a HC in 1957, both as a border plant.

'DESMOND' This is a name that Allwood seem to have missed. However, it is a modern pink selected and named by Jack Gingel from seedlings of unknown parentage raised by Mrs Desmond Underwood of the old Ramparts Nursery, Colchester. It is somewhere between a semi-double and a double. The colour is a dusky velvet crimson (53A) with a duller reverse. The duskiness is particularly noticeable towards the margins of the petals, which are slightly fringed. The colour is somewhat spoilt by the occasional white spotting. The flower is fragrant, 4.5 cm (1.75 in) across and carried on 20 cm (8 in) stems. It was introduced in about 1978 and although still around, does not appear to be offered commercially. One border carnation also has the same name.

'DEVON BLUSH' One of a series of modern pinks that has appeared in recent years. The double flowers have a rose-pink (56D) ground with a wide bright red (52A) zone that diffuses with spots into the ground. They are carried on shortish stems on 12 cm (5 in) long above a light green foliage. The petals are fringed and the flower has a slight fragrance. It was raised from unknown parents by H.R. Whetman of Houndspool in 1985. It is available.

'DEVON CREAM'   Probably the most popular of the series, this plant has double flowers with a yellow (12D) ground, flushed with magenta (68D). It is unfortunately not fragrant. The margins of the petals are fringed and the whole flower resembles a carnation rather than a pink. The flower stems are 15 cm (6 in) long. It was raised from unknown parents by H.R. Whetman of Houndspool in 1985. It is currently available.

'DEVON FLAME'   Another double in the same series. This one is a mandarin red self. As with the others it was raised by H.R. Whetman of Houndspool, this time in 1988. It is currently available.

'DEVON GLOW'   This member of the series has flowers of an almost luminous mauvy-purple (74B) fading to a lighter colour towards the margins. It is a flattish double with slightly fringed edges to the petals. There is a strong scent. It has a long flowering season. It was introduced from unknown parentage by H.R. Whetman of Houndspool in 1985. It is currently available.

'DEW'   A dwarf plant for the rock garden or border's edge. It is a single with deeply fringed petals and of a pale pink colour with a greenish eye. The flowers are very fragrant and carried on 23 cm (9 in) stems. The flowering season is a long one, from July into autumn. It was introduced by Allwood in about 1932 but seems to have disappeared, more is the pity, as it seems a good plant to have.

'DEWDROP'   Allwood have the habit of choosing names similar to those they have already used (and in some cases even using the same name twice). It must not be confused with 'Dew', although it is again a plant for the rock garden or front of border. This one is also a single, but has white flowers with a pale yellowish green eye. The flowers are very fragrant and are carried on upright 15 cm (6 in) stems over a long period, from June until late autumn. It was introduced around 1932 and is still available, although the plants I have seen are very similar to those in circulation (probably incorrectly) as 'Wink'.

'DIANA'   (1) An Alan Bloom plant from the 1930s. It is a deep rose-pink with a crimson central zone. Its flower stems are about 15 cm (6 in) high. The flowering season is mainly in June and July, but some blooms continue to appear into the autumn. It seems to have disappeared from cultivation.

(2) Allwoods introduced an alpine pink with this name in the 1950s. It is a single with a magenta ground and a darker eye.

(3) C.H. Herbert of Acocks Green raised a double 'Diana' in the early 1920s with a white ground, crimson zoning and lacing. It does not now seem to be around.

(4) There were three other pinks with this name, all of which must surely have disappeared. For the record they were a rosy-pink double introduced by R.P. Brotherston of East Lothian at the turn of the century, one with a white ground and purple lacing, introduced by Parker in the middle of the last century, and another with a white ground but with bright rose lacing, introduced by Smith at about the same time.

(5) There were also nine border carnations and five perpetual-flowering carnations with the same name.

'DIANA JOY'   A semi-double pink for the rock garden. The flowers have a pinkish purple ground and a purple (59A) central zone fading at the edges. They are 2.5 cm (1 in) across and are carried on 10 cm (4 in) stems. There is a slight fragrance. The plant was raised by S.T. Byatt of Hampton. The RHS awarded it a HC as a rock garden plant in 1971.

'DIANE'   A very popular modern pink from the Allwood stable. This double has a dark salmon pink (39A) ground, noticeably paler towards the centre. It pales and becomes a bit blotchy as the flower ages, particularly towards the margins. The reverse is paler becoming white at the base of the petals. The petal margins have small serrations. The flowers are up to 6.4 cm (2.5 in) across and are carried over a long season on somewhat floppy stems 30 cm (12 in) long. The foliage is typical of modern pinks, somewhat unrefined. It was introduced by Allwood in 1964 as a sport from that mother of many modern pinks, 'Doris'. Curiously their catalogue lists it as deep red, which is not borne out by any of the plants they offer. There is another pink bearing this name, although it has probably been long since forgotten, at least in

'Diane'

Britain. According to the *IDR* it was introduced by Rivoire of Lyons in about 1910 and was a lilac pink self. There are also four border carnations and one perpetual-flowering carnation bearing the same name. 'Jessica' is one of its offspring.

'DIPPER' One of Douglas' bird series. This is a double with apple-blossom pink flowers and a central zone of deep blood red (*IDR* waxing lyrical for once calls it 'ox-blood red'). The margins are very serrated. The flowers are large and carried on 38 cm (15 in) stems during June and July. Introduced in about 1950 but, alas, it seems to be no more.

'DOCTOR DANGER' A curiously named pink briefly offered by Hopleys in 1990.

'DONIZETTI' A once popular single pink in the composers series. The flower colour is a lovely bright red with a darker eye. The large flowers darken as they age. They are fragrant and have fringed margins to the petals. The flowering stems are about 23 cm (9 in) long. The foliage is fine and grey-green in colour. According to the *IDR* it was raised by R.V. Pritchard of Bayswater, Australia in about 1922. The RHS awarded it an AM in 1922. It is still just in cultivation, but is not very easy to propagate, probably due to its age.

'DORIS' This is almost certainly the most widely-grown pink, used both in the garden and in the cut-flower trade. It is a modern variety raised by Allwood in 1945, when it was selected from a batch of seedlings of unknown parentage. The story goes that Montague Allwood did not think that the plant was worthwhile when he first saw it and so threw it on the compost heap. It was rescued by a member of staff and multiplied up until there were sufficient to plant up a drift in the nursery. When Mr Allwood saw it in this quantity he at last realised its true value and to emphasise this he named it after his wife. The flowers are double and coloured pink (38C) with a darker, salmon pink (44D) central zone. The flowers are about 5 cm (2 in) in diameter and are borne on 30 cm (12 in) stems that tend to be a bit floppy. The petals have slightly fringed margins. It has a good scent and goes on flowering for a very long time, from June until winter. The foliage is a silver grey and has the coarseness typical of most modern pinks. The true 'Doris' is sterile and produces neither pollen nor seed, but 30 years after its introduction it started giving rise to a number of sports. Examples of these include 'Barker's Beauty', 'Houndspool Ruby', 'Jester' and 'Laura', as well as those carrying Doris as part of their name. It is very widely available and, although often sneered

'Doris'

at by devotees of old-fashioned pinks, it is still an extremely good plant. It is also very tough; there are records of it even surviving after being submerged under 60 cm (2 ft) of sea water for a couple of hours, which is not usually considered the best of conditions for growing pinks. The RHS awarded it an AM in 1954 and a FCC in 1956, both as border plants. Allwood did introduce another 'Doris' in the early 1930s. This was a salmon pink single, zoned with pale crimson.

'DORIS ELITE'   A variant of 'Doris'. This semi-double to double is a very pale pink, almost white, with a salmon (47B) eye, fading to a pale pink as it disappears down the throat. The flowers are 5 cm (2 in) across and are carried on stems 43 cm (17 in) long. They have quite a strong scent of cloves. The calyx is not very strong and occasionally splits. The foliage is typical of most modern pinks. It was introduced by Allwood in 1978. The RHS awarded it a PC as an exhibition plant in 1980 and an AM as a border plant in 1983.

'DORIS MAJESTIC'   Another sport of 'Doris'. This time it is a semi-double to flat double that is a bright reddish (43D flushed with 43C) pink, very close to the colour of the zone in 'Doris', paling slightly towards the centre. It seems prone to the occasional white flecking and fades to a paler colour as it goes over. The petals are slightly fringed. The flowers are 5 cm (2 in) in diameter and are carried on 30–40 cm (12 – 16 in) stems above quite compact clumps of typical blue-green modern pink foliage. They are slightly fragrant. The calyx is not over strong and occasionally splits. It was introduced by Allwood in about 1980. The RHS awarded it a PC in 1981 and a C in 1983.

'DORIS SUPREME'   This is quite similar to 'Doris' (pink (49C) with a salmon (50B) central zone) except that the eye is more broken and there are occasional flecks and splashes of the deeper colour (54A) on the petals. The flecks are more purple (54A) in colour. The flowers are semi-double to flat double, 5 cm (2 in) across, and borne on slightly floppy, 30 cm (12 in) stems above typical blue-green modern pink foliage. The petals are fringed. There is a slight scent. When newly opened the flower looks quite fresh, but it soon begins to look a bit messy with its two or three colours and its doubleness. It was introduced by Allwood in 1978 and is still available. It was awarded an AM in 1980 as an exhibition plant and a C in 1982, HC in 1983 and an AM in 1984, all as a border plant.

'DORIS VARLOW'   This has a double flower coloured a lovely blush pink (49D) flushed with darker and paler pinks. The reverse is slightly darker in colour, especially towards the margins, and includes the odd stripe. The flowers are slightly scented. The petals are slightly indented. The flowers are about 4.5 cm (1.75 in) across and are carried on 35–40 cm (14–16 in) stems above grey-green foliage typical in habit of the modern pinks. It was raised by E.W. Varlow of Stanford-le-Hope, Essex in 1976 and can still be seen. The RHS awarded it an AM in 1979 and a FCC in 1990, both as an exhibition bloom, and a HC in 1982, an AM in 1983 and a FCC in 1984, all as a garden plant.

'DOROTHEA'   An Allwood modern double pink that has a pink (48D) ground and a central zone of red (47B). The flowers are up to 5.8 cm (2.25 in) across and are carried on 25–28 cm (10–11 in) stems. They have a slight fragrance. The RHS awarded the plant a C in 1969 as a border plant.

'DOROTHY'   Introduced in 1914, this is one of the earliest of the Allwood modern pinks. The flowers are double with a violet red ground and a very dark, almost black central zone. They are scented. It was around after the Second World War but seems to have now disappeared. There are also four border carnations and three perpetual-flowering carnations sharing the same name.

'DOROTHY MANN'   *see 'Whatfield Dorothy Mann'*

'DOUBLE DEVON'   This is a fragrant double with a purple ground and a deep maroon eye. It is still extant.

'DOUBLE RUBY PINK'   This is an old cultivar from Oxford Botanic Gardens that is probably the same as 'Bat's Double Red'.

'DRAKE'   This is one of the Douglas bird series rather than one named after the naval hero. It is a double with an attractive deep red ground and a dark, maroon central zone. It has a moderate scent, and flowers in June and July on 30 cm (12 in) stems. It was introduced in about 1938. There is also one border carnation with the same name.

'DUBARRY'   There are two, or possibly three, pinks with this name.

(1) Raised and introduced by Alan Bloom in 1928, this double-flowered form has a rosy-lilac ground deepening to a crimson central zone. The stems are about 15 cm (6 in) high. It was selected as a seedling from 'Prichard's Variety'.

(2) The other was introduced by Hollycroft Nursery in about 1950. This was a pink self. Unfortunately no further information is available about this plant but it could be the same as (3).

(3) A flat double or semi-double mauvy-pink (73A touched with 75A) self grown as a rock garden plant. The fragrant flowers are 2–2.5 cm (0.75–1 in) across and are held on 15 cm (6 in) stems above thick mats of grey-green foliage. The main flush of flowers is in June and July, but it continues with odd flowers until the autumn. An increasing number of nurseries seem to be offering this plant.

(4) There are also two perpetual-flowering carnations with this name.

'DUCHESS OF ANCASTER'   (1) A pink of historic importance although it has long since disappeared. It was the first pink that could be properly called laced in the modern sense. The flowers were white with a purple eye and lacing. It was raised in 1770 by James Major of Lewisham, the gardener to the Duchess of Ancaster. From it he raised an important laced series of seedlings, including 'Lady Stoverdale', which was one of the first popular laced pinks. It is sometimes misspelt as the 'Duchess of Lancaster'.

(2) The duchess was obviously a popular person as no less than another three pinks and three border carnations were named after her.

'DUCHESS OF FIFE'   This is a single-flowered, rose pink self. The flowers are large and are carried on 30 cm (12 in) stems over a long period, from June into autumn. They are fragrant. The plant was introduced by Ladhams of Godalming around 1940 and is still in existence.

'DUCHESS OF LANCASTER'   *see 'Duchess of Ancaster'*

'DUNLIN'   Another of the Douglas bird series. This one is a double with a white ground and a carmine centre. The flowers were fragrant. It was introduced in 1952.

'DUNNOCK'   Yet another in the Douglas bird series. It is a fragrant double with a blush pink

ground, and a dark red central zone and lacing. It was introduced by Douglas of Great Bookham in 1958.

'DUSKY'   An Allwood introduction, this is a double with a pink (62B) ground and a raspberry red (59B) eye. The flowers are 3.8 cm (1.5 in), or more, across and appear on 30 cm (12 in) stems in June and July. They are fragrant with a clove scent. The petals are quite noticeably fringed. The calyx is weak and has a tendency to split. The foliage is grey-green and the plant is vigorous, yet compact. It was introduced in 1945 and is reputed to be a cross between an Allwood modern pink and the 'Old Fringed Pink'. Plants are still around. The RHS awarded it a HC in 1951 and a AM in 1955, both as a border plant. It has given rise to the sport 'Ice Queen'. There is also one border carnation with the same name.

'DUTCH DOLL'   This is an old pink from Lancashire. The flowers have a white ground striped and slightly edged with pink. They are about 2.5 cm (1 in) across and the petals are fringed. It was extant in the 1950s but has since disappeared.

'EARL OF CARRICK'   Margery Fish's name for 'Prince of Carrick'.

'EARL OF ESSEX'   An old-fashioned pink from the nineteenth century. It is a fragrant double with a lavender pink (75A) ground and a slight trace of a deeper (74B) eye. The flowers turn almost to white as they go over. The petals are deeply fringed, not just on the outer edges, but almost all round, giving the flower a frilly appearance. It is a very blowsy and untidy flower as it erupts from the calyx, making the flower very loose and exposing the greenish white throat. The flowers are 5 cm (2 in) across and carried on 20 cm (8 in) stems. The foliage forms good blue-green mats with not too coarse a leaf. Will Ingwersen erroneously describes it from a catalogue as a single white, vividly splashed with maroon, but admits he did not grow it. This may mean there are plants of this description around that carry the name of the 'Earl of Essex'. Another confusion is that plants of 'Earl of Essex' are sometimes referred to as 'Excelsior' and vice versa. The latter is generally a much larger flower.

'ECHO'   One of the Allwoodii alpines. This is a single with a ground variously described as red magenta, salmon rose and crimson lake, all agreeing that the eye is a darker colour. The flowers are slightly fragrant and have noticeably toothed petals. It flowers over a long period, from June until late autumn, on 15 cm (6 in) stems. The foliage is very silvery. It was introduced by Allwood around 1933 but unfortunately does not seem to be around. There are also two border carnations bearing the same name.

'EDGAR TICKLE'   A modern double self of a shell pink (43D) colour flushed slightly darker (47C). It has a slight clove scent. It was raised by E.A. Tickle of Purley shortly before 1973. The RHS awarded it a PC in 1973 as an exhibition plant, and a C in 1976 and a HC as a border plant in 1981. It is also known as 'Miss Jane'.

'EDNA'   This is a double modern pink much in the mode of 'Doris' except that the colours are darker. The ground is a rose pink (62A touched with 61D) and the eye a red wine stain (60A). It is almost cerise when it first comes out. The petals are only very slightly fringed. The flowers are up to 5 cm (2 in) across. It flowers over a long period, from June into autumn, on 30–38 cm (12–15 in) stems. The flowers are very fragrant. The foliage is blue-green and is typical in form of modern pinks. It was introduced by Allwood in about 1958 and is still grown. The RHS awarded it a HC as a garden plant in 1967.

'EDWARD'   Another of the Allwood modern pinks. This is a double with a crimson-maroon (60A overlaid with 59A) ground touched with a medium pink (52D) and with a fine pink (66D) edge to the petals. They have a clove fragrance and a long flowering period from June into autumn, the 5 cm (2 in) flowers are borne on 30 cm (12 in) stems. The petals are fringed. It was introduced by Allwood in 1944 and is still around. The RHS awarded it a C in 1951, a HC in 1952, an AM in 1953 and a FCC in 1977, all as a border plant.

'EILEEN'   Yet another Allwood modern pink in their name series. This one is a single with very pale pink, almost white flowers, with a central crimson (59A) zone. The flowers are up to 5.8 cm (2.25 in) across and being single tend to flop a bit, particularly as they age. The margins of the petals are serrated. The flowers are very fragrant and appear from June into autumn on 30 cm (12 in) stems. It was introduced in 1927 and is still grown, especially for showing purposes. There is one border carnation with the same name.

'ELF'   One of Allwoodii alpine pinks, it is a single flower with rose-red (57B) petals. The flowers are 2.5 cm (1 in) across and carried on 15 cm (6 in) stems over a long period. The foliage is a good silver-grey. It was introduced by Allwood in about 1946 and first put up for award the same year. Although it seems to have been a good plant, it unfortunately appears to have disappeared. The RHS awarded it a HC in 1948 as a border plant.

'ELIZABETH'   (1) A scented double modern pink with a pale pink ground. The stems are 30 cm (12 in) long. It has a long flowering period, like so many of the Allwood pinks. It was introduced in about 1922.

(2) This is a short stemmed (7.5 cm (3 in)) pink for the rock garden. It is a double with a pale pink (65D) ground and a crimson-maroon (59A) central ring. The flowers are about 3.2 cm (1.25 in) wide. They are strongly fragrant. The broad petals are serrated. The plant was introduced by S.T. Byatt of Chippenham somewhere around 1955. The RHS awarded it a HC in 1955 as a border plant, and an AM in 1956 and a FCC in 1960 as a rock garden plant.

(3) *IDR* lists two other pinks named 'Elizabeth'. Both are simply given as purple and as being introduced pre-1845. One was introduced by Stone and the other by Willmer. If either is still around it will be impossible to identify them from available information. As one might imagine, this is a popular name and there are also nine border carnations and two perpetual-flowering carnations bearing it.

'ELIZABETH HART'   *see 'Whatfield Elizabeth Hart'*

'ELSENHAM SEEDLING'   This single pink has a large flower with a pink ground and a dark inner zone. It flowers in late summer on 30 cm (12 in) stems. It was introduced in about 1949 but seems to have disappeared, at least under this name.

'EMBER'   A modern semi-double pink with a pink (55D) ground overlaid with salmon red (44D). The flowers are up to 4.5 cm (1.75 in) across and carried on 18 cm (7 in) stems. They have a slight fragrance. The plant has a very compact habit. It was raised by Mrs E.L. Todd of Kemsing. The RHS awarded it a C in 1963 and a HC in 1964, both as a border plant.

'EMERALD'   A pink from the middle of the last century. It had a white ground and a red central zone and lacing. It had small leaves. The plant was still in existence in the 1950s but seems to have disappeared since.

'EMILE PARÉ'   Mule pinks are not as popular as they once were, but this plant is still quite commonly grown. It has clusters of double flowers that are a pale pink flushed with a darker, salmon pink (54C), which gives it its main colour. This pink is well set off by the fresh green foliage. One of its attractions is the strong scent. It also has the advantage of a long flowering season, from June well into autumn. The flowers are up to 3.2 cm (1.25 in) across and are carried on branching stems that are about 20–25 cm (8–10 in) long. The petals are fringed. It is not a very long-lived plant and, as with many of the mules, can flower itself to death, so cuttings should be taken regularly. Sometimes odd flowers are magenta or are streaked or splashed with it, possibly as a form of reversion to something in its ancestry. André Paré raised it at his nursery in Orléans, France in about 1840. It is generally assumed that D. barbatus formed one of the parents and, certainly, its influence can be seen in the clustered flowers and the foliage. The other parent is unknown but was likely to have been an old pink derived from D. plumarius. We are fortunate in that this delightful pink is still safely in cultivation.

'EMILY'   A modern double pink with a rose-red (61D) and a ruby red (59A) central zone. The flowers are 5 cm (2 in) across and are carried on 36 cm (14 in) stems. It was raised by F.R. McQuown of London in the 1940s. It was awarded a HC by the RHS as a border plant in 1948.

'EMILY WHELAN'   A modern double pink that is a white self. The flowers are about 5 cm (2 in) wide and are carried on 30 cm (12 in) stems. They are fragrant. The broad petals are fringed. The plant was raised by S.O. Stroud of Freeland in the early 1970s. The RHS awarded it a C as a plant for the border.

'EMMA ALICE'   A modern semi-double pink with a very pale pink ground, spotted and streaked with pinkish red (50A to 50B). The flowers are about 4.5 cm (1.75 in) across and are carried on 36 cm (14 in) stems. The broad petals are very slightly fringed. The flowers are not fragrant. The plant was introduced by Steven Bailey of Sway in

about 1985. When the plant was first introduced it was known as 'Emma Bailey' but was changed as this was an invalid name (there was already a perpetual-flowering carnation with this name).

'EMMA BAILEY'   see 'Emma Alice'

'EMPEROR'   (1) A double pink that is a deep crimson self. The fragrant flowers are deeply fringed and are carried on 30 cm (12 in) stems. They flower in June and July. It was in existence after the Second World War but seems to have disappeared.
   (2) Another plant of this name was introduced by Ladhams of Godalming. This is a semi-double with a rose red ground and a maroon central zone. The flowers are 4.5 cm (1.75 in) across and are borne on 30 cm (12 in) stems. It was introduced in about 1937. The RHS awarded it an AM as a border plant in 1939. This plant no longer seems to be in cultivation, although it was in the past thought to be the same plant as 'Bat's Double Red', which is still to be seen in gardens.
   (3) The IDR lists two other pinks with this name. One is given as 'laced' and introduced by Girdham sometime around 1798; the other as introduced by T. Davey of Chelsea in about 1820 without any description. The chances of either of these re-appearing and muddying the waters seem very remote indeed.
   (4) There are also eight border carnations and one perpetual-flowering carnation all sharing this name.

'ENID'   (1) One of the Allwood modern pinks. This is a single blush-pink with maroon lacing. It was introduced in about 1930 and was sent to Wisley for trial in 1938, but appears to have failed to achieve an award. It does not seem to be around.
   (2) There is a rock garden plant with the same name. This is also a single but this time with carmine-rose flowers on 12.5 cm (5 in) stems. It flowers over a long period. This too seems to have disappeared from cultivation.
   (3) There are also one border carnation and one perpetual-flowering carnation with this name.

'ENID ANDERSON'   This is a sprawling plant with upright flowers that are between semi-double and double, with quite deeply fringed petals that give them a frilly appearance. They have a crimson (53A) ground with a dark maroon (187A) eye. The flowers are up to 4–5 cm (1.75 in) in diameter and carried on 30 cm (12 in) stems. The calyx is weak and occasionally splits. There is no detectable scent. The foliage is a blue-green tinged with purple. The date of origin is unknown, but it is thought to be this century. It is a pretty flower and luckily still available. In some respects it is similar to 'Old Clove Red', except that it is redder, slightly smaller and lacks the distinct perfume of the older plant.

'ERNEST BALLARD'   A double named after a great plantsman who introduced many valuable garden plants. This one was thought very highly of, but seems to have unfortunately disappeared. It had deep rose-pink (pinker 63B) double flowers with a very strong clove scent. It was floriferous, the 2.5 cm (1 in) blooms flowering on 15–23 cm (6–9 in) stems during June and July. The silver-grey foliage is held in stiff tufts forming dense mats. It was raised by Ernest Ballard at Colwall, near Malvern in about 1943. It was awarded an AM in 1943.

'ESTHER'   (1) Yet another of the Allwood name modern pinks. This one is between semi-double and double. The colour is a pinky-white ground and a maroon eye. Towards the margins the ground is flushed with a darker pink. The flowers are very fragrant and appear from June until the autumn on 30 cm (12 in) stems. It also goes under the name of 'Bedales', or rather went under the name, as it does not seem to be around any more.

(2) There was also a pink of this name introduced by C. Turner of Slough (of 'Mrs Sinkins' fame) in about 1852. The only details now known about it was that it was rose in colour.

(3) There are also five border carnations and two perpetual-flowering carnations with the same name.

'ETHEL HURFORD'   This is a double pink with cerise-pink flowers carried on 30 cm (12 in) stems. It flowers in June and July.

'EVA'   (1) A double flower with a rose-pink (pinker 63B) ground and a crimson (185B) central zone. It is a compact plant with flowering stems only growing to about 23 cm (9 in) above the silver-grey foliage. The flowers are 5 cm (2 in) across. It is very fragrant. It was introduced by Allwood prior to 1947 but seems to have disappeared. It flowers in June and July. The RHS awarded it a HC as a border plant in 1949.

(2) There was a plant with a reddish purple

flower introduced by C. Turner of Slough in about 1867 that also bore the name 'Eva'. There are also two border carnations and three perpetual-flowering carnations with the same name.

'EVE'   Not to be confused with the previous entry, Allwood also produce this plant. It is also double, short-growing and has salmon-pink (49C) flowers, but this time it has deeper colour veining. The flowers are up to 5.8 cm (2.25 in) across and carried on 30–36 cm (12–14 in) stems. They have a slight fragrance. It was introduced prior to 1969 and is still available. The RHS awarded it a HC as a garden plant in 1969. There is also one border carnation and one perpetual-flowering carnation with the same name; it is surprising that this name has not engendered more.

'EXCELLENT'   A semi-double pink from the middle of the nineteenth century. It has a white ground and a red central zone and lacing. It has small leaves. It was in existence in the 1950s but has now disappeared from cultivation as far as I know.

'EXCELSIOR'   (1) 'Mrs Sinkins' has produced a few sports and this is one of them. It is a light mauve self that changes to pale green as it descends into the throat, which is readily exposed as the calyx splits. Sometimes there is a narrow band of purple in the centre of the flower. The flower is double with deeply fringed petals that gives the head a frilly look, especially with the split calyx. In fact, the flower opens so wide that individual petals are displayed almost in the manner of *Centaurea montana*. It is fragrant, like its parent. The flowers are up to 7.5 cm (3 in) wide when split and are carried on 23–25 cm (9–10 in) stems in June and July. The plant is still widely cultivated. Confusion reigns as to whether this is the same as 'Pink Mrs Sinkins'. There do seem to be several versions of the latter currently in cultivation, and the large ones with the slightly dark central band could well be the same as 'Excelsior', whereas the smaller version (same size as 'Mrs Sinkins') with or without the central band could well be the true 'Pink Mrs Sinkins'. Further confusion is caused by the plant's similarity to the 'Earl of Essex', which has a smaller flower. With so many versions around it is unlikely that there will ever be any consensus, and many will continue to use 'Excelsior' as a synonym for 'Pink Mrs Sinkins'.

(2) There were two other pinks with this name, neither of which are likely to still be around, or if

they are, not under these names. A laced-red one was introduced by R. Marris of Leicester in 1871, and a double with a rose ground and a maroon centre was introduced from France in the 1920s. There are also two border carnations and one perpetual-flowering carnation with the same name.

'EXQUISITE'   see *'Show Exquisite'*. (There are also four border carnations, three perpetual-flowering carnations and one malmaison carnation with this name.)

'FAIR ALEX'   A double with white ground and scarlet markings. The flowers are scented and have serrated petals. The plant is up to 36 cm (14 in). It was raised by D.F. Fairweather of Chelmsford in 1987 from unknown parents.

'FAIR BECCY'   A flat double or semi-double with a very pale pink ground overlaid with a shell pink. It pales towards the centre. The flowers are about 5 cm (2 in) in diameter and are carried on 30 cm (12 in) stems. They have slightly serrated petals. It is fragrant. It was raised by D.F. Fairweather of Chelmsford in 1988 as a cross between 'Jenny Wyatt' and 'Christopher'. It is in cultivation. Sometimes the name is spelt 'Fair Becky'.

'FAIR CARL'   A double white self carried on up to 38 cm (15 in) high stems. The flowers are scented and the petals are serrated. It was raised by D.F. Fairweather of Chelmsford in 1987 as a cross between 'Show Enchantress' and 'Show Glory'. It is still in cultivation.

'FAIR FOLLY'   This is an old pink, possibly with seveeenth century origins. It is a single-flowered form with a white or occasionally pale pink (56C) ground, and a crushed raspberry (58C) central zone and narrow lacing, the two being joined by a very narrow bar creating two large white or pink eyes on each petal. The red is dotted with pale pink giving it a dry speckled appearance. The flowers are quite wide for a single pink, being 3.8 cm (1.5 in) across. The petals are only very slightly fringed, almost unnoticeably so. The flower stems are from 20–25 cm (8–10 in) tall and are upright in growth. In spite of its age it is still in cultivation. Sometimes spelt 'Fair Folley'.

'FAIR FREYA'   A double with a rose pink ground and a maroon central zone. The flowers are 3.8 cm (1.5 in) across and carried on 23 cm (9 in) stems. The petals have smooth margins. The flower is scented. It was raised by D.F. Fairweather of Chelmsford in about 1988 from unknown parents. It is in cultivation.

'FAIR JAIME'   A semi-double with a rose-pink ground, and a central zone and lacing of maroon. The flowers are scented and petals are serrated. It is about 30 cm (12 in) tall. It was raised by D.F. Fairweather of Chelmsford in 1980 from unknown parents and is still in cultivation.

'FAIR JESSICA'   A double pink with a pale salmon ground and deeper salmon flecks and lines. The petals are only slightly indented and the flowers are scented. They are carried on 30 cm (12 in) stems. It was raised by D.F. Fairweather of Chelmsford in 1987 as a cross between 'Show Enchantress' and 'Show Glory'. It is still in cultivation.

'FAIR JOHN'   Another in the name series from D.F. Fairweather. This one is a double orange-scarlet self. The flowers are about 5 cm (2 in) across and are carried on 36 cm (14 in) stems. It is scented and the petals have smooth margins. It was raised in about 1988 with 'Christopher' and 'Allen's Huntsman' as parents. It is in cultivation.

'FAIR LACE'   A low plant with semi-double flowers of a white ground, covered by a deep maroon central zone and a very thin lacing of the same colour. The flowers are 3.8 cm (1.5 in) across and are carried on 20 cm (8 in) stems. The petals are serrated and the flowers are scented. It was raised in 1987 by D.F. Fairweather of Chelmsford as a cross between 'Dad's Favourite' and 'Fair Tina' and is still in cultivation.

'FAIR LADY'   This is a double pink for the rock garden with a light cerise (57C) ground, splashed with a deeper colour (57A), with a dark maroon centre. The flowers are up to 2.5 cm (1 in) wide carried on 7.5 cm (3 in) stems. They have a slight scent. The plant was raised by S.T. Byatt of Hampton in the 1960s. The RHS awarded it a C in 1966, an A in 1967 and a FCC in 1971, all as a rock garden plant.

'FAIR LOUISE'   A double pink with a red ground flushed with purple when it first opens. The flowers are up to 4.5 cm (1.75 in) across and borne on stems 25 cm (10 in) high. They are scented and the petals are serrated. It was raised by D.F. Fairweather of Chelmsford in 1988 as a cross between 'Christopher' and 'Allen's Huntsman'. It is still in cultivation.

'FAIR MAID OF KENT' A very old variety mentioned by Parkinson in 1629. This has a white ground and is powdered purple. It is also called 'Russling Robin'. It does not appear to still be in cultivation.

'FAIR ROSAMUND' This is a single flowered dianthus with a salmon pink ground decorated with a red central zone and lacing. It is very fragrant and has a long flowering season from June into autumn. It was introduced by Douglas of Great Bookham in 1924 but, alas, is not still in cultivation, which is a pity as it would be worth growing for the name alone.

'FAIR TINA' The final plant in D.F. Fairweather's 'Fair' series. This is a double white self that turns cream as it opens. The petals have smooth margins and the flowers are scented. The flowers are carried on 30 cm (12 in) stems. It was raised in 1987 as a seedling of 'Allen's Ballerina' and an un-named seedling, and is still in cultivation.

'FAITH' Another case of Allwood using the same name for two different plants. They are both modern pinks.

(1) This is a double flower with a dark pink ground, a maroon zone and red lacing. The flowers are fragrant and the petals fringed. This is a small flowered form, but it was the first of the laced pinks that Allwood introduced (in 1946). It flowers from June well into autumn. The RHS awarded it an AM as a border plant in 1951. It is not now commercially available.

(2) This was a semi-double, creamy pink in colour. It was introduced by Allwood in about 1932.

(3) There is also a perpetual-flowering carnation carrying this name.

'FAITH RAVEN' A mule pink of possible ancient lineage that Monksilver Nursery has rediscovered and introduced under the name for want of the original one. Being a mule it has clustered flowers and green foliage influenced by *D. barbatus*. The double flowers are pink, darkening to a deeper pink as the flower ages. They are carried on 20 cm (8 in) stems. It is currently available, having been reintroduced in 1990.

'FALCON' (1) This is one of the Herbert pinks. It is a floriferous double with a rose colour darkening towards the centre. The flowers are very fragrant and appear from June into autumn on 30 cm (12 in) stems. It was introduced by C.H. Herbert of Acocks Green around 1930, but does not seem to be any longer around.

(2) C.H. Herbert appears to have produced another pink with the same name some seven years earlier, in about 1923. This was also a double, but with a white ground, a deep crimson-maroon central zone and red-purple lacing on the margins of the petals. Like its stablemate, this has also disappeared.

(3) It is curious how this unlikely name for a pink appealed to growers. It is perhaps more understandable that Douglas would choose the name as one of the pinks in their bird name series. This is a double with a white ground, a dark red central zone and crimson lacing, not too different from the previous. The flowers are fragrant. It was introduced by Douglas of Great Bookham in 1957, but seems to have gone the way of far too many pinks.

(4) Two border carnations (one from Douglas!) also share this name.

'FANAL' The *IDR* gives this as a single crimson self, but all the plants around, while being single, are a reddish purple (74A) with a definite darker crimson (reddish 59A) central zone that pales as it enters the throat. The flowers are 3.2–3.8 cm (1.25–1.5 in) across and are carried on stems that vary in length, being only 10 cm (4 in) in pots in the alpine house but up to 25 cm (10 in) in the open garden. The flowers are fragrant and the petals are quite deeply fringed. It was introduced prior to 1974. It is still in cultivation and commercially available. There is one perpetual-flowering carnation of the same name.

'FARNHAM REX' A modern semi-double pink with a pink (62C) ground, flushed with darker pink (62A) and a crimson (60A) central zone. The flowers are up to 5 cm (2 in) across and are carried on 48 cm (19 in) stems. They have a strong clove fragrance. The plant has a spreading habit. The RHS awarded it a HC in 1967 and an AM in 1968, both as a border plant.

'FARNHAM ROSE' This is a delightful pink very close to, if it is not the same as, 'Constance Finnis'. It has large single flowers with overlapping petals. The ground colour is white and there is a purply-pink central eye and lacing. These two are joined down the centre of each petal with a bar of the same colour, creating two white eyes. The purply-pink is not a pure colour, but is speckled with a paler colour. It is floriferous with flowers that are 3.8 cm (1.5 in) across and are carried on 25–30 cm (10–12 in) stems, during June and July. The petals are slightly fringed and the flower is fragrant. There seems to be no information as to its origin. It is in cultivation and commercially available.

'FARRAR'   Jack Drake introduced this floriferous plant in the early 1960s. It is a semi-double with a bright rosy-red colour. It has a long flowering season but no longer seems to be available.

'FAVOURITE'   Not surprisingly there are several pinks with this name, none of which seem to be around.

(1) This is a compact plant with semi-double or double flowers with a rose-pink ground with a maroon central zone. It was introduced by B. Ladhams of Shirley Nurseries, Southampton in about 1923.

(2) A double with a rose-pink colour. It is fragrant. Apparently an old cultivar.

(3) Another old cultivar, possibly introduced by Batten in the 1970s. Nothing else is known.

(4) This stems from the same period and was possibly introduced by Pope. It is laced.

(5) More information is available about one introduced by Hill in the middle of the nineteenth century. This had a white ground and was laced with red.

(6) Also from the middle of the last century came a dark cultivar introduced by F. Hooper of Vine Nursery near Bath.

(7) There are also nine border carnations and four perpetual-flowering carnations all jostling for the same name.

'FAVOURITE LADY'   A plant with semi-double to double flowers pure white in colour, although they tend to have a slight buff tinge towards the centre, particularly when they age. In some years there is the slightest trace of purple in the centre. The petals had a deep but coarse toothing. The flowers are about 3.8 cm (1.5 in) across and are carried on 30–38 cm (12–15 in) stems. They are fragrant. The grey-green foliage is quite wide, but not coarse. It was raised in 1982 by Michael Williams as a cross between 'Highland Fraser' and

an unknown partner. It is still grown. The RHS awarded it a HC in 1991 as a border plant.

'FAY'   One of Allwood's famous alpinus series for the rock garden. The small single flowers are magenta pink. They are fringed and well scented. They are floriferous over a long flowering season, from June well into autumn. It was probably introduced in the early 1930s and is still in cultivation. The RHS awarded it a HC in 1933 as a plant for the rock garden.

'FELICITY'   This is one of the Allwood modern pinks in their name series. This double is a pale magenta with a very dark, almost black eye and magenta lacing. It is fragrant and flowers from June into the autumn. It was introduced in about 1956, but has since vanished.

'FENBOW NUTMEG CLOVE'   A very old cultivar with a recorded history back to at least 1652. It has a semi-double flower that is rich crimson red (43A) self. It is quite a late flowerer (July) and has a delicious scent of nutmeg. The foliage is a good blue-green, but slightly coarse in the manner of a modern pink. Family records show that the plant was introduced to the Fenbow's garden by Julian Fenbow in 1652, according to his diary to allow him to give his wine a nutmeg flavour without going to the expense of importing it. The plant was rediscovered still growing in the garden in 1960 by Mr Sanderson of Leeds. Sometimes it is just called 'Fenbow Clove'. The plant seems to be safely in cultivation.

'FETTES MOUNT'   An old variety with dense heads of double flowers. These are pink but darken as the flower ages. It is a floriferous plant with very fragrant blooms. The flowers are carried on stems that are up to 30 cm (12 in) tall in June and July. According to the *IDR* it was introduced by Potts before 1928. It was once commonly grown, but by the end of the Second World War it was dying out, fortunately it was rescued and is still available from a small number of nurseries.

'FIELD MARSHALL'   (1) A pink with a semi-double flower that is coloured rose pink and has a central zone of red. It was introduced by Prichard in 1947, but does not seem to be around any longer.

(2) There was also another pink introduced by Hale around 1854. This had a rose flower.

(3) Six border carnations and one perpetual-flowering carnation also carried this name.

'FIMBRIATUS'   An old variety from the nineteenth century. This has double flowers that are an ivory white. The flowers are large and have a tendency to split their calyces. They are carried on 30 cm (12 in) stems. It has a wonderful perfume. In spite of its age it is still in cultivation. It is sometimes seen named as 'Fimbriata'. There are still some plants going under the specific name of *D. fimbriatus*, although this is now strictly *D. orientalis*. This is a single with pale pink flowers with deeply fringed petals.

'FIONA'   Another of the Allwood modern pinks in their name series. This one is a double with a pale salmon pink (48D) colour, striped in a deeper pink (50B). The reverse is somewhat paler. The petals are serrated. The flowers are about 5 cm (2 in) across and are born on 30–38 cm (12–15 in) stems. Occasionally it splits its calyx, making it look untidy. It was introduced by Allwood in about 1971 in which year it was awarded a PC as a border plant by the RHS. It is still in cultivation. Two perpetual-flowering carnations bear the same name.

'FIRE KING'   This is a double-flowered plant with large flowers that are a brilliant scarlet. It was introduced by C.H. Herbert of Acocks Green in about 1927. It does not seem to have survived. There was another pink with the same name but all the *IDR* can report is that it was in existence before 1839. It is doubtful whether this will ever cause any confusion. There are also two border carnations and one perpetual-flowering carnation with the same name, as well as one annual, *D. chinensis* 'Fire King'.

'FIRECREST'   Another of the Douglas bird series of pinks. This one is a double with blush pink ground and a central zone and lacing of a deep red shading to a rose pink. The flower are fragrant. It was introduced in 1959 but seems to have disappeared.

'FLAME'   An imperial pink from Lindabruce Nurseries. This one is a flat double of a strong pinky-scarlet (46D) colour with a paler ground colour which shows as the flower goes over. The flowers are 5 cm (2 in) in diameter, perhaps a bit bigger as they age. It has a long flowering period from June into the autumn. The RHS awarded it an AM for exhibition in 1964, and a HC in 1966, an AM in 1969 and a FCC in 1976, all as a border plant. It is one of the several imperials still in cultivation. There are three perpetual-flowering carnations that also have the same name.

'FLANDRIA'   A mule pink resembling 'Emile Paré'. It has clustered heads of bright crimson, double flowers. They are slightly fragrant and flower from June into the autumn. As with most mules, it has *D. barbatus* somewhere in its past history. Also like most mules, it needs constant propagation to ensure its continuance, but this one seems to have been neglected as it looks as though it disappeared in the 1950s. It was possibly introduced by C. Engelmann of Saffron Waldon, sometime before 1939 when it was put up for trial at Wisley. It does not appear to have won any award.

'FLEUR'   An Allwood modern pink. This one is a double with a pale pink ground and a darker pink flecking. The flowers are about 3.8 cm (1.5 in) across and are carried on 30 cm (12 in) stems. The petals have very slight fringing that is almost unnoticeable. The blue-green foliage is typical of modern pinks. It was introduced in about 1971 and is still in cultivation.

'FLORA'   With a name like this one could be forgiven for thinking that this was yet another of the Allwood modern pinks, but this seems to be one they have not yet got round to. However, there are seven pinks, eleven border carnations, two perpetual-flowering carnations and one malmaison carnation all bearing this name. There appear to be no extant pinks bearing this name, but one or more of the more recent ones could be hiding somewhere.

(1) The most recent was introduced by E. Ladhams of Godalming in about 1940. It is a semi-double with rose pink petals.

(2) The other main contender for rediscovery is that introduced by Douglas of Great Bookham in 1927. This is a dark pink self, although Mansfield seems to think it has crimson-maroon central zone. It has a clove scent.

(3) The others are a rose pink introduced by T. Looker in about 1853; one of unknown colour by N. Norman of Woolwich around 1846; another by Miln in about 1832 and a laced red form, also called 'Lady Flora Hastings' introduced by Miles in about 1793. The *IDR* also list a seventh that may or may not have been a pink. It was introduced in about 1845 and had a pink ground, edged with white in the manner of a 'painted lady' type. Does anyone know of any of these?

'FLORIBUNDUS'   Another of the floriferous mule pinks, possibly with *D. barbatus* in its blood. This has dense heads of double, rose-pink flowers. It has a strong scent. The flowers appear for a long period over the summer on 36 cm (14 in) stems. Like many mules, it is prone to flower itself to death (which may account for its possible demise) and, annually, one plant should have its flowers sacrificed by sheering it over to provide cutting material so that the variety can be perpetuated. Introduced by R.D. Brotherston in about 1903.

'FORBE'S VARIETY'   A plant for the rock garden that was around in the 1930s. It has large flowers of a deep pink on 10 cm (4 in) stems above a dark-green mat of foliage.

'FORD BRILLIANT'   This is a double show pink suitable for the open border. The flowers are pale red (46D) selfs. They are up to 5 cm (2 in) wide and are borne on 23–30 cm (9–12 in). The petal margins are slightly serrated. The plant was raised by H. Jayes of Dagenham in the early 1970s. The RHS awarded it an AM in 1974 as an exhibition plant in 1974 and a HC as a border plant in 1975.

'FORD PINKS'   A series of pinks of which the previous and following are probably the most important.

'FORD SYMMETRY'   Another double, this time a pale pink self. The flowers are up to 5.8 cm (2.25 in) across. The petals are slightly waved and have serrated edges. It was raised by H. Jayes of Dagenham in the late 1960s. The RHS awarded it an AM as an exhibition plant in 1971.

'FORSTERI'   Probably a mule type pink with possible parents of *Dianthus barbatus* and *D. pavonius*. The flowers are single, with a fierce magenta-crimson ground and a blue. The flowers are clustered on 15 cm (6 in) stems during July and August. It seems to be very free-flowering and can flower itself to death, so needs regular propagation by keeping one plant especially for cutting material. It was probably introduced before the Second World War but has since disappeared.

'FORTUNA'   One of the older Allwood modern pinks that is still available. This is a flat double with luminous rose-pink (68A) petals, the reverse being paler. The flower fades as it ages and the colour noticeably splits into a darker rose flushing and a pale pink undercolour. The flower is about 5 cm (2 in) across, fringed and fragrant. It was introduced by Allwood in about 1945. There are also two perpetual-flowering carnations with the same name.

'FORTUNE'   This is one of the imperial pinks introduced by C.H. Fielder of Lindabruce Nurseries. It had semi-double flowers with a soft rose pink ground and a deeper central zone. The petals were toothed and the flower very fragrant. It flowered over a long season from June onwards on 30 cm (12 in) stems. The plant was first introduced in about 1946, but seems to have vanished. There is also one perpetual-flowering carnation with the same name.

'FOSTERI'   This is another mule pink, probably derived in part from *D. barbatus*. This one has clusters of rose-crimson flowers set off by rich bronze leaves. The flower stems are only about 15 cm (6 in), which makes it shorter than most other mules. Will Ingwersen said in 1949 that it was of a poor constitution and required frequent propagation to keep it going. Like so many other of this type, it had a tendency to flower itself to death. Presumably the attention that it required was neglected as it seems to have disappeared.

'FOUNTAINS ABBEY'   (1) This is a very old cultivar reputed to have its origins in the sixteenth century although it is more likely to be of Victorian origin. It hovers between being a semi-double and a double. The petals have a white ground and a very dark maroon, almost black lacing. The flowers are quite small, being only about 2.5 cm (1 in) across and the pattern is said (Genders) to resemble that of the 'Queen of Sheba' with two strong white 'eyes' in the middle of each petal.

(2) Another plant with the same name and claiming to have the same origin on the walls of Fountains Abbey is a single with pale lilac (75B flushed paler pink) fading to a greenish white in the centre. The flowers are about 3.8 cm (1.5 in) across and are deeply fringed. They are carried on 30 cm (12 in) stems. This is a wonderfully simple plant but is a bit floppy, especially after rain. There are usually gaps between the petals. It is a bigger version of 'Old Fringed' but has green calyces. This is more likely to be the original sixteenth century plant or, at least, one descended from it, and somehow I feel this should be the true bearer of the name.

'FRAGRANT LACE' Bare information on this plant from the *IDR* indicates that it has a white ground and is laced with maroon. Introduced by H. Jayes in 1966, it is still around.

'FRAGRANTISSIMA' A truly delightful pink distributed by Robinson's Hardy Plants of Swanley for many years under a specific name. It was claimed to have been collected by a customer in Turkey, but there is no specific name *D. fragrantissima* in the *Flora of Turkey* nor have I been able to track it down as a species from that country. It is a white single with deep fringing and a wonderful scent. As the flowers age they sometimes take on a slight trace of a central band of reddish purple. They are about 3.2 cm (1.25 in) across and are carried on 25 cm (10 in) stems above mats of narrow, stiff foliage. They have a long slender calyx. It flowers in June and July. It is still in cultivation and has much to commend it.

'FRANCES ISABEL' A frilly double from the Allwood stable. The colour is a pink (65B) ground with a maroon (redder 59A) eye and lacing. The lacing is quite narrow, but on the occasional flower it becomes quite wide, reducing the pink ground to a small eye in the centre of each petal; sometimes the lacing breaks down leaving flecks of maroon on the paler ground. The reverse is pale pink. The flowers are 4.5 cm (1.75 in) across and are carried on 25–30 cm (10–12 in) stems. They flower from early summer right through to the end of autumn and have the benefit of being fragrant. The foliage is the typical blue green of the modern pink. It was raised by H.V. Calvert of Lupset near Wakefield in 1972 and is still available. It produced a sport that became known as 'Laced Treasure'. The RHS awarded it a HC in 1979 and an AM in 1983, both as a border plant.

'FRANK'S FRILLY' This is an attractive double pink. The flowers are a purple pink (74C) with maroon (187A) zoning and a white throat that shows when the calyx splits. As the name implies, the petals are deeply fringed. The plant flops outwards leaving a dead centre. It is very floriferous. The Frank of the name appears to be the late Frank Waley of Sevenoaks. The *IDR* gives this plant as a crushed strawberry self, giving the Parker-Jervis catalogue as source of the information. In fact the catalogue gives it an eye, so the *IDR* must be considered wrong here. The plant is still available.

'FRECKLES' This is one of the C.H. Fielder imperial pinks and I glad to say that this is one that is still in existence. It is a double with a dusky rose-pink (52C) colouration striped with red (47A). The reverse is the same colour and includes the stripes. The fragrant flowers are up to 5 cm (2 in) across and are carried on 25 cm (10 in) stems. The petals are slightly fringed. It has a long flowering season from June well into autumn. It was introduced by Fielder at the Lindabruce Nurseries in 1948. The RHS has awarded it an AM in 1955 and in 1962, both as a border plant, and an AM in 1962 as an exhibition bloom. It has been used very successfully for breeding purposes, 'Gwendoline Read' being an example of its progeny. 'William of Essex' is a sport from it. There are two perpetual-flowering carnations with the same name.

'FREDA' An Allwood modern pink of some vintage. This is a double to semi-double mauve pink (68A) in colour but noticeably much paler towards the centre. Actually, the ground colour consists of a pale pink with a dark mauve flushed and striped over it. It often opens quite dark in colour with the central petals standing upright like a crown. The petals have serrated margins, which gives the flower a frilly appearance. The 5 cm (2 in) flowers are very fragrant and borne on 30 cm (12 in) stems. The foliage is the typical blue-grey of the modern pink. It was introduced sometime about 1924 and is still available. It was awarded a HC as a border plant by the RHS in 1946. There are also two border carnations and one perpetual-flowering carnation with the same name.

'FREYA' A single given by Mansfield as a Winteri pink. The fragrant flowers have a pale blush-pink ground and a chestnut maroon centre. It has a long flowering season, from June until the autumn. It does not seem to be around.

'FRINGED PINK' see 'Old Fringed'

'FUCHSIA' see 'Whatfield Fuchsia'

'FUSILIER' This is one of S.T. Byatt's military series for the rock garden. It has single flowers with a rose red (61C overlaid with 60B) ground and a deep crimson (59A) central zone. The flowers are about 3.2 cm (1.25 in) across and carried on 12–15 cm (5–6 in) stems. They are fragrant. The plant has a bushy habit. It was introduced sometime before 1955, the year in which the RHS awarded it an AM as a border plant. It received a FCC as a plant for the rock garden in 1967. It is still a popular plant. There are plants being sold under this name that are about the same size and appearance but whose colour is a rich magenta self. There are two border carnations with the same name.

'F.W. MILLARD' This has a large double flower of a crimson colour. They are borne on 30 cm (12 in) stems above tight clumps of grey-green leaves. It seeds itself quite freely and many of the seedlings come true. Because of this tendency, it is probably better to call this a strain, as the direct vegetative link with the original plant may well have been lost. Indeed, it now looks as though even the seedlings may have been lost. It was originally found in Ireland and introduced by F.W. Millard sometime around 1949.

'GAIETY' (1) The main contender for this name is a fully double pink. The colour of the flowers is a rose pink (63B), fading slightly (63C) towards the edges, and with a crimson (59A) central zone. The reverse is the same. The flowers are up to 4.5 cm (1.75 in) across and are carried on 30 cm (12 in) stems. In spite of the flower's fullness they are not frilly, the petals are only slightly cut. They appear over a long season from June well into October and are fragrant. The foliage is a blue-green and typical of a modern pink. It was introduced by Lindabruce Nurseries in about 1955, and appears to have had 'Bridesmaid' as one of its parents, as did so many of their plants. The RHS awarded it a HC in 1958 and an AM in 1961, both as a plant for the border. It is still in existence, although not commercially available.

(2) One with a blush rose-pink ground and a crimson centre, introduced by Barr & Sons of Covent Garden in about 1921.

(3) An earlier pink with this name is one listed by Fellowes in 1885. This was a rosy red.

(4) There are five border carnations with this name and one annual pink, *D. chinensis* 'Gaiety'.

'GALATEA' A Winteri pink. This is a single pink with a pure white ground and a bright maroon zone. It is very fragrant. The petals are fringed. The flowering period is long, from June until the autumn. There are also five border carnations of the same name.

'GARLAND' This is a single pink with overlapping petals. They are pink flushed with a darker pink and with a slight trace of an even darker pink

central zone. When the flower first opens it is a much darker colour, almost a purple pink. It is slightly fragrant. The flower is up to 3.2 cm (1.25 in) across and carried on 36 cm (14 in) stems above clump-forming, blue-green foliage. The petals are deeply but not finely fringed. It is floriferous. Introduced in about 1950, it is still a popular plant. There was another pink with this name in the nineteenth century, which is listed simply as red. It was introduced by Brown in about 1845.

'GARNET' (1) The one I know with this name is a single with a dark pink to magenta ground and a brownish maroon central zone. The reverse is a deep purple pink. The petals are slightly fringed and the flower is fragrant. The flower is up to 3.2 cm (1.25 in) across and held on 15–20 cm (6–8 in) stems above a grey silver foliage. This plant is still in cultivation.

(2) Lindabruce Nurseries introduced, in about 1959, a plant with this name that is a dark red double. It does not now seem to be around.

'GEM' *see 'Whatfield Gem'*

'GERTRUDE' (1) This is a pink with large double flowers of a rosy mauve with a dark purple central zone borne on a tall vigorous plant. It was introduced by C.H. Herbert of Acocks Green in about 1923 but now seems to have disappeared.

(2) At about the same time there was a double white introduced by B. Ladhams of Shirley Nurseries, Southampton.

(3) Much earlier, in about 1867, there was a rose-pink form introduced by C. Turner of Slough, the introducer of 'Mrs Sinkins'.

(4) There are also four border carnations and one perpetual-flowering carnation with this name, as well as one sweet william.

'GERTRUDE ELLIS' A semi-double with a soft, bright pink (67D) ground with a small central zone of rose red (redder 57A). The flowers are up to 5 cm (2 in) across and are carried on 30 cm (12 in) stems. The petals are broad and have serrated margins. The plant has a somewhat straggly habit. It was introduced by Messrs A.V. Ellis of Warmsworth in 1946 but has since seemed to have disappeared. It was awarded a HC in 1953 and an AM in 1955, both as a border plant, by the RHS.

'GERTRUDE TAYLOR' A double with a rose purple (74B) ground, a purple (between 71A and 71B) central zone and cyclamen purple (between

'Garnet'

80B and 80C) lacing. The flowers are up to 5 cm (2 in) across and appear on 38 cm (15 in) rigid stems. The petals are broad and serrated. It was introduced by G.M. Taylor of East Lothian and awarded a C as a border plant by the RHS in 1953.

'GINGHAM GOWN' This is a very good laced single. The ground is pink (69A) with crushed raspberry (71A) lacing and central zone. The lacing and the zone are joined down the centre of each petal by a bar of the same colour, creating two pink 'eyes' on each petal. As the flower ages, so the lacing shrinks, and the eyes increase in size until they cover almost all of the petal. The petals are fringed and overlap each other. The fragrant flowers are about 3.8 cm (1.5 in) across and are borne on 20 cm (8 in) stems above a good compact clump of short, blue-green foliage. The plant was raised by W.J. Archer of Wrecclesham and introduced by Reginald Kaye at Waithman Nurseries, Carnforth, sometime around 1964 and it is still very much in existence. The RHS awarded it a PC in 1964, a HC in 1965 and an AM in 1977, all as a rock garden plant.

'GLADYS CRANFIELD' A somewhat floppy plant with large single flowers. They have a pink

ground and a maroon central zone and are very fragrant. Mansfield reports that the petals are curiously waved. It flowers from June into the autumn on 30 cm (12 in) stems. It was introduced sometime around 1928 but does not now seem to be in cultivation.

'GLEBE COTTAGE WHITE' A semi-double flower with pure white petals and a slight trace of a pink eye. The flowers are about 3.2 cm (1.25 in) across and are carried on 20–25 cm (8–10 in) stems above mats of a green foliage. They are fragrant. It is a sturdy plant with the flowering stems standing upright. The plant was a chance seedling amongst a batch claimed to have come from seed of 'Waithman's Beauty' at Glebe Cottage Nursery, in North Devon, although the flower of this plant is quite different in colour and shape. (It is interesting to note that in 1954 an un-named seedling was introduced that was a reputed cross between *D. tatrae* and 'Waithman's Beauty' that had taken place in H. Roger-Smith's garden. This cross had fringed white flowers with a central carmine central band, so the chances of 'Waithman's Beauty' producing a white offspring is not as far-fetched as one might imagine.) This seems to be identical to another plant called 'Checkley'.

'GLENDA'   An Allwood modern pink. The double flowers are pure white and scented. The flowers are about 5 cm (2 in) wide and are carried on 38 cm (15 in) stems. It was introduced in about 1972 and is still in existence. The RHS awarded it a HC in 1973, an AM in 1975 and a FCC in 1977, all as a border pink.

'GLORIA'   (1) An Allwood modern pink. This one has a double flower with a salmon pink ground and darker, crimson eye. It was introduced in about 1945 but seems to have disappeared.

(2) It is also a synonym for 'Glory' (*qv*).

(3) There are also two border carnations and three perpetual-flowering carnations that share this name.

'GLORIOSA'   (1) A lavender self introduced by J.E. Dixon in about 1946. It seems to have disappeared from cultivation.

(2) A much earlier plant, being introduced in the late eighteenth century. This was a flat double or semi-double and had a dark pink (73A) ground and a crimson (redder 187C) eye. The very fragrant flowers are 3.8 cm (1.5 in) across and are carried on 25 cm (10 in) high stems above a fine blue-green foliage, which forms good mats. The petals are slightly fringed. The calyx splits. It is reputed to be of Scottish origin and is still in cultivation.

(3) Moreton describes a pink with this name that might be the same as (2) as his description could be incomplete. He describes it as a carnation cross pink, with large full flowers with serrated edges. The colour is given as blush and the flowers are extremely fragrant. He states that it is of eighteenth century Scottish origin. It was still in existence in the 1950s and, if it is not the same as (2), it has since disappeared.

(4) There are also three border carnations and one perpetual-flowering carnation with the same name.

'GLORIOUS'   An imperial pink from C.H. Fielder at the Lindabruce Nursery. This one is a double with an apple-blossom (65B) ground and a crimson (185B) eye. The flowers are about 5 cm (2 in) wide and are carried on 45 cm (18 in) stems. The broad petals are fringed. The flowers have a clove fragrance. It is a floriferous plant that flowers from June into the late autumn. It was introduced in about 1957. The RHS awarded it a HC in 1959 and an AM in 1961, both as a plant for the border. There are also two perpetual-flowering carnations with the same name.

'GLORY'   Three plants that are similar enough, at least in written descriptions, to be the same plant. Unfortunately, apart from the first, they do not seem to have survived (unless of course it is the second that survived or perhaps even the third). Margery Fish describes one of them as having a 'wonderful scent'.

(1) From the mid-nineteenth century comes a double or semi-double with a rose-pink ground with a maroon central zone and carmine chocolate lacing. The plant is somewhat straggly and inclined to split the calyces. It was also called 'Gloria'. This is the one that is assumed to still be in cultivation. However, it must be said that Moreton states in the mid 1950s that there is also a modern form of 'Gloria' (possibly (3)) with stronger growth but inferior flowers. Let us hope that it is the older form still in cultivation.

(2) J. Keynes of Salisbury introduced another similar plant also in the mid-nineteenth century. This is described as rose pink with purple lacing.

(3) The most recent was introduced sometime in 1923. This is a double with a rose-pink ground and a central zone and lacing of crimson. It is clove scented.

(4) There are also four border carnations with the same name, as well as a strain of sweet williams.

'GLORY OF LYONNAISE'   This has large double flowers with a soft pink ground and a cream centre changing to pale green in the throat. They flower from June until late summer on 30 cm (12 in) stems. It has a tendency to split its calyx. Kew currently has two large clumps labelled with this name but the plants ('Old Fringed') have single white flowers that open a pale pink and then fade. From all other descriptions this is obviously not the correct plant.

'GOBLIN'   An Allwoodii alpine pink for the rock garden, with single flowers of a deep pink (73B) ground and a deep maroon (187B) central zone. The flowers are about 2.5 cm (1 in) across. They are fragrant and flower over a long period from June until the end of autumn on 15 cm (6 in) stems. The broad petals are serrated. It was introduced by Allwood in about 1941 and is still around. It was awarded a HC as a border plant by the RHS in 1954. There is also a border carnation with the same name.

'GOLDFINCH'   An unusual name for an Allwood pink but this was given because of its colour: an apricot ground with a deeper flush. This is due to its parentage of a *D. alwoodii* cross with *D. knappii*, the latter imparting the yellowness and also the tendency to bear flowers in trusses. It has a double flower. Allwood introduced it in about 1940. Roy Genders maintained that it was a more vigorous plant than 'Yellowhammer' but it now seems to have disappeared. Perhaps somebody should reattempt the cross. There are also four border carnations and one perpetual-flowering carnation with the same name.

'GRACE MATHER'   A double pink for the rock garden or edging. The flowers are a salmon pink and are carried on 20 cm (8 in) stems over neat blue-grey foliage. They are well scented. The plant was introduced by G. Mather of Sidcup in 1960 and it is still in existence.

'GRANDAD'   A modern semi-double with a deep candy pink (61D) ground and an indistinct crimson (60A) central zone. The flowers are up to 4.5 cm (1.75 in) across and carried on 36 cm (14 in) stems. The broad petals are fringed. The flowers are slightly fragrant. The plant was raised and introduced by Stephen Bailey of Sway in 1983. The RHS awarded it a HC in 1986 and an AM in 1987, both as a border plant.

'GRAN'S FAVOURITE'   A popular plant introduced by Mrs D. Underwood of Rampart's Nursery, Colchester. The flowers are double with a white ground and a bright dark pinkish purple (66A) central zone and paler (59B) lacing that fades towards the edges. The lacing is not very wide giving a good expanse of the white ground. The flowers are 5 cm (2 in) across and are carried on 35 cm (15 in) stems that tend to be floppy and may need support. The petals are fringed and the whole flower fragrant. The foliage is grey-green. It was introduced in about 1966 and is widely available. The RHS awarded it a PC as an exhibition plant in 1981, an AM in 1982 as a plant for the border (when it inexplicably recorded it as being single) and a FCC in 1984 for the same purpose.

'GRAVETYE GEM'   A pink for the rock garden or edging. It has single flowers with a rose-pink ground and maroon markings. The flowers are about 1.25 cm (0.5 in) across and are carried on 12 cm (5 in) stems. It was introduced by Ingwersens, possibly in the 1950s, and is still in cultivation. The name is probably not a valid one as there is a border carnation of the same name from the last century.

'GREBE'   One of the Douglas bird series. This is a double with a deep rose ground and a dark central zone. It is fragrant. The introduction was made in 1960 but it seems to have vanished.

'GREEN EYE'   *see 'Musgrave's Pink'*

'GREEN LANES'   Introduced by Cecil Wyatt of Colehayes, Bovey Tracey. It is a double white with a green centre and is still available. It has coarse modern foliage. Also listed as 'Green Lane'.

'GREENSIDE'   A large double pink for the rock garden or edging. It has pink flowers. They have a very strong fragrance. The flowers are carried on 20 cm (8 in) stems. It is a vigorous plant. Its current status is unknown but it was extant in the mid 1970s.

'GRENADIER'   This is one of S.T. Byatt's military series of pinks for the rock garden. It is a semi-double with a dark red (53B) ground and a darker central zone. The flowers are about 2.5 cm (1 in) wide. It has a clove scent. The stems are up to about 10 cm (4 in) above the grey-green foliage. It was introduced in about 1963 and is still in cultivation. The RHS awarded it a PC in 1964, a HC in 1966, an AM in 1967 and a FCC in 1968, the last three as a plant for the rock garden. There are also eight border carnations and three perpetual-flowering carnations with the same name.

'GUSFORD'   This has a large double flower with a soft pink ground and a few reddish marks. These are borne on 30 cm (12 in) stems. It has a strong fragrance and was introduced by Thompson and Morgan in about 1961.

'GWENDOLINE'   *see 'Betty Norton'*

'GWENDOLINE READ'   A very fine double with a rose pink (48D) flushed with paler pink, which shows especially towards the margins. It becomes darker, almost salmon pink as it ages. As it goes over it fades to a pale pink. The flowers are about 5 cm (2 in) across and are borne on stiffly erect 15 cm (6 in) stems. The petals are serrated. It is fragrant. This is a very compact, floriferous plant, flowering in June and July. The plant was introduced by Hayward's Carnations of Purbrook in 1991 as a seedling from 'Freckles'. It was named after one of their employees and is also known as 'Gwen Read'. It is a first-class plant and one of the best introductions of recent years.

'HAKEM'　This is single with a white ground and a few light mauve spots around the centre. It has a slight scent and fringed petals. The flower stems are about 15 cm (6 in) tall. It was a chance seedling that was raised by T.J. Wood at Southcombe Gardens in Devon, in about 1986.

'HARLEQUIN'　There does seem a bit of confusion with this name and an increasing number of nurseries are stocking plants using it. These seem mostly to be alpine forms.

(1) A rock garden pink with flowers that have a dark pink ground and maroon central eye and lacing. The flowers are carried on 20 cm (8 in) stems and appear in June. Allwood has offered a similar plant except that it is bright pink with a large maroon eye (no mention of lacing, but then this would not be the first time that it would have been omitted from a catalogue). The flowers are carried on 7.5 cm (3 in) stems and the petals are heavily fringed. Neither, if they are different plants, appears to be in the *IDR*.

(2) Roy Genders also mentions a rock garden plant not listed in the *IDR*. This is a brick red single 'beautifully marked', whatever that might mean. It could conceivably be the same plant as the above. The flowers are carried on 15 cm (6 in) stems. One nursery currently offers a pink with single rich red flowers marked with pale pink, which ties in with Genders' description.

(3) Another Allwood contribution is also a puzzle because *IDR* suggests that it might be the same as 'Show Harlequin'. The description it gives is of pale pink ground flushed with rose pink. It was introduced in 1958. Why this should add up to 'Show Harlequin' I am not certain.

(4) There are two other, much older, pinks with the same name. One is given as being laced and introduced by Major before 1798 and the other as a red, introduced by McLean of Colchester in about 1867; neither of which, I would think, are likely to surface. There is also the annual strain of sweet william, *D. barbatus* 'Harlequin'.

(5) There are also five border carnations and two perpetual-flowering carnations with the same name.

'HARMONY'　A medium sized double flower that has a tendency to split its calyx. It has a white ground with crimson central zone and flushed and specked with crimson. It was introduced by C.H. Herbert of Acocks Green around 1931. There are also three border carnations and three perpetual-flowering carnations with the same name.

'HAROLD'　This is one of the earliest of the Allwood modern pinks. It is a double with a white ground and a cream eye. The petals are fringed and the flower very fragrant. The stems are about 30 cm (12 in) long. It is a perpetual-flowering from June through to the autumn. Allwood introduced it in about 1914 but it seems to have long disappeared. The RHS awarded it an AM in 1920. There are also one border carnation and one perpetual-flowering carnation with the same name.

'HAROLD II'　The reason that the original 'Harold' disappeared was probably because of the introduction of this improved form by Allwood. It is also a double but is a pure white self. Like its predecessor it is also very fragrant. The flowers are 6.4 cm (2.5 in) across and borne on 38 cm (15 in) stems. The petals are broad and have smooth margins. The plant has a spreading habit and is free-flowering. It was introduced before 1941 but now seems to have gone the same way as 'Harold'. The RHS recognised it with a HC in 1951 and an AM in 1954, both awarded as a border plant.

'HART'S DELIGHT'　*see 'Whatfield Hart's Delight'*

'HASLEMERE'　A fragrant pink with a large double flower that has a pure white ground and a chocolate central zone. It was introduced by Thompson and Morgan in about 1962 but seems to have disappeared.

'HAWFINCH'　One of the Douglas bird series of pinks. This one is a double white with a crimson central zone and lacing. It was fragrant and had stems of 30–35 cm (12–15 in) stems. The flowers appear over a short period in June and July. It was introduced in 1955 but does not now appear to be around.

'HAYTOR ROCK'　This modern pink has a double flower with a very pale pink ground and streaked with scarlet (47D). The fragrant flowers are up to 5.8 (2.25 in) across and are carried on 35 cm (15 in) stems. The petals are fringed and the calyx has a tendency to occasionally split. It was introduced by Cecil Wyatt of Colehayes, Bovey Tracey in 1979 and it is still quite widely available. The RHS awarded it a PC in 1981 and a HC as a border plant in 1982.

'HAYTOR WHITE'　A very popular modern pink (that tends towards a carnation both in ap-

'Haytor White'

pearance and constitution) whose name is usually abbreviated to 'Haytor'. It is a double with pure white flowers, although they occasionally have crimson flecks. The flowers are 5–6.4 cm (2–2.5 in) across and are carried on 30–35 cm (12–15 in) stems above a blue-green foliage. The petals are coarsely, but evenly, toothed in a very distinct manner. The flowers are fragrant and have a long season. It is not a long lived plant and needs regular propagation. Cecil Wyatt of Colehayes, Bovey Tracey, introduced it in about 1971. The RHS awarded it an AM in 1980 and an AM as a border plant in 1982. It is sometimes called 'White Doris' but it does not have any relationship with 'Doris'. I have seen 'Haytor White' offered as 'Mrs Sinkins' from which it is very distinct.

'HEATH'   This is a modern pink very much in the style of a small carnation. It has double flowers that have a white ground with a very pale green central zone that sometimes flushes outwards to cover most of the flower. They are only 3.8 cm (1.5 in) across but are carried on long 45 cm (18 in) stems. The petals are cut rather than fringed. It flowers in June and July. The calyx can split. The foliage is wide and coarse more in the nature of a carnation than a pink.

'HELEN'   (1) One of Allwood's double modern pinks that resembles a slightly larger and darker 'Inchmery'. It is a medium pink, flushed with both a lighter and darker pink, the variations of which give the flower a very three-dimensional quality, especially as they appear deeper towards the centre where the petals are bunched. The average colour is probably 52D. They are slightly fringed and are fragrant. The flowers are about 5 cm (2 in) across and are carried on 30–35 cm (12–15 in) stems. They appear over quite a long season from June until the autumn. It was introduced by Allwood in about 1948 and is still widely available. The RHS has awarded it a HC in 1959, an AM in 1960 and a FCC in 1966, all as worthy plants for the border.

   (2) Perhaps of little significance now, but Allwood introduced another 'Helen' in about 1932. This was a deep, dull rosy red semi-double. It is doubtful if it is still in existence.

   (3) Historically there was also red form introduced by McLean of Colchester in about 1867.

   (4) There are also four border carnations and one perpetual-flowering carnation with the same name.

'HELEN'S FANCY'   A fancy semi-double verging on double with a dry rose-pink ground with occasional distinct purple stripes and flecks. The flowers are 4.5 cm (1.75 in) across. The petal margins appear smooth although they have a very slight indentation. It is in cultivation.

'HELGA'   An Allwood pink for the rock garden. The flowers are single with a light reddish-purple (between 63A and 63B) ground, which is veined in a slightly darker (63A) colour, and a crimson-maroon (59A) central band. They are about 3.2 cm (1.25 in) across and are borne on 10–12.5 cm (4–5 in) stems. There is a slight fragrance. The RHS awarded it a HC for the rock garden in 1963.

'HENRY OF ESSEX'   This is a fully double pink with cup-shaped petals that are turned up slightly at the margins revealing the paler undersurfaces. The upper colour is a pink (63C) ground suffused with the crimson (59A) of the lacing and central zone, which cover most of the petal except for two small 'eyes' showing in the middle of each petal. The irregularity of the fringing and the upturned petals give the flower a very frilly appearance. The petals are finely indented but this is hardly noticeable. The flowers are 3.8 cm (1.5 in) across and are fragrant. It was introduced by Jack Gingell of Ramparts Nursery as a seedling from 'Gran's Favourite' in the 1980s. He wanted to name it 'Prince Henry' in honour of the royal baby, but as this was not possible as it had been used before, he named it 'Henry of Essex' to match his previously named 'William of Essex'.

'HER MAJESTY'   A popular double pink from the end of the last century, which, according to Roy Genders, was often confused with 'Mrs Sinkins' although it is smaller and more fringed. It is a double with white flowers, very fragrant and free flowering. It was introduced sometime before 1891 by F. Hooper of Widcombe Hill, Bath and, although it was possibly still in cultivation after the Second World War, it seems to have disappeared. However, it is possible that Genders is right and some of the smaller versions that one sees under the name of 'Mrs Sinkins' could in fact be 'Her Majesty'. One imagines that the plant was named after Queen Victoria. The RHS awarded it a HC in 1891, an AM in 1893 and a FCC in 1898, all as a plant for the border.

'HERBERT SUTCLIFFE'   A pink for the rock garden presumably named after the famous cricketer. It was a single (an offence, perhaps, to somebody who had hit so many boundaries) with a rose ground and a darker, crimson eye. The flowers were carried on 15 cm (6 in) stems. It was introduced by Holden Clough Nurseries in about 1951.

'HERBERT'S PINK'   A semi-double tending towards a double with a pale pink flushed with a darker rose pink (68A). It is especially pale towards the centre and when going over. The 3.2 cm (1.25 in) flowers are fragrant and are carried on 15 cm (6 in) stems. The reddish brown calyces tend to split. It was raised by Herbert Exton. It is still in cultivation.

'HERMANRIC'   A large single flowered pink with a very pale pink ground and a deep velvet red central zone. The petals are fringed at their margins. The flowers are carried on stems up to 30 cm (12 in) tall. It was raised as a chance seedling by T.J. Wood at Southcombe Gardens, Devon, in 1986.

'HIDCOTE'   A popular pink for the rock garden. It is a flat double or semi-double with cerise (60B) flowers. The flowers are about 2.5 cm (1 in) across and are carried on stems that vary from 7.5 to 16 cm (3–6 in) in height. They are strongly scented. The foliage is a deep blue-green. Some growers have found that it flowers best on a spartan diet. It also has the synonym 'Lawrence Johnston' who was, of course, the owner of Hidcote. It was he who introduced the plant at some time before 1964. The RHS awarded it a PC in 1964 and a C in 1966 and a HC in 1969, both as a worthy rock garden plant. Some plants of 'Hidcote' have been sold as 'Constance Finnis' which, doubtless, will cause some confusion at some point.

'HIDCOTE PINK'   *see 'Annie Macgregor'*

'HIGHDOWN'   A single-flowered pink for the rock garden with a very bright pink (68A) ground and a darker central band and a pale throat. The flowers are sweetly scented. They are carried on 15 cm (6 in) stems. The foliage is a neat bun of glaucous green leaves. It was raised by Frederick Stern at Highdown in Sussex. The RHS awarded it an AM as a plant for the rock garden in 1951.

'HIGHLAND'   P.S. Hayward of Treasure Holt Nurseries, Clacton-on-Sea, raised an enormous number of pinks, mainly in the 1930s, with names beginning with 'Highland', the most famous and one still in existence is 'Highland Fraser'. Although they were distinct and sold as named plants, they were also sold as seed, giving rise to differing plants for the same name, 'Highland Fire' for example being variously described as ruby red with a dark zone and as a pale pink self! They were all sold as plants for the rock garden or front of border, certainly some were much bigger than the conventional alpinus type of rock garden plant and would have done well in the border (I have two growing as border plants). Brief descriptions are given below of the main varieties with separate entries for the few still in cultivation. **'H. Adventure'** dwarf, white ground and a crimson central zone; **'H. Amulet'** ruby purple; **'H. Angus'** dwarf red; **'H. Beauty'** rose pink; **'H. Ben Alder'** dwarf, white blotched crimson; **'H. Ben Lomond'** cerise fancy; **'H. Blaze'** salmon-rose ground and a dark red central zone; **'H. Brigadier'** reddish crimson ground and a pale central zone and lacing of a pale rose pink; **'H. Brilliance'** reddish crimson ground and a pale rose central zone; **'H. Cairn Beauty'** a pale pink ground, blotched a deep rosy purple; **'H. Captain'** a dark crimson self; **'H. Charm'** dwarf, shining pink; **'H. Chieftain'** not a Haywood plant, see below; **'H. Claymore'** a crimson ground spotted pearl pink; **'H. Clove'** a rosy carmine ground with a central zone of crimson maroon; **'H. Countess'** tall-stemmed, salmon rose ground and a central zone of dark crimson; **'H. Crimson Fraser'** a darker version of the popular 'H. Fraser'; **'H. Crimson Velvet'** a deep lustrous crimson; **'H. Crofter'** a soft cerise red; **'H. Crown'** a strawberry red; **'H. Delight'** large-flowered white marked with red; **'H. Destiny'** red; **'H. Dimity'** a white ground and a scarlet eye; **'H. Duchess'** a rose madder ground and a crimson central zone; **'H. Dundonald'** vermilion; **'H. Enchantress'** white changing to blush pink; **'H. Exquisite'** a rosy cerise; **'H. Fairy'** fancy red and white; **'H. Fire'** either a ruby red with dark zone or a pale pink self; **'H. Firebrand'** a red fancy; **'H. Flame'** vivid red; **'H. Fort William'** no description; **'H. Fraser'** see below; **'H. Gallant'** ruby; **'H. Gay Gordon'** brilliant scarlet; **'H. Gem'** see below; **'H. Glencairn'** blush pink with dark crimson eye; **'H. Glory'** red; **'H. Glow'** a dwarf crimson; **'H. Greetings'** no description; **'H. Gwenda'** dwarf salmon; **'H. Heather'** a pink to purple self; **'H. Inspiration'** glowing cerise red; **'H. Isobel'** a pink fancy; **'H. Jeanie'** dwarf brilliant red; **'H. Jewel'** a rose-pink ground and with a central zone and lacing of a deep crimson (it won a HC in 1933 as a rock garden plant); **'H. King'** rich scarlet crimson, see also 'H. Chieftain' below; **'H. Laddie'** dwarf brilliant red; **'H. Lassie'** charming pink; **'H. Love Song'** charming pink; **'H. Loy-**alty'** a deep rosy carmine ground with a central zone of crimson; **'H. Lustre'** no description; **'H. McFarland'** pretty flecked red; **'H. McLachlan'** fancy variety; **'H. Maid'** white ground and a scarlet; **'H. Margaret'** a salmon pink self or vivid rose self; **'H. Marjorie'** deep red with picotee edges; **'H. Marksman'** scarlet red; **'H. Mary'** a white with a crimson centre; **'H. May'** bright salmon pink; **'H. Meg Merilees'** gipsy shadings of red; **'H. Melody'** no description; **'H. Minstrel'** ruby, jewelled white; **'H. Nell'** dwarf vermilion; **'H. Pearl'** a white with red zone, won HC as a border plant in 1933; **'H. Pink Pearl'** shell pink with red zone; **'H. Piper'** deep red; **'H. Pixie'** a pale pink; **'H. Prince Charlie'** brilliant cherry-scarlet; **'H. Princess'** pretty pink; **'H. Prosperity'** red and white fancy; **'H. Queen'** see below; **'H. Red Opal'** a pale rose ground with a central zone and lacing of a rose red, awarded a HC as a border plant in 1933; **'H. Reel'** no description; **'H. Robert Bruce'** a deep crimson ground with a central zone and lacing in a pale rose pink, awarded a HC as a border plant in 1933; **'H. Rob Roy'** rosy carmine ground that has a crimson maroon central zone and flakes of the same colour near the margins; **'H. Rose'** a brilliant rose self; **'H. Royal Scot'** very dwarf, crimson and pearl; **'H. Salmon'** salmon pink; **'H. Shepherd'** fringed grey-pink; **'H. Silver Lace'** silver and pale pink; **'H. Snowfall'** white; **'H. Star Shower'** jewelled red and white; **'H. Stella'** a white ground and a scarlet eye; **'H. Stormer'** a white ground with a scarlet eye; **'H. Stuart'** fine jewelled variety; **'H. Sylph'** pale pink; **'H. Tam O'Shanter'** purplish red, flecked pink; **'H. Tartan'** no description other than pretty variety; **'H. Thistle'** thistle purple with rich purple tones; **'H. Treasure'** a salmon pink self; **'H. Veteran'** no description; **'H. Victory'** a crimson ground with white spots; **'H. Visionary'** dwarf rosy carmine with dark zone; **'H. Wallace'** no description; **'H. Warrior'** rose red; **'H. Welcome'** in a long list of plants that appear, unfortunately, to have a scarlet to crimson self; **'H. Willie Mille'** fringed fancy.

'HIGHLAND CHIEFTAIN' This breaks the sequence as, although from the same stock as the above, it was raised by another nurseryman. Like most of the others it is a single pink for the rock garden. The flowers have a white ground and a red central zone and lacing. The petals are not fringed. It was raised with 'Highland Fraser' as one of its parents by Reginald Kaye at Waithman's Nursery at Silverdale near Carnforth. It was originally called 'Highland King'.

'HIGHLAND FRASER'   This is still a popular rock garden pink. It is a single with unique markings that give it a tartan effect. The ground is a purple pink (73A). This is decorated by a velvety purple crimson (61A) central zone and lacing, which are laid in such a way as to produce the tartan markings. It has some scent and flowers over a long season. The stems are up to 15 cm (6 in) high, sometimes taller. It is a good strong plant that increases well. It also produces good quantities of seed, the seedlings of which often bear a resemblance to the parent. Because of this many plants have been raised and distributed from seed, which has led to quite a variation in the plant as it is now grown. Regretfully it has become a strain rather than a cultivar. This explains why different written sources give differing colour descriptions of the plant. The name is sometimes spelt 'Highland Frazer'. The plant in my possession, whose lineage can be traced back to the 1930s, has quite a dark pink ground, which is more in keeping with the descriptions by Ingwersen, Hills and Mansfield than by other authorities including the *IDR*, but since seed was distributed by the original nursery, who can say what the correct form is. It was produced by P.S. Hayward of Treasure Holt Nurseries, Clacton-on-Sea in about 1930 and is still widely available. There is a larger growing plant with very similar, although darker, flowers called 'Betty Buckle'. It could be that this plant was derived from seed of 'Highland Fraser'.

'HIGHLAND GEM'   This is another Hayward plant, this time a pale pink self according to the *IDR*, but Hayward's catalogue lists it as very dwarf ruby red. Until quite recently there was a third form of this plant still in cultivation. Unfortunately the nursery is no longer trading and their last catalogue simply gives it as a single laced pink for the rock garden, which ties in with neither of the above. This variation may, again, be due to Haywards distributing seed as well as plants. It was originally introduced by P.S. Hayward of Treasure Holt Nurseries, Clacton-on-Sea in about 1930. The last-mentioned plant is likely to still be in cultivation but I have unfortunately not seen it.

'HIGHLAND QUEEN'   Another of the 'Highland' series from P.S. Hayward. This is a single with large flowers, up to 5 cm (2 in) across, which are a rich crimson pink carried on 20–25 cm (8–10 in) stems. It is a bigger and more vigorous plant than 'Highland Fraser'. It was introduced by Hayward at the Treasure Holt Nurseries, Clacton-

on-Sea in about 1932. *IDR* lists another pink with the same name. It describes it as a single bright crimson self introduced in about 1952 by an unspecified person. It is quite likely, knowing the variation in people's interpretation of colour, that this could be the same plant as the above or possibly a seedling from it. The one in circulation still fits Hayward's original plant. A further form seems to be in cultivation that is a single dry brick red (51A) with a dark maroon (187A) central zone. The petals have a very slight fringing. Yet another is also a single, this time with a lilac pink (75C) ground with a purple (61A) central zone that extends almost to the coarsely fringed margins of the petals. There are two small pink 'eyes' in the middle of each petal. The flowers are 3.8 cm (1.5 in) across and are carried on 30 cm (12 in) stems. One of these may be the true 'Highland Queen', the other being possibly a sport or seedling from it (as with all this series Haywards distributed seed as well as plants) or simply a misidentification at some point.

'HOLLYCROFT FRAGRANCE'   A small double-flowered pink suitable for the rock garden or front of border. The flowers are a dark pink (63C) flushed with a darker pink (63A) and with a crimson central zone (59A). With age the flower fades to a muddy colour and it is best to do a bit of dead-heading. The margins of the petals are fringed giving the flower a frilly look. The reverse of the petals is a paler version of the ground colour, especially towards the calyx. They are about 2.5 cm (1 in) across and are carried on 15 cm (6 in) stems. They are very fragrant. It was introduced in about 1979 by the Hollycroft Nurseries (hence the name). It is still in cultivation. A printer's error (one assumes) in one nursery catalogue calls it 'Hollyhock Fragrance', but I have not seen any plants put around under this name.

'HOLLYCROFT ROSE'   Another plant from the same stable as 'Hollycroft Fragrance'. This is a double that is deep rose self. It was introduced in about 1979.

'HOLLYHOCK FRAGRANCE   *see 'Hollycroft Fragrance'*

'HOLMSTED'   A large-flowered, single pink for the rock garden. The flowers are a soft rose pink. The petals are fringed and are overlapping. The overall size of the flower is about 5 cm (2 in) and they are carried on 15 cm (6 in) stems. It appears that this was a very floriferous plant that was discovered in a garden in Surrey in the 1930s, but now seems to have disappeared.

'HOPE' (1) A double Allwood modern pink with a pale pink (65D) ground and maroon (187C) zoning and lacing. The flowers are up to 5 cm (2 in) across and appear on 38 cm (15 in) stems. It was introduced by Allwood in 1946 having earlier used the name for another plant (see (2)). It is still in cultivation. The RHS awarded it an AM in 1951 and a FCC in 1952, both as a border plant.

(2) It would appear Allwood also introduced another plant with this name in about 1932. This was a double, scarlet self. This plant does not seem to be still in cultivation.

(3) Two more pinks bear this name, one undescribed plant introduced in about 1841 by Neville of London, and the other, with a white ground with red lacing, was in existence around the middle of the last century.

(4) Four border carnations also carry this name.

'HORTON' A flat double or semi-double pink with quite a coarse fringing to the petals, which gives the flowers a frilly look. The flowers are white with a red zone (61A) that takes up nearly a third of each petal. Within this there is a white eye where the petals disappear down the throat, which is particularly noticeable as the calyx splits on most flowers. The flowers are about 5 cm (2 in) across and are borne on 30 cm (12 in) stems above a blue-green foliage. The splitting of the calyx gives the flower an overblown, blowsy look. It was discovered in the village of Horton by Sue Farquhar in the 1980s and is still in cultivation.

'HOUND TOR' A striped double sport of 'Bovey Belle' with very pale pink (65D), almost white, ground heavily flecked with purple (67A) stripes and flecks. The flowers are 5 cm (2 in) across and are fringed. It was introduced by R. Hubbard of Landscove in 1988. It is still in cultivation.

'HOUNDSPOOL CHERYL' A double modern pink with velvety red (46A) petals with a slight dusky appearance. The flowers are about 5 cm (2 in) across and appear on stems that are 38 cm (15 in) above the blue-green foliage. The petals are slightly fringed and the whole flower has a slight clove perfume. It was found and introduced as a sport from 'Houndspool Ruby' by J. Whetman of Houndspool (hence the name) near Dawlish in 1980. It is still in cultivation. The RHS awarded it

a C in 1982, a HC in 1985 and an AM in 1987, all as a worthy border plant.

'HOUNDSPOOL RUBY' A popular modern double pink. The flowers are coloured a bright pink (61D) with a ruby red (53A) central zone. The ground colour pales towards the edges of the fringed petals. The flower is slightly fragrant. It is 4.5 cm (1.75 in) across and are carried on 33 cm (13 in) stems. It was raised as a sport from 'Doris' by J. Whetman of Houndspool (hence the name), near Dawlish in 1977 and is still widely available. It is sometimes called 'Ruby' or 'Ruby Doris' (*qv*). The latter name also refers to a variety from Allwood. It is one of the parents of 'Saint Bertram', 'Saint Botolph', 'Saint Eata', and 'Saint Kenelm'. The RHS awarded it a PC in 1981, a HC in 1982, an AM in 1986 and a FCC in 1987, all as a border plant.

'HOUSTON HOUSE' An old form from Houston House near Paisley in Strathclyde (previously Renfrewshire). This is a deeply fringed semi-double that makes a frilly, even untidy, flower, especially when going over. The colour is a bright mauvy pink (pinker 75A), darkening towards the centre, giving the suggestion of an eye. The flowers are carried on 20 cm (8 in) stems above fine leaves of a blue-green. The *IDR* lists it as 'Houstan House', which would seem to be incorrect as the house plus the village near which it is situated are definitely Houston. The date of origin is unknown but it is still in cultivation.

'HUGH' One of Allwood's earliest modern pinks. It is a double with a rich crimson purple colouration. It was introduced somewhere around 1918 but seems to have now disappeared, perhaps because of the introduction of 'Hugh Improved'.

'HUGH IMPROVED' A double modern pink from Allwood that one assumes was introduced to replace the previous plant. It is again a double and is a crimson purple self. It is very fragrant and flowers over a long period from June into the autumn. It was introduced by Allwood in about 1929, but it has now disappeared.

'HUMMING BIRD' One of the Douglas of Great Bookham's bird series of double pinks. This one is a very pure white with a cyclamen purple central zone. The flowers are fragrant. It was introduced by Douglas in about 1955 but like the rest in this series, it seems to have disappeared.

'HUNTSMAN'   *see 'Allen's Huntsman'*

'HUZZAR'   A single pink for the rock garden. It has a light red (53C) ground flushed with a darker red (53A), and a maroon (187A) central zone. The flowers are about 3.2 cm (1.25 in) across and are carried on 10 cm (4 in) stems. They have no scent. The plant was introduced by C.E. Lucas-Phillips in the late 1960s. The RHS awarded it a HC as a rock garden plant in 1971.

'IAN'   A double (varying to semi-double) modern pink from Allwood that was introduced in 1938 and is still going strong. It is a bright crimson red (53A) flushed with a sheen of a darker, duskier red. The reverse is the same colour but duller, changing to almost white where it enters the calyx. The petals have serrated margins. The flowers are up to 5 cm (2 in) across and are carried on 30 cm (12 in) stems for a long period, from June into the autumn. It was originally very fragrant with a clove scent, although I have not noticed this on any of the flowers I have examined. The foliage is finer than in most modern pinks but is of the typical blue-green colour. There is one perpetual-flowering carnation with the same name. It is still widely grown.

'IBIS'   This is listed in *The Plant Finder* (UK) as a pink but it is a border carnation.

'ICE QUEEN'   A modern double introduced by Allwood in about 1948. The flowers have a white ground and a narrow central zone of deep rose pink (57C). The flowers are 3.8 cm (1.5 in) across and are carried on 30 cm (12 in) stems. The petals are fringed and the flower is fragrant. It has a long season, from June into late autumn. The plant has a compact, bushy habit. It was raised as a sport from 'Dusky'. The RHS awarded it a C as a worthy border plant in 1953. It is not certain whether it is still in cultivation.

'ICEBERG'   One of the imperial pinks that has managed to survive, indeed the number of nurseries stocking it seems to have increased. Its flowers are large semi-doubles, verging on doubles. They are a pure white and are up to 5 cm (2 in) across and were carried on stems that can be up to 51 cm (20 in) long. The broad petals are indented but not as much as 'Haytor'. The flowers are fragrant and are carried over a long season, from June into autumn. It was introduced by C.H. Fielder of Lindabruce Nurseries in about 1950. The RHS

thought it a good plant and awarded it a PC in 1953, a HC in 1954, an AM in 1955 and a FCC in 1956, all as a plant for the border. There are also two border carnations and a perpetual-flowering carnation with the same name.

'ICOMB'   A rock garden plant raised before the Second World War as a seedling of *D. gratianopolitanus* by Simpson Hayward of Icomb (hence the name). It is a smaller plant than the species but it retains the pink colour and good fragrance. The flowers are notably large. It flowers in June and July and is floriferous. The *IDR* records it as 'Icombe Hybrid'.

'THE IMP'   A double pink with very large ruby red flowers that have a clove fragrance. It was introduced by C.H. Herbert of Acocks Green in about 1923 but no longer seems to be in cultivation.

'INA'   A pink for the rock garden. The flowers are single with a pink ground and a darker pink central zone. They are fragrant. It was raised in Canada in about 1983.

'INCHMERY'   This is one of my favourite pinks. It is quite a flat double of the most beautiful clear shell pink (56A), suffused with a paler pink as it ages. The flowers are about 3.8 cm (1.5 in) across and are carried on 20 cm (8 in) stems above a good blue-green, mat-forming foliage. It is very fragrant, but not as cloying as 'Mrs Sinkins' nor does it split its calyx. The petals are only slightly fringed. It was introduced in the eighteenth century. This is a very good old fashioned pink, it flowers slightly later than many of the others and has quite a long season. When it goes over it does so gracefully. It does well on heavier soils. Do not stop young plants otherwise they will not flower that year. The RHS awarded it an AM in 1946 and then an AGM in 1962. This is one pink that should be in every garden.

'INCHMERY WHITE'   *see 'White Inchmery'*

'INDIAN'   A double pink with a small button of a flower. These are a rich reddish purple (nearest is 64A) with a white, suffused with pink, edging which bleeds over from the reverse of the petal. It splits its calyx, often while still in bud, revealing its white throat. The flowers are 3.2 cm (1.25 in) across (more with split calyx). The petals are fringed and somewhat curled, which together with the split calyx gives the flower a frilly look. The

'Inchmery'

reverse is a white tinged with pink. The flowers are fragrant. The plant was found growing in gardens on the Oxfordshire Buckinghamshire border where it was known locally as an Indian.

'INGLESTONE'   A dwarf single pink for the rock garden. It has a dull cerise (67A) ground flecked with red at the centre, which noticeably fades as it enters the throat. The colour contrasts well with the white styles. There is a slight trace of a beard with red hairs. The petals are fringed. The plant is about 15 cm (6 in) tall.

'INSHRIACH DAZZLER'   A magnificent rock garden pink whose flowers have a wonderful freshness and clarity about them. They are single with a magenta ground (67B) and a steely blue eye (116A). The reverse is a strong buff colour, which may suggest that D. pavonius has blood in it somewhere. The petals are perfectly shaped and make a good rounded, flat flower with no overlapping or gaps between the petals. They are fringed. The flowers are 2.5 cm (1 in) across and are carried on 10 cm (4 in) stems above a good clump-forming, green foliage. It is a floriferous plant, with the flowers appearing in May and June. It was introduced by Jack Drake at his Inshriach Alpine Nursery (hence the name), Aviemore, sometime

around 1979. It is still widely available.

'INSHRIACH STARTLER'   A floriferous single pink with cherry-red flowers. They are fragrant and appear in June and July on 15 cm (6 in) stems. It was introduced by Jack Drake of Inshriach Alpine Nursery (hence the name) near Aviemore in about 1983. It is still in cultivation.

'IPSWICH MULBERRY'   A straggly, mat-forming plant with single flowers of dark rose and a maroon (53A) centre. The dark rose is not a pure colour but consists of darker colour (60D) streaked over a paler pink. The reverse is a paler version of the same. The flowers are 3.2 cm (1.25 in) across and are borne on 15–18 cm (6–7 in) stems. The petals are slightly fringed and are turned up at the margins. The flowers are fragrant. The leaves are flat and quite wide. They are of a grey-green colour, often with blotches of purple. It is still in cultivation.

'IPSWICH PINK'   Unlike 'Ipswich Mulberry', this is a flat double, slightly fuller than a semi-double. The flowers are small and pink. They are fragrant and the petal margins are slightly fringed. It flowers in June and July on 23 cm (9 in) stems. It was introduced before 1951, which was when

'Inshriach Dazzler'

Mansfield records it. It is doubtful whether it is still in cultivation. Thompson & Morgan are re-introducing a seed-strain of mixed colours called 'Ipswich Pink' that is supposed to have derived from the original introduction.

'IRISH PINK'   A contentious plant as the different written authorities variously claim it to be single, semi-double and double.

(1) However, the plant still in existence is a single with a purplish pink (the nearest is 62A but the flushing from the eye makes it difficult to assess) ground heavily overlaid with a velvety crimson (bright 60B), with a paler ground showing through around the margins of the petals. The fragrant flowers appear in June and are carried on 30 cm (12 in) stems. The foliage is a blue green, the leaves being quite narrow. It is still in cultivation.

(2) Another plant with this name is the one mentioned by Moreton as being in existence in the 1950s. This is a semi-double with a crimson ground and white stripes and markings. The flowers are about 3.2 cm (1.25 in) across and the petals have fringed margins. It is an old variety found in a garden in Cork in 1937. With a bit of imagination it could be said that these two plants are one and the same (few-petalled semi-doubles often appear

single and vice versa, and the heavily flushed white marks might appear purplish pink). Moreton says that it originally had another name but that this has now been lost, therefore there is the outside possibility that the plant may also exist under its other name.

'ISLE OF WIGHT PINK'   Another mule pink from André Paré of Orléans, France. This one is a cerise colour. Its name derives from the fact that the plant was discovered in a garden on the Isle of Wight by Moreton. It was originally introduced in about 1840. As with all these mule pinks, they need constant propagation to ensure that they survive. It was in existence in the 1950s but does not appear to now be around.

'ISOBEL'   An Allwood modern pink. It is a semi-double verging on a flat double with a cherry pink (55A) ground with a golden sheen to it and a narrow central zone of crimson brown (59C). The flowers are very fragrant and bloom from June into the autumn on 30 cm (12 in) stems. They are 5 cm (2 in) across. It was introduced about 1947 but no longer appears to be in cultivation. The RHS awarded it a HC in 1949 and an AM in 1953, both as a plant suitable for the border.

'ISOLDE' A semi-double with a white ground tinged with a very pale pink, a red (59A) central zone and purple (74B) lacing. The flowers are 4.5 cm (1.75 in) across and are carried on 18 cm (7 in) stems. The broad petals are serrated. The plant is vigorous but compact. It was raised by G. M. Taylor of East Lothian in about 1938 but it does not appear to be still extant. The RHS awarded the plant a HC in 1950 and an AM in 1954, both as a border plant.

'JACQUELINE' A double Allwood modern pink with rose-vermilion (45D overlaid with 45C) flowers. The flowers are up to 5 cm (2 in) across and are carried on 28 cm (11 in) stems. The petals have serrated margins and the flowers have a slight fragrance. This is a compact plant with short stems. The RHS awarded an AM as an exhibition plant in 1967 and a HC in 1968 and an AM in 1969 as a border plant.

'JACQUELINE'S DELIGHT' A double-flowered pink with cerise petals carried on 40 cm (16 in) stems. It is not scented. It was introduced as a sport from 'Pink Delight' by J.R. Armstrong of Staindrop, Co. Durham in 1986. It is still in cultivation.

'JANE' One of the Allwood modern pinks to which they have given forenames. Unfortunately there is confusion as the *IDR* says it is a double while Genders and Mansfield maintain that it is a single. Unfortunately the plant is not around to settle the argument. There seems to be consensus that it has a rose-pink ground and a crimson central zone although the *IDR* goes on to give it lacing of the same colour. It was introduced in about 1924.

'JANE AUSTEN' An interesting old-fashioned single pink that has a very long flowering season. When they first come out the flowers are a rich reddish-purple pink (61A) with two very pale pink (62C) eyes in the centre of each petal and a fine line of the same colour round the margins. As they age the darker pink fades slightly and breaks down in an irregular manner leaving fragments of the purple in the centre and scattered around the flower. It is often possible to see as many as six completely different-looking flowers on one plant. Certainly anyone given a newly open flower and an older flower would never guess that they were the same cultivar. However, this breakdown of the pattern does nothing to detract from the plant, indeed it adds to its charm. The petals are toothed

and the whole flower fragrant. The flowers are about 2.5 cm (1 in) across and are carried on 25 cm (10 in) stems. Although old-fashioned in appearance it is a twentieth century plant and is available.

'JANE BOWEN' This is a double-flowered pink with dark-red (60A) petals. The flowers are very fragrant. It was raised as a sport from 'Bovey Belle' by David Bowen of Dawlish in about 1983 and is still in cultivation.

'JANET' A double with an apple-blossom pink ground and a maroon central zone. It flowers in June and July on 38 cm (15 in) stems and was introduced by Douglas of Great Bookham in 1927. A plant of this name is still in circulation but I am not certain whether it is the same one. There are also two border carnations and one perpetual-flowering carnation with the same name.

'JANET WALKER' A single-flowered pink with a deep pink ground and a darker centre. It is fragrant. The flowers are carried on 10 cm (4 in) stems over neat cushions of silver-grey leaves. It has a long flowering season. The plant occurred as a chance seedling of *D. gratianopolitanus* and was introduced by Joe Elliott of Broadwell Nursery in about 1955. It is still in cultivation.

'JEAN' One of Allwood's modern pinks. As with so many it borders between a flat double and a semi-double. The flowers have a white ground and a crimson-purple (74B) central zone. They are up to 4.5 cm (1.75 in) in diameter and appear on 30 cm (12 in) stems and have a long flowering period, from June into the autumn. The plant has a spreading habit. It was one of Allwood's original introductions of about 1916 but it seems to have now disappeared. The RHS awarded it an AM in 1920 and a HC in 1949.

'JENNY WYATT' A very full double pink with large flowers of a pale pink (49D) akin to that of 'Inchmery'. The flowers are up to 6.4 cm (2.5 in) across and are borne on 25 cm (10 in) stems. They are a bit floppy and they tend to split their calyces. It is strongly fragrant. It was introduced by Cecil Wyatt of Colehayes, Bovey Tracey in about 1983. It is still widely grown. It is one of the parents of 'Fair Beccy'. The RHS awarded it a C in 1987.

'JEREMY WELLS' A dwarf pink for the rock garden. The flowers are single and deeply fringed.

They are a deep rose-pink colour, flushed with a soft red. The flower stems grow up to 20 cm (8 in). It was introduced by S.P. Wells & Son of Moordown, Bournemouth somewhere around 1949. The RHS awarded it a C as a border plant in 1950. It does not seem to be in current cultivation.

'JESSICA'   A modern double pink with a salmon pink ground and rose-pink streaks. The flowers are fragrant. The plant was raised from 'Diane' by Barkers of Whipley Nurseries and was introduced in 1985.

'JESSIE'   A double pink with a deep rose pink (63B) flushed with a brighter pink (58B) and paling towards the centre of the flower. The flowers are up to 5 cm (2 in) across and are carried on 30 cm (12 in) stems. The broad petals are slightly fringed. It was raised by E.A. Tickle of Purley in the 1970s. The RHS awarded it a HC as a border plant in 1977.

'JESTER'   (1) The original plant with this name is a double modern pink introduced by C.H. Herbert of Acocks Green. It is a dark scarlet self and is clove scented. It was introduced in about 1930 but does not seem to be around now.

(2) A more recent introduction is a plant introduced by Lindabruce Nurseries, Lancing. This is also a double but with a deep pink ground striped and flaked with carmine. The flowers are up to 5 cm (2 in) across and are carried on 38 cm (15 in) stems. The petals are slightly fringed. It is scented. It was raised as a sport from 'Doris' and is still in cultivation. The RHS awarded it an AM as an exhibition plant in 1981.

'JOAN'   An early flat double, bordering on a semi-double, from Allwood. It has a candy pink (73A) flushed with a lighter pink (68C) ground and a purplish red (redder 57A) central zone. It is very fragrant and the 5 cm (2 in) flowers appear on 30 cm (12 in) stems from June into autumn. The plant is free-flowering and has rigid stems. It was introduced in about 1917. The RHS awarded it an AM as a border plant in 1949 since when it seems to have gone out of cultivation.

'JOAN'S BLOOD'   A wonderful cultivar of *D. alpinus* for the rock garden. It is single with a deep blood-red ground with a very dark red central zone. The flowers are up to 2.5 cm (1 in) in diameter and appear on 7.5 cm (3 in) stems over a dark green foliage. It was introduced by Joe Elliott of

'Joan's Blood'

Broadwell Nursery in the mid-seventies. His wife, Joan, selected the seedling from a batch of *D. alpinus*. As she picked it out of the bed Joe noticed that her finger was bleeding and gave it the temporary memory-jogging name 'Joan's Blood'. The name stuck. The seedlings from this plant showed little variability and with selection Joe soon produced a plant that nearly always came true from seed. It is still very much in cultivation.

'JOHN BALL' An old-fashioned, flat double or semi-double pink resembling 'Beauty of Healey'. The large flowers have a white ground centred in a deep crimson (59A) and lacing of a paler purple (64A) colour that often appears broken. Its flowers are 3.8 cm (1.5 in) across and appear in June and July on 30 cm (12 in) stems. They are very fragrant. The foliage is blue-green and is narrow but upright. It was raised by Allan McLean of Colchester and introduced by Turner of Slough, who also introduced 'Mrs Sinkins'. John Ball worked as foreman in the latter's nursery. It is still in cultivation but Moreton was already warning in 1955 that plants of this name were not always true.

'JOHN GRAY' This is a frilly double pink often regarded as a double 'Musgrave's Pink'. The flower has a white ground with a pale green (145A/B) eye. This eye is noticeable before the calyx splits and once it does it is even more in evidence. The flowers are about 3.8 cm (1.5 in) across and have a fine deep fringing. They are fragrant. The plant is mat forming and has good fine leaves of a green-blue colouration. Margery Fish used to grow this on top of a wall taking advantage of its occasional tendency to flop. In spite of its habit of splitting its calyx and flopping it is still a very good plant. It is still in cultivation. The name is sometimes spelt 'John Grey'.

'JOHN STREET' This is mainly a show pink but can be grown in the border. It is a double with a light salmon pink (48D) with a trace of darker salmon pink (47D) central zone. The flowers are up to 5.8 cm (2.25 in) across and are carried on 45 cm (18 in) stems. The petal margins are quite smooth. The flower are fragrant. The plant was raised and introduced by E.A. Tickle of Purley. The RHS awarded it a HC in 1973 as a border plant, and a PC in 1973 and an AM in 1973, both as an exhibition plant.

'JOHN TURK' *see 'Whatfield John Turk'*

'JORDANS' A single with a cerise ground and green eye for the rock garden. The reverse of the petals is a buff colour suggesting *D. pavonius* somewhere in its makeup. *D. alpinus* is suggested as another parent. The flowers are carried on 15 cm (6 in) stems in June and July. It is likely to flower itself to death so cuttings should be regularly taken. It was discovered in the garden of the Jordan's Meeting House, Buckinghamshire but, alas, it does not seem to still be around.

'JOY' (1) One of the Allwood modern pinks, which do not seem to be as prolific this far into the alphabet as they were towards the beginning. This is a double with a dark pink (52D) ground that is darker when it first opens and towards the margins. It is paler towards the centre, especially when it goes over. There is occasional orange streaks on some flowers. It is quite coarsely fringed. The flowers are up to 5 cm (2 in) across and appear above the typical blue-green, coarse foliage of a modern pink. It was introduced sometime around 1965 and is still a very popular plant. The RHS awarded it a C in 1965 and a HC in 1966, both as a border plant. It should not be confused with 'Laced Joy'. It produced the sport 'Rose Joy' and was the seed parent of 'Benjamin Barker'.

(2) It was preceded by another modern pink, with the same name, from the Allwood stable. This was also double, this time with a salmon pink ground and a brown eye. This one has disappeared. This was exhibited at the RHS in 1936 but failed to get an award.

(3) There are also one border carnation and three perpetual-flowering carnations with the same name.

(4) See also 'Whatfield Joy'.

'JUBILEE' (1) This is a large flowered double that arose as a sport from 'Prince of Wales'. It has a salmon pink ground and mauve rosy purple. There are alternative claims to its origin, *IDR* claims it was Hayward in about 1935, while Mansfield attributes it to C.H. Herbert. Either way it probably does not matter as it seems to have quit our gardens.

(2) For the record, there was also a pink with this name introduced by Ward in about 1835, but no more is known of it. There are also five border carnations and two perpetual-flowering carnations with the same name.

'JUDY' An Allwood modern pink with a blush white ground and a scarlet centre. It was introduced in about 1946 and could be around if the current plant with this name is the same one. There are also three border carnations and three perpetual-flowering carnations with the same name.

'JULIA'   (1 & 2) A semi-double modern pink with a tuft of petals in the centre. The flowers are a white, heavily speckled with purple (68B). They are up to 6.4 cm (2.5 in) across and borne on 33 cm (13 in) stems. The petals are fringed and slightly incurved. They make bushy, free-flowering plants. Mansfield saw the plant through tinted glasses and has it as silver pink, splashed with rose red. It is possible that either he made a mistake or was referring to an earlier Allwood pink with this name. *IDR* has it that the plant was introduced in 1953 at the time that the plant was awarded a HC as a border plant by the RHS. But there was already a plant of that name introduced by Allwood in the 1930s that could have been the same plant or the one to which Mansfield was referring. As well as the HC it also received an AM in the following year.

(3) There was one introduced by 'Mrs Sinkins' nurseryman, C. Turner of Slough, in about 1867. This was a dark red.

(4) An earlier one was a light purple form introduced by Young sometime around 1851.

(5) There are also six border carnations with the same name.

'JULIAN'   A modern double pink with a creamy-white ground heavily flushed with salmon pink (48C to 48D) paling towards the centre. The flowers are carried on 51 cm (20 in) stems. They have a slight fragrance. The plant was introduced by Mrs Desmond Underwood of Ramparts Nursery, Colchester in 1969. The RHS awarded it a PC as an exhibition plant in 1981 and a HC in 1982, an AM in 1984 and a FCC in 1986, all as a border plant. It is still in cultivation.

'JUNO'   (1) This pink has a single flower with a deep red-pink ground streaked with a darker red and having a reddish-brown central zone. It is fringed and very fragrant. It flowers from June to the autumn.

(2) There is another pink, introduced by Dean, that had a white ground and a red centre. It was awarded a HC as a border plant by the RHS in 1894.

(3) Prior to that was another plant with this name, which was deemed to be purple. It was

introduced by T. Looker of Oxford in about 1852.

(4) One that I would be surprised to see rediscovered is that introduced by Russell in about 1793. All that is known about it is that it is laced.

(5) There are also ten border carnations and one perpetual-flowering carnation with the same name.

'JUPITER'   (1) One of the Allwood alpinus group of rock garden plants. This one is a double and has a pink (68A) ground and a slightly deeper eye. The flowers are 2.5 cm (1 in) across and are fringed. It only grows 10 cm (4 in) high and has a good silver foliage. The plant has a long flowering season with the main flush of flowers in May and June but continuing fitfully until the autumn. It was introduced by Allwood in about 1939 and is still in cultivation. The RHS awarded it a HC in 1957 as a border plant and an AM in 1960 as a plant for the rock garden.

(2) There were two earlier pinks with this name, both of which have doubtless vanished and even if they, by some miracle, are still around, it is doubtful if their descriptions will lead to their identification: W.R. Bragg of Slough introduced a purple one in about 1853 and Stockwell produced an undescribed plant in about 1819.

(3) There must be something that attracts dianthus growers to this name as there have been at least 16 border carnations and four perpetual-flowering carnations that have been dubbed with it.

'KALI'   A single-flowered pink with a creamy pink ground flushed with rose and with a reddish-brown central zone. It is very fragrant. It has a long flowering period from June into the autumn. As far as I know, this plant is no longer in cultivation.

'KATHERINE LEIGH'   An imperial pink introduced by C.H. Fielder of the Lindabruce Nurseries. It is a double with a magenta pink ground with a dark red central zone. It is a free-flowering form that blooms from June until well into the autumn. It was introduced in 1948 but it seems to have disappeared.

'KATHLEEN HURST'   A modern double with a deep pink (52C) ground flushed and striped with carmine (darker 57B). The flowers are up to 5 cm (2 in) across and are carried on 28 cm (11 in) stems. The broad petals are finely serrated. The flowers are fragrant. The plant is bushy and has a good, erect habit. It was raised by H. Hurst in the 1950s.

The RHS have awarded it a HC in 1957 and an AM in 1958, both as a border plant.

'KATHY'   A dwarf plant for the rock garden. It is a semi-double with noticeably fringed margins. The ground colour is purple (64A) and there is a slight trace of a crimson (59A) eye. The flowers are about 2.5 cm (1 in) across and are carried on 10 cm (4 in) stems. It is in cultivation.

'KESTEVEN ANNEMASSE'   One of a series of pinks introduced by A.E. Robinson of Enfield. This double is a deep mauve (75B touched with 73B) self that pales towards the centre of the flower. The flowers are about 3.8 cm (1.5 in) wide and are carried on 15 cm (6 in) stems. The petals are fringed. The flowers are fragrant. It has a clove scent. It was introduced in 1971 and was awarded a HC as a border plant by the RHS in 1977.

'KESTEVEN BELVEDERE'   Another of Robinson's introductions. This one has a brick red ground and darker central zone. It was introduced in 1971.

'KESTEVEN CHAMBERY'   A good mat-forming, floriferous plant with single flowers. Their colour is a very pale pink ground, almost white with a rose purple central zone and lacing. The darker colour is not pure and tends to be spotted giving the lacing a dry look. The petals are quite deeply fringed. The flowering stems are about 15 cm (6 in) in height. It flowers in May and June. It was introduced by A.E. Robinson of Enfield in about 1979 and is still in cultivation.

'KESTEVEN CHAMONIX'   A single-flowered plant with a deep pink (73A) ground with a central zone and lacing of a deep purple (61A). The lacing has a central bar and produces two 'eyes' on each petal of the lighter colour. The flowers are about 2.5 cm (1 in) across and borne on 15 cm (6 in) stems. The margins of the petals are smooth. The styles are a prominent feature of the flower. The plant was introduced by A.E. Robinson of Enfield in about 1971 and is still in cultivation. The RHS awarded it a HC in 1972 and an AM in 1973 as a rock garden plant.

'KESTEVEN KIRKSTEAD'   A single flower of wonderful clarity brought about by the velvety, crimson (59A) central zone being set off by the pure white ground. The zone is quite wide 0.7 cm (0.25 in) and fades to a purple as the flower ages.

Beyond the central zone the throat fades to white. The flowers are 5 cm (2 in) across and recurving slightly as they age. The margins are slightly fringed. They are fragrant. The blue-green foliage is typical of a modern pink. It was raised by A.E. Robinson of Enfield as a seedling from 'Laced Romeo'. The RHS awarded the plant an AM in 1983 as an exhibition plant and a HC in 1979, an AM in 1987 and a FCC in 1988, all three as a plant for the border. It is still in cultivation. A good plant.

'KESTEVEN SHAW'   Another single-flowered plant, this time with a light pink ground with crimson lacing. It was introduced by A.E. Robinson of Enfield in about 1972.

'KESTEVEN WAVERLEY'   The last of this group of plants introduced by A.E. Robinson. This is a single with a pink ground and a deep red eye. It was introduced in about 1970.

'Kesteven Kirkstead'

'KESTOR'   A flat double or semi-double that is a bright, dark rose pink (61D) self with just a slight trace of a red central band. The flower is about 5 cm (2 in) across and a toothed margin. The flowers have a clove fragrance and are carried on 35 cm (14 in) stems. It was raised as a seedling from 'Haytor' by Cecil Wyatt of Colehayes, Bovey Tracey in about 1979. It is still in cultivation. The RHS awarded it an AM as a border plant in 1982.

'KESTREL'   One of the Douglas bird series of pinks. This is a double with a white ground, a deep red central zone and slightly lighter lacing. It is fragrant and was introduced by the Great Bookham firm in 1952, but seems to have disappeared. There is one border carnation with the same name.

'KING HENRY'   An old single with a flesh-pink ground and a maroon centre. The margins are smooth. It was around just after the Second World War but seems to have since disappeared.

'KINGSBROOK CRIMSON'   A modern double with a bright rose pink (darker 66C) ground overlaid with a darker pink and with a maroon (187C) central zone. The flowers are up to 5 cm (2 in) across and are carried on 30 cm (12 in) stems. They have a clove fragrance. The broad petals are slightly fringed. The plant has a somewhat spreading habit. It was raised by A.T. Barnes of Kingsbrook Gardens (hence the name), Bedford in 1949. The RHS awarded the plant a C in 1961 as a border plant.

'KINGSTONE COTTAGE'   This is a flat, only just a semi-double with turned up petal tips and irregular splashes of crimson (brighter 59A) on a purple pink ground (a lilac pink (70D) over-flushed with crimson (59A)). The flowers are about 3.2 cm (1.25 in) across and carried on 25 cm (10 in) stems. They are heavily fringed. It was introduced by Sophie Hughes of Kingstone Cottage near Ross-on-Wye. It is still in cultivation.

'KITTY JAY'   A single pink with large flowers of lavender pink. They are fragrant. It was introduced by R. Hubbard of Hill House, Landscove in about 1987 and is still in cultivation.

'LACED AVOCA'   An old eighteeenth century double variety from Avoca in Eire. It has a creamy rose-pink ground with a maroon central zone and lacing. The flowers are carried on 25 cm (10 in)

stems. It is still in cultivation but its age is beginning to show as it is now difficult to propagate.

'LACED CHARM'   An Allwood modern pink with, as its name suggests, a laced appearance. This is an extremely double flower with a lavender pink ground, a maroon central zone and a slightly paler, red lacing. It is heavily fringed and very fragrant. The stems are 30 cm (12 in) high. The flowering period is long, from June into the autumn. It was introduced in 1947 and it seems a pity that it has disappeared.

'LACED CONQUEROR'   Another of the All-wood laced pinks. This one is a double with a lilac pink ground with a central zone and lacing of purple. As with most Allwoods it has a long flowering period from June into the autumn. It was introduced in 1948 but seems to have vanished.

'LACED HERO'   Another Allwood laced pink but this is one that has definitely survived. This is a semi-double-cum-double that has a white ground shown off quite brilliantly against the very dark purple (187A) central zone and slightly lighter (59A) lacing. The lacing has a very clear-cut quality. The flowers are 3.8 cm (1.5 in) across and are only slightly fringed. They are carried on 30 cm (12 in) stems. It has a long flowering season, from June into the autumn although its main flush is at the beginning of the period. It was originally introduced by Allwood in 1947 but in 1951 they introduced a form called 'Laced Hero Improved'. It would seem that this is the form in existence and the 'Improved' epithet has been dropped.

'LACED JOY'   Another one of this series that is still in existence, indeed it appears to be one of the most popular of the laced pinks. Again it is between a double and semi-double but this time the ground is a rose pink, composed of a dark pink (73A) against a paler pink (65D). When the flower first opens the darker colour dominates. The central zone and the lacing are maroon (a redder 59A). As with most pinks the colour and degree of lacing varies with age, the latter disappearing almost entirely in some flowers. When the lacing is present it is quite a narrow band, close to the margins of the petals. The margins of the petals are slightly indented. Flowers are about 3.8 cm (1.5 in) across, larger as they age. They have a clove fragrance. The flowering stems are up to 30 cm (12 in) high and the foliage is that of a typical modern pink. The plant was raised and introduced

'Laced Joy'

by Allwood in 1947. The RHS awarded it a C in 1966, an AM in 1968 and a FCC in 1984, all as a border plant.

'LACED MONARCH' One of this popular series of Allwood's. It is a double with a dark pink (74A) ground and a brownish maroon (189A) central zone and lacing. The size of zone and degree of lacing diminish and become redder as the flower ages. The flowers are 3.8 cm (1.5 in) across and are slightly fringed. There is a slight fragrance. The flowers are carried on 30 cm (12 in) stems. It was introduced by Allwood in 1972 and was awarded a HC in 1975 and an AM in 1978, both as a border plant, by the RHS. Erroneously being sold under this name is a large double with a white ground and a maroon (59A) central zone and lacing that splits its calyx.

'LACED PRUDENCE' *see 'Prudence'*

'LACED ROMEO' A semi-double with a white ground into which is diffused the brownish maroon red (187C) of the central zone and lacing. The reverse of the petals is white suffused with pink. The flowers are 3.8 cm (1.5 in) across and are carried on 30 cm (12 in) stems above a typical blue-

green foliage of the modern pink. It was introduced by Allwood in 1963 and is still very much in cultivation.

'LACED TREASURE' An Allwood double in the same series as those above. This has a pale pink (65D) ground that only shows up on the extreme edge of the petals and on the reverse, which often shows as the petal can be curled inwards when they first open (similar to 'Camilla'). The central zone is crimson (59A) and comes almost to the margins of the petals. The edge of the zone is irregular, emphasising the slight fringing on the petal. As the flower goes over, the zone pales and becomes broken, and the margins widen, giving the flower a pinker look. The flowers are 3.8 cm (1.5 in) across and are carried on 25 cm (10 in) stems and have a long flowering season from June into the autumn. The petals are very wide and ruffled, which gives them a frilly look. The calyx splits, allowing the petals to flop out, but this causes the flowers to look pretty rather than untidy. It was raised as a sport from 'Frances Isabel' by Mr Calvert and was introduced by Allwood in 1981. It is still in cultivation.

'LADY DIANA'   This is a Reg Kaye plant for the rock garden. It is a single with a white ground and cerise markings. It was introduced from his Waithman's Nurseries in about 1982 and is still in cultivation.

'LADY GRANVILLE'   An old semi-double pink from the middle of the nineteenth century. It has a white ground, a very distinct crushed raspberry central zone (60A) and a brighter lacing (67A), the white ground taking up more than half of the petal. The lacing can be broken and on some flowers, especially the older ones, it may be absent altogether. The flowers are 4.5–5 cm (1.75–2 in) across and are carried on 30–35 cm (12–15 in) stems. The petals are quite coarsely fringed. The flowering season is in June and into July. The good foliage is a blue green, with individual blades being short, but the plant is a bit sprawling. The Lady Granville in question is thought to be either the first wife of the first Earl of Granville or the wife of the second Earl, whose marriage took place at about the time (1840) that this plant was possibly introduced. It is still in cultivation.

'LADY SALISBURY'   This is a full single that could be considered semi-double at times. The flowers have a white ground, laced with purple (near 61A) and crimson (59A) central zone. The lacing is quite thin and disappears or becomes irregular when the flower ages. It was introduced by S.E. Webb of Oxford in about 1980. It is still in cultivation. It is very similar to 'London Lovely' with which it could be confused. The latter has a more sombre colouring and its central zone and lacing is wider. It is also more semi-double.

'LADY STOVERDALE'   A long-lost pink but one of historical importance in that it was one of the main precursors of the laced pinks as we know them today. It was introduced by James Major of Lewisham, gardener to the Duchess of Ancaster, in about 1772 as a seedling from 'Duchess of Ancaster'. It had a white ground and more distinct red lacing than ever before seen on a pink and sold widely for many years.

'LADY WHARNCLIFFE'   A delightful old pink from about 1835. It is a double with a pure white ground and a deep purple (purplish 187A) central zone and lighter purple (60C) lacing. The edges of the lacing are jagged giving the flower a frilly look, although the margins of the petals are not deeply indented. The backs of the petals are white with just a hint of the purple showing through. The flowers are 3.8–4.5 cm (1.5–1.75 in) across and are carried on 30 cm (12 in) stems. It is also known as 'Revels' Lady Wharncliffe' and, more recently, as 'Camelford A'.

'LAMBROOK BEAUTY'   A double verging on semi-double with a magenta/cerise pink ground and a darker centre. The petals are smooth edged. It was introduced by Margery Fish in about 1966 but seems to have now vanished.

'LANCING JESTER'   An imperial pink introduced by C.H. Fielder of the Lindabruce Nurseries. This is a double with a white ground and dark pink (68B) markings. It has a clove scent and flowers from June until well into the autumn. The flowers are about 5 cm (2 in) in diameter. The broad petals have a finely serrated margin and are evenly arranged. It was introduced in about 1949 but seems to have now disappeared. Lancing of the plant's name was where the Lindabruce Nurseries were situated. The RHS awarded it an AM as an exhibition plant in 1952.

'LANCING LASS'   This is one of the imperial pinks in the Lancing series that is still certainly in cultivation. It is a double with a delicate rose pink (73C) ground and a reddish pink (73B) central zone. The flowers are 5.7 cm (2.25 in) across and are carried on 30–36 cm (12–14 in) stems. The petals are broad and slightly serrated. It has a clove scent and flowers from June until the end of the autumn. As with the others, it was introduced by C.H. Fielder from his Lindabruce Nurseries at Lancing, in about 1949. The RHS awarded it a HC in 1953 as a border plant and an AM as an exhibition plant in 1964.

'LANCING SUPREME'   Another imperial pink. This one has large double flowers with a dark pink (55D) ground and a red (52B) central zone and lacing. The broad petals are slightly fringed and evenly arranged. The flowers 6.4 cm (2.5 in) in diameter. As with the others in the series it flowers over a long period, from June until the end of autumn. It was introduced by C.H. Fielding of the Lindabruce Nurseries, Lancing, in about 1949, but no longer seems to be around, unless someone has a plant tucked away somewhere. The RHS awarded it an AM in 1952 and FCC in 1954 as an exhibition plant and an AM in 1953 as a border plant.

'LANCING WHITE' The last of these series of imperial pinks. This is a double with pure white flowers. They have a clove scent and flower from June until the end of autumn. It was introduced by C.H. Fielder of the Lindabruce Nurseries, Lancing in about 1949, but seems to have disappeared.

'LASSIE' An imperial double with a white ground and a crimson central zone. The flowers are about 3.8 cm (1.5 in) across and are heavily fringed at the margins. The flowering stems are about 25 cm (10 in) high. They are slightly fragrant. It was introduced by C.H. Fielder of Lindabruce Nurseries in about 1948 when it was first submitted for award. It seems to have disappeared.

'LAURA' (1) An Allwood modern pink. It is a flat double or semi-double that has a pale scarlet red (50A) colour fading towards the centre and margins, especially when going over, and with a slight streaking of a darker red. The fading as it ages gives it a bit of a washed-out appearance. The flowers are about 5 cm (2 in) across and are slightly serrated at the margins. It was raised as a sport from that ever-obliging 'Doris' by Allwood in about 1952 and is still in existence. The RHS awarded it a PC in 1960 as a cut flower, exhibition flower and as a border plant.

(2) C. Fellowes of Shotesham Rectory introduced a double pink with a white ground and purple central zoning and lacing in about 1908. It was clove scented. It seems to have now vanished.

(3) An earlier one with a white ground and purple lacing was introduced by Willmer in about 1848.

(4) There are also six border carnations and two perpetual-flowering carnations with the same name.

'LAURA JANE' A semi-double or flat double modern laced pink with a white ground and crimson central zone and pinker lacing. The central zone covers nearly half of the petals. The petals are indented and the lacing follows it, giving it a scalloped effect. The flowers are fragrant. The plant was raised by S.E. Webb of Oxford in 1980.

'LAURIE BELLE' A double modern fancy pink with a white ground and luminous purple-pink (74B) stripes that occasionally coalesce to produce patches. The flowers are up to 5.8 cm (2.25 in) across and carried on 36 cm (14 in) stems. They are fragrant. The petal margins are slightly fringed but the striping makes it difficult to see. It was

raised as a sport from 'Bovey Belle' by L.A. Ryman of Othery in about 1986 and is still in cultivation. This is not my sort of pink, brash and almost vulgar; it would be very difficult to fit it into a border although it must be said that the plant has a reasonable upright habit. The RHS awarded it a HC and an AM in 1991, both as a border plant.

'LAVENDER LADY' A semi-double pink with a white ground and a central zone and lacing of a maroon (redder 187A). The flowers are about 4.5 cm (1.75 in) across and are carried on 40 cm (16 in) stems. They are fragrant. The broad petals are fringed. The plant was raised by Mrs Desmond Underwood of Ramparts Nursery in the early 1960s. The RHS awarded it an HC in 1962 and an AM in 1964 as a border plant.

'LAVEROCK' A large-flowered pink from the House of Douglas. The flowers are double with a rose pink ground and a deep crimson central zone. They are slightly fragrant, the scent being of cloves. The flowering stems are up to 38 cm (15 in) long. It flowers in June and July. It was introduced in about 1950 but seems to have disappeared. There are also two border carnations with the same name.

'LAWLEY'S RED' This is a bit of an enigma in that it is so similar to 'St Nicholas' that it could be the same plant; the slight differences that exist could be due to variations of soil and situation. This plant has double flowers that are a deep purple pink (61B) with a crimson (59A) central zone. There are a few minute yellow or gold spots sprinkled over it. In the plants I have examined the flower seemed slightly smaller than 'St Nicholas' and of a slightly paler colour. The central zone is not so well defined and the main colour pales as it reaches the central zone. It flowers a week or so later than 'St Nicholas', flowering being in June and July. The flower is quite a small compact one being only 2.5 cm (1 in) across and is carried on 20 cm (8 in) stems. The petals are slightly fringed. It is fragrant. It is supposedly an old plant although its origins are unknown. The confusion is not only with 'St Nicholas' as there is another very similar plant currently being sold under the name 'Mr Neville' that again could well be the same plant.

'LAWRENCE JOHNSTON' *see 'Hidcote'*

'LEADER' This is one of C.H. Fielder's imperial pinks. It is a semi-double (occasionally double) with a mauvy-rose (72D) ground and a crimson

(187C) central zone. The broad petals are fringed and the flower has a very strong clove scent. It flowers from June until the end of autumn on 36 cm (14 in) stems. This plant is vigorous and spreading. It was introduced at the Lindabruce Nurseries in about 1946 but seems to have now disappeared. The RHS awarded it an AM in 1949 as an exhibition plant, and a HC in 1951 and an AM in 1952 as a border plant.

'LEDA'   One of G. Winter's single pinks. This one has an ivory white ground and a red central zone. The ground is tinged pink from the centre eye. It has quite a long flowering season, from June until autumn. The flowers are fragrant and carried on 25 cm (10 in) stems. It seems to be lost to cultivation.

'LEMSII'   A plant for the rock garden that is widely available, although it is not one of the best plants. It hovers between being single and sparsely semi-double; sometimes with more and sometimes with less petals. Either way the flower is quite flat. It is pink flushed with purple. The centre of the flower is paler and with a single purple fleck on each petal in the middle of this paler area, giving the notion of a inner zone. The flowers are up to 2 cm (0.75 in) wide and are carried on 12.5 cm (5 in) stems. The margins of the petals are serrated and there is a slight fragrance. They flower in June and July with the occasional later bloom. Its origins are obscure but it seems to have been introduced in the 1980s. The *IDR* declares that 'Lemsii' is an invalid name (presumably because it is cultivar with a Latinized name, a form that was deemed ineligible after 1959) but the name has been generally accepted and is widely sold under it.

'LEN HUTTON'   A companion to 'Herbert Sutcliffe' that was also produced by Holden Clough Nurseries. This one is single with a bright red ground and a white edge. It grows to about 20 cm (8 in) and is a plant for the rock garden. Surely someone somewhere still grows this plant.

'LEONORA'   (1) A Douglas pink. This is a single that is a salmon pink self. The flowers are produced on 25 cm (10 in) stems over a long period from June into the autumn. It seems to have vanished.

(2) C. Fellowes of Shotesham Rectory, Norfolk also used this name in 1908 to describe his introduction that was a laced dark red.

(3) Allwood seem to have missed this name but there are two border carnations and one perpetual-flowering carnation that have also used it.

'LETITIA WYATT'   This has a large, double flower of a blush pink (55D) deepening towards the centre. The flowers are about 5.8 cm (2.25 in) across and are carried on 28 cm (11 in) stems. The petals are fringed. The flowers are strongly fragrant with a clove scent. The foliage is typical of that of a modern pink. It was introduced by Cecil Wyatt of Colehayes, Bovey Tracey in about 1981. The RHS awarded it an AM as a worthy border plant in 1984.

'LILAC MUSGRAVE'   An Allwood plant with single flowers. The ground is lilac (68B) and there is an amber central zone encircled by a crimson band. The flowers are about 5 cm (2 in) across and are carried on 25 cm (10 in) stems. It was introduced by Allwood in the 1940s, possibly as a sport from 'Musgrave's Pink'. The RHS awarded it a HC in 1949 as a plant for the border. It is, sadly, no longer around.

'LILAC TIME'   Another of C.H. Fielder's imperial pinks. This one is a double with a lilac mauve colouration. The flowers have a strong clove scent and flower from June until the late autumn. It was introduced from the Lindabruce Nurseries in about 1957. It was awarded a PC as an exhibition plant by the RHS in 1959.

'LILIAN'   An Allwood modern pink. It is a double white self with a strong clove fragrance. The flowers are 5 cm (2 in) wide and are borne on 36 cm (14 in) stems. It was introduced in about 1953 but does not seem to be in cultivation, although plants of 'Rose de Mai' have been mistakenly sold under this name. The RHS awarded it an AM in 1960 and a FCC in 1963, both as a border plant.

'LILY COLLINS'   A large ivory-white self that hovers between being double and semi-double. The flowers are 5 cm (2 in) across and are carried on 23 cm (9 in) stems. It is a free-flowering form. It was raised as a sport from 'Inchmery' by A. Collins of St Albans before 1947, when it was first exhibited at the RHS, but it seems to have now vanished. It was awarded an AM as a border plant in 1948.

'LINCOLNSHIRE LASS'   An old variety from the early nineteenth century or before. The flower is a lilac pink and has a sweet fragrance. It is fringed. It used to be found growing in gardens of Lincolnshire and East Lothian. It was certainly still around in the 1950s but its present status is not certain. The plant is also known as 'Lothian Lass'.

'LINCOLNSHIRE LIFE' This has a semi-double flower with a light mauve-pink ground (69A) and a wide deepish red (bright 60A) central zone. The flower pales as it ages and the red zone becomes duller. The flower is about 5 cm (2 in) across and is slightly fringed at its margins. It is fragrant. The flower stems are up to 30 cm (12 in) long above a blue-green foliage. It was raised from unknown parents by J.H. Pepper of Cleethorpes in about 1987 and is still in cultivation. It was awarded a PC in 1989 and a HC in 1990 by the RHS.

'LINCOLNSHIRE POACHER' From the same stable as 'Lincolnshire Life' comes this single-flowered pink. It has a mauve-pink ground (69A) darkened by a flush of a deeper pink and a wide purple-maroon (61A) central zone inside which is a white eye disappearing into the throat. The flower is 4.5–5 cm (1.75–2 in) wide. The margins of the petals are deeply fringed and somewhat reflexed, particularly as the flower ages, because of its large diameter. It is fragrant with a clove scent. The flower stems are up to 40 cm (16 in) high above a blue-green foliage not quite as coarse as the typical modern pink's. It was introduced by J.H. Pepper of Cleethorpes in about 1982 and is still in cultivation. The RHS awarded it a HC in 1986, an AM in 1987 and a FCC in 1991, all as a border plant.

'LINDA' One of Allwood modern pinks. This one is a double, salmon pink self. It was introduced around 1970 and is still in cultivation. The RHS awarded it a HC in 1970, an AM in 1971 and a FCC in 1972, all as a border plant. There are also three border carnations and two perpetual-flowering carnations with the same name.

'LINNET' This is another of the vanished bird series from the House of Douglas. It is a blush pink with a crimson centre. It was introduced from Great Bookham in about 1955.

'LITTLE BURNETT' This is a modern semi-double pink with a white ground and a maroon (redder 187A) central zone and lacing. The flowers are up to 3.2 cm (1.25 in) across and are carried on 28 cm (11 in) stems. The broad petals are deeply serrated. The flowers have a strong scent. The plant is bushy with a spreading habit. It was raised by T.T. Burnett of Petersfield in the 1950s. The RHS awarded it a HC in 1957 as a border plant.

'LITTLE DORRITT' (1) The C.H. Herbert plant of this name is a double, ruby red self. It was introduced in about 1933.

(2) There was also a Douglas plant introduced in the mid-1920s. This was a soft blush pink with a blood red centre.

'LITTLE JOCK' One of the mainstays of the rock garden dianthus. It is a semi-double with a rich mauvy-pink ground and a crimson central zone. The flowers are about 2.5 cm (1 in) across and have a scent. They are carried on 7.5–10 cm (3–4 in) stems. The petals are fringed. Their main period of flower is in June and July, although there may be a few odd flowers later in the season. It was a chance seedling raised as a cross between *D. gratianopolitanus* and *D. plumarius* by John Gray (always known as Jock, hence the name) of Benhall, near Saxmunden in the 1920s. It is still very much in cultivation although plants offered under this name do vary in appearance. The RHS awarded it an AM for the rock garden in 1930. It is a very good plant for the rock garden, trough or edging.

'LITTLE MISS MUFFETT' A rather unusually coloured pink that tends to have a washed out look and an air of going over, even when it first opens. The reason for this is that the flower has a pale pink, almost white (56D) ground and a dark rose pink (55A) reverse that bleeds irregularly over the petal margins onto the front, giving a strong contrast to the ground colour. The flowers are semi-double and about 3.8 cm (1.5 in) across. They seem to have no or just a slight trace of scent. The flower stems are about 30 cm (12 in) tall. It was raised from unknown parents and introduced by R. Hubbard of Landscove, near Ashburton, in 1987. It is still in cultivation. In spite of the washed-out effect, the flowers are quite pretty when viewed close to.

'LITTLE OLD LADY'   *see 'Chelsea Pink'*

'LITTLE TONY' A flat semi-double that is a pink self. Little else seems to be known about it except that it has disappeared from cultivation where it was known to be after World War II.

'LODER'S PINK'   A double pink with a floppy habit. The flowers are a rose red and have a very long season (Will Ingwersen claimed to have seen it growing through snow). It appears to be no longer in cultivation.

'LONDON BEAUTY'   (1) The first of a series of London pinks. This is a semi-double with a pink ground, zoned and laced with purple. It has a clove scent. It was introduced by F.R. McQuown in about 1960. I have not seen it and do not know if it is still around.

(2) There was also a much earlier pink with this name, introduced by Barr sometime around 1798. It was described as simply 'laced', so the chances of this turning up are remote.

'LONDON BROCADE'   Another McQuown pink, this time one definitely still around. The flowers of this are semi-double with a white ground and a crimson (59A) centre and lacing. The margins are quite noticeably fringed. It is fragrant. The stems are about 25 cm (10 in) high above a good silver blue-green foliage. It was introduced in about 1961. The RHS awarded this plant a HC in 1962, an AM in 1970 and a FCC in 1971, all as a worthy plant for the border. It was one of the parents of 'Becky Robinson'.

'LONDON CONQUEROR'   This is a double with a pink ground and a purple centre and lacing. This one is an early member of the series, introduced by McQuown before 1950. It does not appear to be in cultivation.

'LONDON DELIGHT'   This flat double or semi-double has a pink (73B) ground, tinged with a darker purple-pink (57C) from the lacing, and with a maroon (59A) zone and purple (57C) lacing. The lacing can be intermittent or broken. The reverse is a pale pink. The petals are only very slightly fringed. The flowers are fragrant. The width of the flowers is 3.8–4.5 cm (1.5–1.75 in) across and they are carried on 30–38 cm (12–15 in) stems. This is another McQuown plant and was introduced sometime around 1960. It is still widely cultivated. The RHS awarded it an HC in 1960 and an AM in 1963, both as a border plant.

'LONDON DREAM'   Another in the series but one that has disappeared. This is a semi-double with a pale pink ground and a red zone. It was introduced by F.R. McQuown in about 1947.

'LONDON GEM'   This one is a double with a white ground with a crimson central zone and lacing. It is fragrant. F.R. McQuown is again the raiser, this time around about 1944. I have not heard of it still being in cultivation.

'LONDON GIRL'   Another semi-double with a white ground and a central zone (187C) lacing of purplish crimson (61A to 61B). The petals are smooth around the margins. The flowers are up to 5 cm (2 in) across and are borne on 36 cm (14 in) stems. They are fragrant and have a long season from June onwards. The plant has a bushy habit. It was introduced by F.R. McQuown in about 1944 and was awarded an AM by the RHS in 1949 as a border plant. It is doubtful if this is still in cultivation.

'LONDON GLOW'   This is a double with a very dark, almost black, velvety crimson (59A) ground, and narrow lacing of pale pink (65B) that looks almost white in the contrast to the dark ground. The flowers are 5 cm (2 in) across and are carried on 30 cm (12 in) stems. It is a very fragrant flower. It was introduced by F.R. McQuown in about 1944 and is still in cultivation. The RHS awarded it an AM as a border plant in 1948. There is a wrongly attributed plant going round with this name that has a pink ground and maroon centre, and lacing that flushes into the pink. The lacing breaks down as the flower ages.

'LONDON HERO'   This is thrown in to confuse everyone as it is not a McQuown plant but a much earlier one, introduced by Barr in about 1798. All that is known about it is that it was laced. There is also a border carnation of about the same time with the same name.

'LONDON JEWEL'   The *IDR* describes this as a semi-double with a white ground overlaid with magenta, and blotched and edged with garnet lake. It was raised by F.R. McQuown in about 1963 but now seems to have disappeared. It was awarded a C in 1964 as a border plant by the RHS.

'LONDON LADY'   Another F.R. McQuown pink, this time a double with a pink (65D) ground and a crimson (60B) central zone and lacing. The flowers are 5 cm (2 in) across and are carried on 36 cm (14 in) stems. It was introduced in about 1944. It might still be around but I have not seen it. The RHS awarded it an AM in 1948 as a border plant.

'**LONDON LOVELY**' This has a semi-double flower that sometimes has so few petals that it is almost a single. The ground is pure white and there is a dark purple crimson (61A) central zone that covers half the petal and gets paler as the flower ages. There is lacing of the same colour, but this fades and becomes irregular, sometimes almost disappearing, especially in older flowers. Occasionally there is a slight trace of purple lacing on the margins. The flowers are 3.8 cm (1.5 in) across and toothed at the margins. They are fragrant. It was introduced by F.R. McQuown in about 1944 and is still very much in cultivation. It is similar to 'Lady Salisbury' except that the crimson zone is more sombre in colour and that the lacing is also wider. It is also more semi-double.

'**LONDON MAGIC**' Another one of F.R. McQuown's pinks. Its description relies on previously written sources: a double with a rose Bengal ground and a garnet lake central zone and lacing. It was introduced in about 1947 but seems to be no longer around.

'**LONDON POPPET**' This one is definitely still in cultivation. It is a semi-double with a white touched with pink ground and a ruby red (59A) central zone and lacing. The lacing is quite wide, about the same width as the central zone. Beyond the lacing is a white, flushed with red from the lacing. The flowers are up to 5 cm (2 in) wide and carried on 30 cm (12 in) stems. It does not appear to be scented. The plant is compact and bushy. It was introduced by F.R. McQuown in about 1946. The RHS awarded it a HC in 1949, an AM in 1951 and a FCC in 1962, all as a border plant.

'**LONDON SUPERB**' A F.R. McQuown double with a white ground with deep purple central zone and a slightly paler lacing. The petals are fringed. The flowers are borne on 25 cm (10 in) stems and have a long flowering period. It was introduced in 1944 but appears to have disappeared from cultivation.

'**LORD LAMBOURNE**' A large double-flowered pink. The flowers are a cherry red with a maroon central zone. They are very fragrant. It has a long flowering period from June into autumn. The flowering stems are about 30 cm (12 in) tall. It was introduced by C.H. Herbert of Acocks Green in about 1922, in which year it was awarded an AM by the RHS. It does not seem to still be in cultivation.

'**LOTHIAN LASS**' *see 'Lincolnshire Lass'*

'**LOUISE'S CHOICE**' This is a semi-double with a dark rose pink (67D) ground and a good-sized maroon (187A) central zone (at least half the width of the petal) and a somewhat lighter, purple (61A) lacing. Some flowers have the hint of a central bar from the apex of the lacing to the central zone creating two pink 'eyes'. These eyes can also be flushed or flecked with the colour of the lacing. As the flower ages so the pink ground and purple lacing fades, and the maroon zone loses its velvety appearance. The petals are only very slightly fringed so that they appear smooth. The 5 cm (2 in) flowers are fragrant and appear on 30 cm (12 in) stems. The flowers are a bit floppy but the leaves are a good blue-green and are not as coarse as most modern pinks. It was raised as a cross between 'London Brocade' and 'Laced Joy' in 1983 by J.W. Radcliffe of Romford. It is still in cultivation. The RHS awarded it a PC as an exhibition plant in 1989, and a HC in 1990 and an AM in 1991 as border plants.

'**LOVE BIRD**' This is a large double with pale pink, almost white ground, and a dark red centre. The flowers are fragrant. It was introduced by the House of Douglas of Great Bookham in about 1960, but seems to have since disappeared. There is one border carnation with the same name.

'**LOVELINESS**' A strain of annual pinks raised by Allwood by crossing 'Sweet Wivelsfield' and *D. superbus* (*D. speciosus*).

'**LOVELY ANNE**' Another Douglas pink. This time a rose ground with crimson centre and lacing. It was introduced in about 1951 but is no longer to be found. There is also one border carnation sharing the same name.

'**LUDFORD PINK**' A dwarf pink with small rose pink flowers. It is a semi-double with a strong scent. It was found in Ludford, Lincolnshire (hence the name) at some time around 1955. It is not available at the moment.

'**LYRIC**' A C.H. Herbert pink. This is a large double with a deep purple colouration. It was introduced sometime around 1927.

'**MAB**' This is one of the original Allwoodii alpinus types for the rock garden. It is a single with a reddish pink ground and a deep crimson eye. It is moderately fragrant and after its main flush of flowers in June it goes on with odd blooms until the end of the autumn. The flowering stems reach about 15 cm (6 in) high. It was introduced by Allwood in 1931 but I have not seen it in cultivation recently. There is one perpetual-flowering carnation with the same name.

'MABEL VARLOW' A modern semi-double pink with a pale pink (56D) ground, a crimson (59A) central zone and lacing of the same colour. The flowers are about 4.5 cm (1.75 in) across and carried on 40 cm (16 in) stems. They have a slight fragrance. The plant has a bushy habit. It was raised by E.W. Varlow of Chadwell St Mary in the late 1950s. The RHS awarded it a C in 1960.

'MAB'S PINK' A single pink from the eighteenth century or possibly earlier. This has a pale pink ground with a band of crimson dots near the centre. The flower is quite small in diameter and has a long, slender calyx. The petals are deeply fringed. It is of Scottish origin. The plant was still in existence in the 1950s but seems to have now disappeared.

'MACAW' Another of the pinks in Douglas' series with bird names. This is a double with a bright cherry-red ground and a darker red central zone. It is fragrant. The House of Douglas introduced it in about 1960, but it seems to have gone the same way as many of their pinks and disappeared.

'MADONNA' This pink is either an old old-fashioned pink or possibly a more recent one that gives that impression. It is a blowsy double that splits its calyx with the petals cascading out. It has a white ground and a narrow band of mauve-purple (71A) near the centre. The flowers are 3.8–4.5 cm (1.5–1.75 in) across with deep, fine fringing and carried on 25 cm (10 in) stems. It is very similar in appearance to 'Bridal Veil' but if the two are placed together they can be seen to be distinct. 'Madonna' has a slightly smaller flower with finer fringing and a noticeably darker zone. 'Sally's Mauve' is another very similar but this also has a paler zone. One nursery showed a plant of 'Madonna' at a recent Chelsea Show that had paler (and quite disjointed) markings and was probably 'Bridal Veil', so there must be plants of the former being sold as the latter, which should thoroughly confuse the issue in a few years. (There were also blooms marked 'Bridal Veil' that were paler than

they should have been, which might indicate, as they were likely to have been grown in tunnels or under glass, that the colours had faded – either way they were not typical of the named type.) Just to add to the confusion there are also three border carnations and one perpetual-flowering carnation with the same name.

'MAGENTA' (1) Although this plant is still in cultivation I know little about it except that it is a single with magenta flowers with two white 'eyes' in the middle of each petal.

(2) See also 'Whatfield Magenta'.

'MAGPIE' (1) As one would expect, the House of Douglas issued a pink with this name. It was a double with a white ground with a rosy purple lacing and central zone.

(2) Genders (in a reference that I cannot now trace) mentions a double with a dwarf habit with flowers of a rose cerise ground and maroon central zone, but I can find no other reference to this.

(3) More recently, in 1971, E.A. Tickle of Purley introduced a single form with a white ground and a maroon centre that had been raised as a sport from his own 'Valerie'. This is the only one likely to still be in cultivation.

(4) There is also one border carnation and one perpetual-flowering carnation with the same name.

'MANDY' Back on surer ground, this is an Allwood modern pink. It is a semi-double verging on a double. This is a plant that is distinctive to the eye but difficult to describe as it is a fusion of colours. The central zone, which is wide, taking up a half to two-thirds of the petal, is a crushed strawberry (53A) colour. The ground is a pale pink that is so diffused and striped with the colour of the eye that it is almost impossible to say where one starts and the other ends, and it is certainly impossible to code it. The flowers are 5 cm (2 in), or slightly more, across and are carried on 38 cm (15 in) stems. The petals are quite deeply toothed. The flowers have a strong fragrance. It was introduced by Allwood in about 1959 and is still in cultivation. The RHS awarded it an AM in 1969 and a FCC in 1984, both as a border plant.

'MANDY'S CHOICE' A double modern pink with a red (53A) ground that becomes pinker (57B) towards the base of the petals. The flowers are about 5.8 cm (2.25 in) across. They are scented. The margins of the petals are serrated. It was raised by J.W. Radcliffe of Romford in about 1970. It was awarded an AM by the RHS in 1971 as an exhibition plant.

'MANNINGTREE PINK'   *see 'Cedric's Oldest'*

'MARGARET'   There appears to be three plants with this name although the *IDR* only lists the second two.

(1) Both Genders and Mansfield list a double, soft-pink self that fades white towards the edge of the petals. It is fragrant and long-flowering. They claim it to be an Allwoodii modern pink, but not necessarily introduced by Allwood as the *IDR* lists (2) as an Allwood.

(2) A double with a white ground with a carmine rose (52C) central zone and slightly paler lacing. The flowers are up to 5.8 cm (2.25 in) wide and are carried on 40 cm (16 in) stems. The broad petals are deeply cut. Allwood introduced it in about 1940. It was awarded a HC as a border plant in 1956.

(3) Probably of no consequence now, but there was another pink bearing this name introduced by Bradshaw sometime before 1849. It is simply described as black and white.

(4) 'Margaret Met' (*qv*) was originally distributed under this name.

(5) There are also four border carnations and two perpetual-flowering carnations listed with the same name.

'MARGARET CURTIS'   A single-flowered form of the Winteri group. It has a white ground and a dark maroon (187A) eye. It is very fragrant and has a long flowering season. It is quite a good mat-forming plant with a blue-green foliage. It was introduced by G. Winter in 1929 and is still in cultivation.

'MARGARET MET'   A rather attractive semi-double with a frilly appearance. The main colour is a crimson maroon (187A) that has a pale pink to white edge of about 0.3 cm (0.125 in) wide. The edge of the main colour is very jagged, matching the fringing on the petals, which gives it its frilly appearance. The flowers are about 3.8 cm (1.5 in) across and are carried on 38 cm (15 in) stems. The foliage is a light-blue green, almost silvery, forming good mats. It is a chance seedling of unknown parentage raised at Church Hill Cottage by Margaret Metianu in the late 1980s. It was originally distributed as 'Margaret'. It is still in cultivation.

'MARGOT'S PINK'   A single pink from the eighteenth century or possibly earlier. It has very small flowers with feathered petals. The plant is of Scottish origin and although extant in the 1950s, seems now to have vanished.

'MARG'S CHOICE'   This is mainly seen as a show pink although it recently (1991) received a HC as a border pink. It is a flat double or semi-double with a blush pink comprising a pale pink (49C) overlaid with a brighter, almost salmon-pink (52C) that tends to be the dominant colour. The colour appears darker when the petals are bunched towards the centre. The fringed flowers are about 4.5 cm (1.75 in) across and are carried on good upright stems of about 40 cm (16 in) in height. The RHS awarded it an AM for exhibition in 1990, and a PC and a HC as a border plant in 1991.

'MARIA'   *see 'Allen's Maria'*

'MARJORIE'   This has a pink ground and a central zone and even lacing of bright crimson. In spite of its name it was not introduced by Allwood but by the House of Douglas in about 1929, but does not seem to be still around. There are also one border carnation and one perpetual-flowering carnation with the same name.

'MARJORY PERFIELD'   This is a single-flowered pink with a dull red ground and a darker central zone. It is fragrant and carries its flowers on stems up to 23 cm (9 in). It has a few flowers after the main flush. It was introduced by Amos Perry of Enfield in about 1941, but seems to have now vanished unless someone still has plants of it tucked away somewhere.

'MARK'   An Allwood double modern pink that is a dark red (46A) self overlaid with a velvety sheen. The flowers are up to 5.8 cm (2.25 in) across and are carried on 40 cm (16 in) stems. They are a clove fragrance. The plant was first introduced by Allwood in about 1957 and is still in cultivation. The RHS awarded it an AM as a border plant in 1966.

'MARS'   A famous dwarf pink for the rock garden or front of border that was first introduced in the early 1930s by Allwood and is still going strong. It is a flat double or semi-double with bright crimson flowers (redder 61B) darkening a bit (to 60A) with age. The fragrant flowers are about 2.5 cm (1 in) in diameter and are carried on 10 cm (4 in) stems. Its main flush of flowers is in June and July, but it continues to flower until the autumn. This plant can flower itself to death, so taking regular cuttings is essential. The tufted foliage is short and a light blue-green or silver. The RHS awarded it a HC as a border plant in 1935. There are three eighteenth century pinks, probably of little consequence, that bore this name, as well as eleven border carnations and five perpetual-flowering carnations. Confusingly, it is also a synonym of 'Brigadier' (*qv*) which 'Mars' closely resembles, although the former's flowers are more purple.

'MARSHWOOD MYSTERY' A semi-double with a candy pink (73C) ground, wine-coloured (60A to 60B) central zone and lacing fading to white in the throat. The flowers are 5 cm (2 in) across and carried on 30 cm (12 in) stems. It has quite a strong fragrance. Raised and introduced by Three Counties Nursery in about 1982. It is still in cultivation. The RHS awarded it a C in 1985.

'MARTIN' This is a double with a very dark red centre on a white ground flushed with pink from the central zone. It is fragrant. The name is after the bird rather than a forename as it is one of the plants produced by the House of Douglas in the 1950s. It seems to have been lost to cultivation. There are also four border carnations and one perpetual-flowering carnation with the same name.

'MARVEL' Another House of Douglas plant produced in the early 1950s. This time it is a deep lilac pink with a maroon centre. It flowers in June and July and is slightly fragrant. Unfortunately, like so many from this nursery, it seems to have vanished. There is one perpetual-flowering carnation bearing the same name.

'MARY' This is a very early Allwoodii pink, introduced in 1914, which must make it one of the first, indeed some authorities state it was the first. It is a double with a lavender pink ground with a maroon central zone. It is very fragrant and flowers mainly in June and July, but continues into September. Alas, this historic plant seems to have disappeared from cultivation. There were two other eighteenth century pinks with the same name: one introduced by Ellis sometime before 1848 that had a white ground and rose lacing, and the other raised at about the same time by Kaye that is described as black and white. There are also five border carnations and two perpetual-flowering carnations sharing the same name.

'MATILDA' An Allwood modern pink. This has a double flower with a rose (69A) ground, and a central zone and the lacing of crimson (59B) on the inner petals is very velvety. The flowers are 6.4 cm (2.5 in) in diameter and are carried on 30 cm (12 in) stems. It is a vigorous, bushy plant. The RHS awarded it a C in 1951.

'MAURICE PRICHARD' A semi-double crimson self. This plant was introduced by Messrs. M. Prichard in about 1949 when it was submitted for trial at Wisley. It is still in cultivation.

'MAVIS' A Douglas double-flowered pink with a maroon centre on a deep rose ground. It has a clove scent and flowers in June and July. It was introduced in about 1927. There was another pink with the same name introduced by J.E. Firth in 1920 which, from its description, could be the same plant. Either way, neither are still in cultivation as far as I know.

'MAY' One of the Allwood modern pinks. This one is a double white self tinged with pink. It is deeply fringed and has a fragrance. The habit is compact. Allwood introduced it in about 1946. It was sent for trial at Wisley in 1947 but does not appear to have had an award. The plant does not seem to be in existence any longer. There are also one border carnation and two perpetual-flowering carnations sharing the same name.

'MAY JONES' This pink has a soft pink ground, spotted with lavender. The foliage is a grey-green and it gets straggly with age. The plant was introduced by N. Ovington of Honeybourne in about 1976. It is still in cultivation. This plant is one of the parents of 'Saint Bertram', 'Saint Botolph', 'Saint Eata' and 'Saint Kenelm'.

'MERCURY' One of the Allwoodii alpinus types for the rock garden or front of border. This has large semi-double flowers with a cherry-red (57B) ground and a darker, cardinal red (46A) eye. The broad petals are noticeably fringed. The flowers are 3.8 cm (1.5 in) across and are carried on 15 cm (6 in) stems. It was introduced in the early 1950s, but like most of the series it has now unfortunately disappeared. The RHS awarded it a HC in 1952 and an AM in 1954 as border plants, and a FCC in 1962 as a plant for the rock garden. A pink with the same name was introduced sometime before 1792 by Hughes. There are also three border carnations sharing this name.

'MERLE'   A double with an almond-blossom pink ground and a deep red centre. It is fragrant. It was introduced by the House of Douglas in 1958, but seems to have disappeared since.

'MERLIN   Another in the same series as 'Merle' from the House of Douglas. This is also a double, this time with a white ground and a purple-crimson central zone and lacing. It was introduced in about 1959 but, again, has disappeared.

'MESSINES PINK'   This is one of the mule pinks probably raised by crossing a *D. plumarius* with *D. barbatus*. Many of these pinks were raised in France and it is generally assumed that this one was as well, especially as it bears a resemblance to 'Emile Paré'. This is a flat double (or possibly a full semi-double) with pale pink (36D) petals. The flowers are fragrant and the margins are fringed. They are up to 3.2 cm (1.25 in) across and are carried on 25 cm (10 in) stems. The foliage is more characteristic of the sweet williams than the usual pinks. They are a pale green and without the usual glaucous bloom. Their main flowering season is in June and July, but they will continue into the autumn. They are very floriferous and, like so many mules, can flower themselves to death, so cuttings should be taken each year, possibly re-serving one plant for just this purpose and sheering it of flowering stems. It is still in cultivation. Mans-field has a delightful tale about this plant: 'A curious story is told of this plant, which may or may not be true. A soldier wounded in the neighbourhood of the Messines Ridge was found holding a piece of a plant in his hand. He was returned to England still holding it; the cutting was duly planted and gave rise to 'Messines Pink'. ' The plant was sent for trial at Wisley in 1933, but does not seem to have had an award.

'MESSINES WHITE'   Identical to the above plant except that it is a white self. It is supposed to be a sport from 'Messines Pink' raised in about 1951. The one currently in existence has been raised from a more recent sport.

'MICROCHIP'   An annual hybrid strain of *D. deltoides*.

'MILLEY'   A semi-double with a dark-red, brown eye on a pale, reddish-pink ground. It is fragrant. The *IDR* finds that this name is not ac-ceptable, presumably because there have been two

border carnations (one in 1884 and the other in 1902) with the similar sounding name 'Millie'. The current plant takes its name from J. Pike's Milley Nursery of Waltham St Lawrence, which in-troduced the plant in about 1972. It is still in cultivation under this name.

'MINI'   *see 'Whatfield Mini'*

'MISS CORRY'   A double flowered pink of which the *IDR* says that it is a dark pink self and Genders that it is a large, rich wine red self. Unfortunately I have been unable to find any plants to see which one or both or these descriptions is correct. It was introduced by Filippi of Holland sometime before 1949.

'MISS JANE'   *see 'Edgar Tickel'*

'MISS SINKINS'   A diminutive version of its better-known relative 'Mrs Sinkins'. This is a double white self with many of the same char-acteristics of Mrs Sinkins except that the scent is not so strong and it is smaller in all its parts. It grows to about 10–12 cm (4–5 in), which makes it suitable for the rock garden or the front of border. It is reputed to have been discovered in a garden in Henfield, Sussex, and was introduced by Allwood sometime around the Second World War. It is still in cultivation.

'MIST'   One of the dwarf Allwoodii alpinus group for the rock garden or front of border. This is a single, soft lilac pink. The large flowers are fragrant and appear in a main flush in June and July with odd flowers until way into autumn. It has the same neat habit as others in the series. The flowering stems are 10–15 cm (4–6 in) high. It was introduced by Allwood in about 1931, but has gone the way of so many of the alpine pinks and disappeared.

'MISTY MORN'   *see 'Whatfield Misty Morn'*

'MODEL'   To many older writers on pinks this was one of the most perfect ever produced and certainly lived up to its name, but, alas, it can no longer be found in any catalogues. It was in-troduced by C.H. Herbert of Acocks Green in the early 1920s. The freely produced double flowers have a soft rose-pink ground and a deep crimson red centre. It is very fragrant and has a long flowering period. The flowers are produced on 30 cm (12 in) stems. It has Herbert's famous 'Bridesmaid' in its makeup. There are one other pink (described as purple and introduced by Brown sometime before 1845), one border carnation and one perpetual-flowering carnation sharing this name.

'MOLLY'   An early Allwood modern pink. This double has a curious colour variously described as purplish crimson or violet, edged and speckled with a pale rose pink or white. It has a compact habit. It was introduced by Allwood in about 1927. There are also two perpetual-flowering carnations with the same name.

'MONICA WYATT'   This is a modern pink with a double flower of a deep pink (65A) ground and red (53A) central zone that diffuses into the ground. The petals are fringed and bunched, which gives the flower a frilly appearance. It is fragrant. The flowers are 5 cm (2 in) across and produced on 28 cm (11 in) stems. Flowering starts in June and continues into the autumn. It was raised as a seedling from 'Valda Wyatt' by Cecil Wyatt of Colehayes, Bovey Tracey in about 1981. It is more vigorous than its parent and was awarded an AM in 1984 and a FCC in 1986. It is still in cultivation.

'MONTY'   An early Allwood modern pink. It has large 7 cm (2.75 in) double flowers with a rose pink (67C) ground and a chocolate maroon (187C) central zone. They have a strong perfume and are carried on 23 cm (9 in) rigid stems. As with most in this series, it has a long flowering period, from June into the autumn. The plant is bushy in habit. It was introduced by Allwood in about 1929 but has since vanished, although it did last at least until 1949 when it was awarded a HC as a border plant by the RHS.

'MORN'   A double pink from Lindabruce Nurseries. The flowers are a light purple (63B) touched with a brighter cerise pink (58B). They are up to 6.4 cm (2.5 in) across and are carried on 28 cm (11 in) stems. They have a slight fragrance. The plants have a spreading habit. The RHS awarded it a HC in 1972 and an AM in 1973, both as a plant for the border.

'MOZART'   This sounds an intriguing flower and one I would dearly love to see. It is described variously as brilliant and glowing in its colour. The flower is a large single crimson self noticeably fringed and borne on 25 cm (10 in) stems. To add to its charms, it is also fragrant and had a long flowering season. It was introduced sometime before 1949. Surely someone must have this gem tucked away somewhere? If any plant was worth rescuing then this must be it, or do the descriptions belie the plant, which is why it has disappeared? There are also two border carnations and one perpetual-flowering carnation with the same name.

'MR NEVILLE'   Here one is treading on slippery ground. The *IDR* simply describes it as purple and pre-1850. Whether this plant is still around or not I do not know. There is a 'Mr Neville' currently being sold, but this is identical to 'Saint Nicholas' (*qv*) and I am convinced that the extant form has been misnamed. For the record, it is a double with dark reddy-pink (60B/C) ground and a crimson (59A) central zone. The flowers are quite small being only 2.5–3 cm (1–1.25 in) across.

'MRS CLARK'   *see 'Nellie Clark'*

'MRS CLIFFORD WOOLEY'   A vigorous plant with double pale salmon pink flowers with a deeper pink for the central zone. This was one of C.H. Herbert's pinks, which he introduced in 1924. It was awarded an AM by the RHS in that year.

'MRS DUNLOP'S PINK'   This is an old Scottish pink with semi-double, verging on flat double, flowers with a maroon (187B) zoning and lacing that covers nearly all the petals except for one or two patches in the middle, which are a dark pink (59D) and occasionally just showing white through the diffused colour. The fragrant flowers are not very wide, being only 2.5–3 cm (1–1.25 in) across. They have an almost smooth margin to the petals. The stems are about 20 cm (8 in) high, above blue-green foliage. Its age is telling and it is not too easy to propagate. Some years the plant will make a good clump and then others, inexplicably, it will be straggly. It was named by Mrs McMurtrie after a friend. In spite of the difficulties in propagation it is still in cultivation.

'MRS F. CLARK   *see 'Nellie Clark'*

'MRS G. WALKER'   Another vigorous C.H. Herbert plant. This is a large double with a bright pink ground and a red central zone. It has a clove fragrance. It was introduced in about 1923 and has since disappeared from cultivation.

'Mrs Holt'

'MRS HOLT' A dwarf single pink for the rock garden. The colour is a pink flushed and veined with a darker pink (overall a pinker 80D) that pales towards the centre. The flowers are fringed and are fragrant. They are about 2.5 cm (1 in) across and are carried on 12 cm (5 in) stems. It flowers mainly in June and September, but has the odd flower well into the autumn. It was introduced sometime before 1939 when it was mentioned in Bloom's Catalogue and is still in cultivation. There is also one border carnation that bears this name.

'MRS J. PERRING' This pink is a double white with a maroon centre and a clove scent. It has a long flowering season, the blooms being carried on 30 cm (12 in) stems. It was introduced by Iden Nurseries in 1944, but seems to have since disappeared.

'MRS JACKSON' A floriferous single pink with a purply-rose (72C) ground and a narrow cerise (64B) central zone. It pales only slightly as the flowers age. They appear in June. The petals are fringed. The flowers are about 3.2 cm (1.25 in) across on 30 cm (12 in) stems above a good blue-green foliage. Mrs Jackson, a customer of Robinson's

Hardy Plants at Swanley, discovered this chance seedling and passed it on to Robinsons who introduced it in the 1970s. It is still in cultivation.

'MRS McBRIDE' This is a semi-double flower with a rose pink (75B flushed 73A) with a maroon (bright 59A) central zone and a white throat. It has a slight fringing on the margins and has a strong perfume. The flowers are about 5 cm (2 in) in diameter and are carried on 20–25 (8–10 in) stems. The plant forms a good clump and has quite large leaves. It was named by Mrs McMurtrie after a friend. It is still in cultivation.

'MRS PRYOR' (listed as 'Mrs Prior' in Mansfield) This is a semi-double with a white ground and a crimson eye. The fragrant flowers appear on 30 cm (12 in) stems in June and July and continue sporadically into the autumn. It was introduced by B. Ladhams of Southampton in the early 1920s.

'MRS SINKINS' This is probably the most famous of the old-fashioned pinks and one known to most gardeners. It is a double white with a light green eye that is particularly noticeable when the calyx splits. This tendency makes it a very untidy flower to which many people, especially some of those who show, object. However, many more love its blowsiness which they, rightly, consider is all part of its character. It has a very strong, almost cloying, scent. The petals are quite deeply fringed, all adding to the general frilliness of the flower. The flowers are about 4.5 cm (1.75 in) across when the calyx is split, but much smaller if calyx rings have been applied. The stems are up to 25 cm (10 in) long. It has a relatively short flowering period in June and July. This plant was originally raised by John Sinkins of Slough in 1868 and named after his wife, Catherine. It was introduced by C. Turner of the Royal Nurseries, Slough (it was incorporated in the Slough coat of arms in 1938). There have been claims that the plant was listed in a nursery's catalogue as early as 1810, but I have not seen evidence for this. Catherine Sinkins claimed that the plant originated as a cross between 'Fimbriatus' and a clove carnation, so it seems likely that it did originate with her husband. Whether we still have the same plant as that of 1868 is a matter of debate. I have seen so many differing plants that purport to be the original, some of them up to 7.5 cm (3 in) across. It is surprising that 'Mrs Sinkins' has managed to keep its vigour for all these years, and one suspects that it has seeded at various times and the stronger growth from the seedling has inadvertently been taken as cutting material and so small changes have taken place. (It is interesting that McQuown, in 1962, was writing that the plant was losing its vigour, but most of the plants now claiming to be 'Mrs Sinkins' are again as vigorous as ever.) Things have been further confused by Thompson and Morgan naughtily marketing seed under the name 'Mrs Sinkins', which has also added to the need for the name to be applied to a strain rather than one specific clone. It is not only size, shape and fringing that vary, I have recently seen plants emanating from a major wholesale pink nursery that have got slight, but distinct, purple markings in the centre of each flower. Although this is unlikely to be the true 'Mrs Sinkins', it is interesting to note that both Catherine Sinkins and her son remember the original flower having either a crimson fringe or a splash of crimson on the petals. Her son also recalled in his old age that the flower of the 1950s had an inferior scent to that of the original. If we consider that our 'Mrs Sinkins' has one of the best fragrances of any pink, what could the original have smelt like? Habit can also vary, some plants having foliage with almost the coarseness of that of the modern pinks. I have even seen

'Haytor' offered as 'Mrs Sinkins'. However, having said all that, most of the variations of the modern 'Mrs Sinkins' are relatively minor and the essential 'Mrs Sinkins' is still there for us all to enjoy, whether it is precisely the same as when it was created or not.

'MULTIFLORUS ROSEUS'   A multi-headed pink of mule origin. There used to be a whole group of Multiflorus pinks and it may be considered a strain, although this one and the next were often picked out as individuals that were perpetuated by cuttings. This is a rose-pink semi-double (Ingwersen says deep rose and Mansfield says with equal conviction pale rose – they likewise disagree over the scent, not strong and very strong respectively). The flowers are carried on 25 cm (10 in) stems with the typical wide, fresh-green leaves of the mule pink. It needs constant propagation to keep them going, and it looks as though this has not been done as it now seems to have vanished.

'MULTIFLORUS SALMONEA'   Similar to the last except that it has soft pink flowers (which makes it very similar to 'Emile Paré'). Although Margery Fish grew it in the 1950s, when she thought it was new, it has now disappeared.

'MURRAY'S LACED PINK'   A mid-nineteenth century pink still in cultivation. It was probably one of the original Paisley pinks, rediscovered by George M. Taylor of Longniddy. It is a semi-double with a white ground and a large maroon (a redder 187B) central zone covering more than half of each petal. It also has a narrow band of lacing of the same colour, but this is not always present. The flowers are about 3.8 cm (1.5 in) across and carried 20–25 cm (8–10 in) stems. They are fragrant and noticeably indented on the margins. The foliage is blue-green but not very attractive, particularly as the whole plant is a bit floppy. However, the attractive flower redeems the plant. Propagation is not very easy, probably due to its age. However, it is still sufficiently accommodating for a large number of nurseries to offer it in their lists. It was awarded a HC by the RHS in 1949.

'MURTON'   A interesting plant found in the village of Murton, after which it was named, by Sophie Hughes, who introduced it through her Kingstone Cottage Nursery in the mid-1980s. It is a double with a pale, purplish-pink (68C) ground with a large crimson (59A) central zone and lacing that take up most of the petal. The pink is really

'Musgrave's Pink'

only round the edge, except when the flower ages, when two 'eyes' appear in the middle of each petal. The flowers are very fringed, which gives it a frilly appearance, aided by the petal spilling out of the calyx, which has a tendency to split. It is still in cultivation.

'MUSGRAVE'S PINK'   A wonderful plant, especially when the flowers are in prime condition. It is a famous plant supposedly dating from about 1730 as a similar plant appears in a painting of that date. The flower is a single with a creamy white ground and a definite pale green (150A) central zone. The flowers droop a little particularly when they are fading, which can give the plant an untidy appearance. The flowers are quite large, up to 3.8 cm (1.5 in) across, and carried on 20–25 cm (8–10 in) stems. They are coarsely fringed at the margins and are fragrant. The RHS awarded it an AM in 1946 as a border plant, although it had failed to win an award when Allwoods first presented it in 1937. The name 'Musgrave's Pink' seems to have been given to it by Allwood when they started to distribute the plant. It was discovered by George Allwood in a Henfield (Sussex) garden, the owner of which had been given the plant by Mr Musgrave. Over the years it has acquired a large number of synonyms including 'Avalon', 'C.T. Musgrave', 'Green Eyes', 'Musgrave', 'Tiverton' and 'Washfield'. Thankfully it is still in cultivation.

'MY CHOICE'   A modern double pink with salmon red (50B) flowers fading a bit towards the centre. The flowers are about 4.5 cm (1.75 in) across and are carried on 38 cm (15 in) stems. They are fragrant. The broad petals are fringed. The plant was raised by J.W. Radcliffe of Romford in the early 1970s. The RHS awarded it a PC both for exhibition and the border in 1974, and an AM as a border plant in 1975.

'MY LOVE'   A single, cerise self introduced by the Holden Clough Nurseries sometime around 1953. The flowers are carried on 23 cm (9 in) stems over a long season. There are also one border carnation and one perpetual-flowering carnation with the same name.

'NAN BAILEY'   A double modern pink with pure white petals with a touch of creamy yellow in the centre when the flower first opens or when the petals are still bunched. The flowers are up to 5 cm (2 in) across and are only slightly fringed. They are carried on 23 cm (9 in) stems, which tend to be a bit floppy. The flowers are slightly fragrant. The plant was introduced by Stephen Bailey in about 1985 and he has Breeder's Rights on it. The RHS awarded it a PC as an exhibition plant in 1985, and a HC in 1986, an AM in 1987 and a FCC in 1989, all three as a border plant.

'NANCY LINDSAY'   The plants I have seen of this name were singles with a white ground dotted with varying intensity of purple (a richer, redder 71A), darker and richer towards the centre, and paler towards the margin. When first open, no eyes in the middle of the petals are showing, but as the flower ages two irregular eyes appear. The deeply fringed petals are lined with white. The flowers are about 3.2 cm (1.25 in) across and are borne on 20 cm (8 in) stems. These plants came from Miss Nancy Lindsay's garden and are claimed to be from the original plants. However, the entry in the *IDR* claims it to be a form of *D. pavonius* with dark pink edged and veined with lavender, which does not seem to agree with the above plants. The RHS awarded it a PC in 1959 as an exhibition bloom, an AM as a plant for the alpine house in 1961, and a HC in 1960 and an AM in 1962, both as a plant for the rock garden. The plants put up for these awards are, however, at variance with the above description. The fact that they are singles is not in dispute. The ground colour is deep candy pink (between 68A and 68B) edged and veined with light purple (between 72C and 72D). The flowers are about 3.8 cm (1.5 in) wide and are carried on 7.5–10 cm (3–4 in) stems. I think we must assume that this is the true plant, in spite of the provenance of the one mentioned above, which is probably a seedling. I am uncertain whether the award plant is still in existence, the first certainly is and as it is a distinctive attractive plant should have its own name. Just to add a final note of confusion, for those who may have seen them, Kew had several plants in a border of 'Paisley Gem' that were labelled 'Nancy Lindsay' for some years.

'NAPOLEON III'   A legendary plant raised in about 1840 that is still in cultivation. It is a mule pink with double flowers of a dark but bright crimson. The flowers are clove-scented and appear mainly in June and July, with occasional later blooms. The plant is about 23 cm (9 in) high when in flower. The foliage is not particularly attractive, being thin and a pale yellowy green. As with most of these mule pinks, it has a tendency to flower itself to death, and so cuttings should be regularly

taken; if necessary one plant should be put aside for this purpose. Ingwersen recommends a rich soil in a cool position for the best chance of survival. It was raised by Emile Paré in about 1840. It was awarded a FCC by the RHS as long ago as 1867. It is still in cultivation, although it could easily disappear. There is also one border carnation bearing the same name.

'NELLIE CLARK'   A plant with double flowers that are a dusky cerise (57A) self. They are 3.8–4.5 cm (1.5–1.75 in) across and carried on 20–23 cm (8–9 in) stems. They appear above a reasonably good mat of blue-green foliage. The plant has a long flowering season from June until the end of autumn. It was introduced by F. Clark sometime before 1946, when it was exhibited at the RHS. It is still in cultivation. Sometimes it can be seen under the name 'Mrs Clark' or 'Mrs F. Clark', and sometimes ends in an 'e' in any of the three versions.

'NICOLA JANE'   A plant for the rock garden raised at Lochside Alpine Nursery. It has single pink flowers that are fragrant. It is the result of a cross between *D. pavonius* and 'Prichard's Variety'. It is still in cultivation.

'NINE STAR'   *see 'Whatfield Nine Star'*

'NIGHTJAR'   A strange name for a pink, but it is one of the House of Douglas' bird name series. The flower is a double with a lilac pink ground, and crimson central zone and picotee edge. It is clove scented and flowers in June and July. It was introduced in about 1949. It is no longer in cultivation.

'NONSUCH'   (1) An old pink from the seventeenth century that was still in cultivation in the 1950s. The flowers are ruby flushed on rose-pink. They are large and deeply fringed. It has now disappeared.

(2) There is another old pink of this name that was introduced about the middle of the last century by R. Marris of Leicester. This is simply described as red.

(3) There are also three border carnations with the same name.

'NORWICH GLOW'   A modern double that is a crimson self. The flowers are fragrant. It was raised by P.A. Fenn of Norwich and introduced by

Ramparts Nursery. It was awarded a PC by the RHS in 1986.

'NORWICH PRIDE'   A modern double that is a rose cerise self. The flowers are fragrant. It was raised by P.A. Fenn of Norwich and introduced by Ramparts Nursery. It was awarded a PC by the RHS in 1986.

'NUTHATCH'   Another odd name, but again it belongs to the series of Douglas' bird names. This double has a shell-pink ground with a crimson central zone. The flowers are fragrant and have a short season in June and July. It was introduced sometime in the early 1950s, but has now disappeared like the rest of this large series.

'NUTMEG CLOVE'   *see 'Fenbow Nutmeg Clove'*

'NYEWOOD'S CREAM'   A dwarf pink for the rock garden that has become popular in recent years, at least with the producers if not their customers. It has single flowers of a white tinged with an ivory-cream. The petals are almost smooth, apart from a couple of small indentations. The flowers are 1.5 cm (0.6 in) across and are carried

on 5 cm (2 in) stems above good compact hummocks of green foliage. It was introduced by E.S. Lyttel of Nyewoods, Chilworth and is still very much in existence.

'NYMPH'   One of the Allwood alpinus group for the rock garden. This one is a single with a blush pink ground finely speckled with a deeper pink. They are fringed and fragrant. It is very floriferous. The main flush of flowers is in June and July, with a few odd flowers following later. The flowering stems are about 15 cm (6 in) high. It was introduced sometime in the early 1930s but has not been seen lately. There are also four border carnations bearing the same name.

'OADBY GEM'   A modern semi-double pink with a bright pink (68A to 68B) ground, and a central zone and lacing of very deep purple (nearest 183A). The flowers are about 5 cm (2 in) across and are carried on 40 cm (16 in) stems. They are fragrant. The plant was raised by E.J. Edwards of Oadby (hence the name) in the early 1960s. The RHS awarded it a C as a border plant in 1964.

'OAKINGTON'   A famous introduction, raised by Alan Bloom in about 1928, that has stood

'Oakington'

the test of time and is still widely cultivated. It is a flat double or semi-double of a purple-pink (74C) colouration. It is a very floriferous plant with a solid mass of flower above a mat of fresh-looking foliage. The flowering stems are up to 15 cm (6 in) high. It was selected as a seedling from 'Prichard's Variety'. It is also called 'Oakington Hybrid' and 'Oakington Rose'. There is another pink (double pink self) raised in the nineteenth century that also carries this name.

'OAKINGTON HYBRID'   *see 'Oakington'*

'OAKINGTON ROSE'   *see 'Oakington'*

'OAKINGTON ROSE SPORT'   A sport from 'Oakington' to which it is very similar except that the flowers are a deeper colour.

'OAKWOOD BILL BALLINGER'   A fancy pink for those who like them. This double has a pink ground streaked, blotched and flecked with a bright red (44A–B). The pink ground changes to a yellowy cream (19C), which is probably its correct colour as the initial pink is flushed out of the red markings. The flowers are 5–5.8 cm (2–2.25 in) and carried on 38 cm (15 in) stems. They are slightly fringed at the margins and are fragrant. Not a very tidy plant, with flowers flopping and dieback forming in the middle of the clump. It was introduced by S. Hall of New Ollerton in 1985. It is still in cultivation. The RHS awarded it a PC in 1988 as an exhibition plant and a HC in 1989 as a border plant.

'OAKWOOD CRIMSON CLOVE'   A double self that is crimson (53A) with a duskiness towards the edge of the petals and paling slightly towards the centre. The flowers get deeper in colour as they age and develop yellow spots. The flowers are very slightly fringed with an even serration. They have a slight fragrance. The flowers are 3.8–4.5 cm (1.5–1.75 in) across and are borne on 40 cm (16 in) stems. This has a good upright growth, but the foliage has a tendency to die back in mid-season. It was raised by S. Hall of New Ollerton in about 1986 as a cross between 'Oakwood Flare' and 'Oakwood Gem'.

'OAKWOOD DAINTY'   A double with a pink ground and laced with a claret red. It is scented. It was raised by S. Hall of New Ollerton in about 1985. It is still in cultivation.

'OAKWOOD DOROTHY'   A sprawling plant that would not be very attractive if it were not for the pretty pink flowers. They are a flat double with a pink (49C) ground flushed with darker and paler pinks. The flowers look a bit sad as they go over and the plants look better for being regularly dead-headed. Some flowers are finely flecked as they grow older. They are about 4.5–5 cm (1.75–2 in) across and are carried on 40 cm (16 in) stems. The narrow petals are fringed. The flowers are slightly scented. The plant was raised by S. Hall of New Ollerton in about 1987 and it is still in cultivation. The RHS awarded it a PC as an exhibition plant in 1988 and a HC as a border plant in 1989.

'OAKWOOD ROMANCE'   A good strong plant with upright growth, and forming a good clump with some leaves dying back by mid-season. The double flowers are a brilliant purple cerise (58A). This is a difficult colour to place in a border and it may possibly be best grown as a cut flower. The flowers turn to a velvety crimson as they age. They are prone to white flecking, as are so many rich-coloured selfs. The flowers are about 5 cm (2 in) across and are carried on 30 cm (12 in) stems. The margins of the petals are fringed and the flowers are fragrant. It was raised by S. Hall of New Ollerton in about 1986 as a cross between 'Oakwood Bill Ballinger' and an unknown seedling. It is still in cultivation.

'OAKWOOD SPARKLER'   This is another in the series from S. Hall. This is a white double with a slight tinge of pinky cream in it. There is a narrow central band of purply-red that is only just able to peep through the bunched petals. The petals are only just slightly fringed and appear smooth, but they are curled and bunched, giving the flower a frilly appearance. The flowers are up to 5 cm (2 in) across and appear on 40 cm (16 in) stems. The *IDR* claims that it is scented, but I have not noticed this on any flowers I have smelt, but I could have just been unlucky. It was introduced in about 1985 from unknown parentage.

'OAKWOOD SPLENDOUR'   This is another double, this time with a purplish pink (62B) ground and a crimson (53A) central zone. The flowers are slightly fringed and are fragrant. They are 4.5–5 cm (1.75–2 in) in diameter and are borne on 25 cm (10 in) stems, which are quite strong and upright. It is a good clump-forming plant. The plant was raised by S. Hall of New Ollerton in about 1985 and is of unknown parentage. It is still in cultivation. The RHS awarded it a PC in 1989.

'OAKWOOD SUNRISE' A double that is a deep, luminous pink (48C) self that, unfortunately, soon becomes patchy and rather washed out. The flowers are about 5 cm (2 in) across and are carried on 30 cm (12 in) stems that have a tendency to flop, showing the paler washed-out underside of the petals. The flowers are slightly fringed and are fragrant. The foliage is not too coarse, but dies back in the centre making the plant look a bit untidy. Raised by S. Hall in 1985 from unknown parents. The RHS has awarded it a PC in 1988 and a C in 1989. It is still in cultivation.

'OBERON' One of the original Allwoodii alpinus group of pinks for the rock garden. This is a single with a pale cerise ground and a pale maroon centre. The flowers are fragrant and appear mainly in June and July, but continue until October. The plant was introduced by Allwood in about 1931, but has since disappeared from cultivation. There are also five border carnations sharing the same name.

'OEILLET PANACHÉE' A mule pink raised as a sport from 'Emile Paré'. Ingwersen knew it as a rich crimson, but the *IDR* just states that it is striped. Perhaps we will never definitely know, unless it is still in existence somewhere in France. It has a dark, typical mule-pink foliage and a good scent. Its origins are obscure, but was probably raised in France sometime around the mid-nineteenth century. Also anglicized and spelt 'Oillet Panache' ('oily panache' does not sound a particularly enticing name for a pink, which may be the reason for its disappearance!).

'OLD CHELSEA' One of the earliest pinks from Douglas of Great Bookham, introduced before 1905. A double with a rose ground and central zone, and a heavy lacing of rose red. It is fragrant and has a short flowering season from June into July. The flowers are carried on 38 cm (15 in) stems. It would appear to be no longer in cultivation.

'OLD CLOVE RED' A very old plant (*IDR* claims it originated in the sixteenth century) with semi-double flowers that have a crimson (53A) ground and a dark maroon (187A) eye. The flowers are quite deeply fringed and very fragrant, with what Margery Fish claimed was the best scent of them all. They are 5 cm (2 in) across and are carried

on 25 cm (10 in) stems. It has a tendency to split its calyx. It is similar in some respects to 'Enid Anderson' except that the latter is redder in colour, smaller in size and the scent is absent. This is a description of the extant plant. The *IDR*, however, claims that it is a crimson self and a border carnation rather than a pink, which it well may be. It matters little either way; the existing plant is worth growing.

'OLD COTTAGE PINK' A double with a white ground and a central zone of deep violet (*IDR* says lilac). The flowers are fragrant and are borne on 30 cm (12 in) stems from June into August. Another plant that no longer seems to be with us.

'OLD DUTCH PINK' This is a well-known old-fashioned semi-double from the seventeenth century with a pink (73A) ground flushed with a paler pink and white, and with a ruby (brighter 185A) central zone that throws out odd flecks onto the pink ground. The petals are deeply fringed which, added to the tendency of the resulting teeth to curl upwards, gives the flower a frilly look. The flowers are up to 3.8 cm (1.5 in) across and are carried on 25 cm (10 in) stems. The plant has good blue-green foliage that is quite broad. 'Old Dutch Pink' can be confused with 'Paddington', but the latter is a more mauvy pink and although deeply fringed, the petals are not curled, and the general appearance is not so frilly. The central zone is more purple and is not as irregular as on the former.

'OLD FEATHERED' *see 'Ursula Le Grove'*

'OLD FRINGED' (1) An elegant simple pink with small (1.25–2 cm (0.5–0.75 in) across) but deeply fringed single flowers of a delicate mauvish-pink (76D), darker when they first open and fading to white as they age. The calyx is a deep mahogany red that makes a good contrast, setting off the fragrant flowers beautifully. This is a very simple, floriferous plant that is a joy to grow, eventually forming quite a large clump. The flower stems are thin and arching, about 20–25 cm (8–10 in) high. It is early coming into flower and the flowers seem to last well. For some curious reason the plants of 'Old Fringed' at Kew were labelled 'Glory of Lyonnaise' for some years, to which this plant bears no resemblance. It is still very much in cultivation. Also known as 'Fringed Pink'.

(2) See also 'Shock White'.

'OLD FRINGED WHITE'   Another delightful plant, this time a 10–12 petalled, semi-double with pure white flowers with a very slight touch of green in the centre. Occasionally they might have a slight tinge of purple as they age. They have quite a distinctive shape as the petals almost form a funnel shape when they first open, flattening as the flowers age. The flowers are deeply fringed and are very fragrant. It is not a very big flower, being only 2.5 cm (1 in) across, but it has a simplicity that makes it worth growing. The flower stems are 30–36 cm (12–14 in) high and, in spite of the small flowers, are a bit floppy. Its main flowering period is June into July, but it does seem to go on quite a bit beyond the normal flowering period of most old fashioned pinks, often flowering into winter. It is reputed to originate from the seventeenth century and is in cultivation, although one doubts whether this is still the original plant.

'OLD IRISH'   This is an attractive, single-flowered cultivar with a deep pink ground (61D) and a speckled crimson (187C) central area, with odd touches up the centre and round the margins of the petal in the manner of a disjointed lacing. The flowers are 3.8 cm (1.5 in) across and are carried on 25 cm (10 in) stems. The margins of the petals are toothed and the flowers are fragrant. It is an old variety of unknown origin but still in cultivation.

'OLD MAN'S HEAD'   A double from the early seventeenth century that was rediscovered in the north of Yorkshire but, once again, seems to have slipped into oblivion. It has a white ground flecked and splashed with a purple and cream. It has a strong perfume. The flowers are carried on 23 cm (9 in) stems and, for an old-fashioned pink, it has a long flowering season.

'OLD MOTHER HUBBARD'   Unlike all the others prefixed with the word 'Old', this is a recent introduction. It is a flat semi-double with a pink (38D) ground and fancy markings, including stripes and flecks, of a darker, salmon pink (43C). The flowers are slightly serrated at their margins and are fragrant. They are 5–5.8 cm (2–2.25 in) in diameter and are carried on 38–40 cm (15–16 in) stems. The growth is strong and upright, and the plant has good blue-green foliage. It was raised as a sport from 'Doris' by R. Hubbard of Landscove in Devon in 1984 and it is still very much in cultivation. The RHS awarded it a HC in 1986, an AM in 1988 and a FCC in 1989, all as a border plant.

'OLD NORWICH'   A small pink with a white ground and a cherry-red central area. The petals are very fringed and the flowers are carried on 15 cm (6 in) stems above thick tufts of fine leaves. It splits its calyx. It was raised by a Norwich nursery in about 1840.

'OLD SQUARE EYES'   A popular plant amongst those who know it. The large (4.5 cm (1.75 in) diameter) single flowers have a white ground and a distinctive pink (36C) central zone. The marking on each petal is triangular, with one corner pointing up the centre of the petal. The combined effect is to give the impression that the central zone is square (closer examination will reveal, of course, that it is a five sided square but, nonetheless, the impression still remains). The zone is quite large and takes up an increasing amount of the petal as the season progresses, so that eventually nearly the whole petal is diffused with the central colour. There is also a lacing on the outer edge of the same colour. These outer edges are inclined to curve upwards. The margins are deeply fringed. The flowers are fragrant and each is encased in a long and elegant calyx. The main season is in June and July, with the occasional later bloom. The flowering stems are quite long and straggly; up to 41 cm (16 in) or more. This is an attractive plant that always causes comment. I know nothing of its origins, but suspect that it is not very old. It is also known as 'Square Eyes'. It is still in cultivation.

'OLD VELVET'   A very firm favourite amongst those that grow it. This semi-double, verging on a flat double, has a rich dark purpled-red (187A), velvet-like colour fading to pink and then white on the extreme edge. The pink is a bit bleached after a cold spring, and the velvet loses its lustre, with occasional patches of white showing through, as the flower ages. The reverse is a silvery white tinged with purple. The petals are only slightly fringed and appear almost smooth. The flowers are fragrant. They are about 3.8 cm (1.5 in) across and are carried on strong 30–36 cm (12–14 in) stems. It flowers in June and July. The foliage is quite large and looks more like that of a modern pink than an old-fashioned one. It is a very old plant of unknown origin. It is still in cultivation.

'OLIVER'   An Allwoodii modern pink. This is a very flat semi-double is a purple-cerise pink (between 63A and 63B) self. There is a very slight trace of a darker central area. The petals are only

'Old Velvet'

very slightly indented, almost smooth. The flowers are 4.5 cm (1.75 in) across and carried on 38 cm (15 in) stems. They are slightly fragrant. It was introduced by Allwood in about 1972 and is still in cultivation. The RHS awarded it an C in 1973.

'ORIEL' One of the House of Douglas' bird series of pinks. As with them all, this is a double, this time a rose pink with a purple central area. It has a clove fragrance. It flowers in June and July on 38 cm (15 in) stems. It was introduced in about 1950, but now seems to have disappeared. Douglas also produced an earlier (1922) pink with a rose centre with this name. There is also a border carnation with the same name.

'ORIENTALIS ALBUS' A mystery plant this, with an odd name traditionally applied to it, but no records of it can be found. It is a double white with a slight trace of a white eye. It is quite small, being only 3.2 cm (1.25 in) across, but has deep, 0.7 cm (0.25 in), fringing. It is fragrant. It has 30 cm (12 in) stems and the flowers appear in June and July. It splits its calyx, The flowers are, in fact, like a small 'Mrs Sinkins', but neater and not so blowsy. It is possible that it is a seedling from the latter. The plant is still in cultivation.

'ORTALAN' Yet another in the vanished series of bird pinks from the House of Douglas. This is a double with an apple-blossom pink ground and a deep crimson central zone and lacing. It is fragrant. It was introduced in about 1957.

'OTHELLO' (1) One of the offspring from C.H. Herbert's famous 'Bridesmaid'. This is a double deep-crimson self that opens quite flat. It is very fragrant and has a long flowering period. It was introduced by Herbert sometime before 1927, but now seems to have disappeared into obscurity.

(2) E. Benary of Germany produced a dark red form with this name in 1928, which does not seem to be around.

(3) Two other pinks are recorded with this name, but they are probably of little consequence. One, introduced by T. Looker of Oxford in about 1852, is simply listed as red. There is even less information about the other, just that it was introduced by Thurtell before 1845. If anyone can find and positively identify it, they deserve to make a fortune out of it. There are also five border carnations and four perpetual-flowering carnations.

'OVINGDEAN' A semi-double, verging on a flat double, with small flowers of a pink (57D) ground and a rose-pink (between 66B and 66C) central zone. The flowers are 3.2 cm (1.25 in) across and are carried on 36 cm (14 in) stems. The broad petals are fringed. It was introduced by L.H. Cox of Newick, Sussex sometime around the Second World War, but has now disappeared, in spite of the RHS awarding it an AM in 1946 as a border plant.

'OWL'   A double with a rose pink ground and blood red central zone and lacing. It is fragrant. The plant was introduced by the House of Douglas of Great Bookham in about 1955.

'PADDINGTON'   A smallish double with a pale purplish pink (68C) ground with a maroon (187B) central zone. It is deeply fringed and fragrant. The flowers are 3.2–3.8 cm (1.25–1.5 in) in diameter and are carried on 23–28 cm (9–11 in) stems. It is reputed to have been raised on the site of the present Paddington Station by Thomas Hogg at the beginning of the nineteenth century and it is still going strong. The RHS awarded it an AM as a border plant in 1946. It can be confused with 'Old Dutch Pink' although the latter has its fringed margins curled upwards giving it a more frilly look. The central area of 'Paddington' is more purple and not so irregular in its appearance.

'PADDINGTON COB'   A double rather like a small 'Pheasant's Eye' with a white ground and a maroon central zone. It was raised in about 1750 by Richard Cob of London. The plant was still in existence in the 1950s but seems to have disappeared since.

'PAINTED BEAUTY'   This is a single with an underlying white ground that shows on the extreme margins and has two white 'eyes' in the middle of each petal. The central area and lacing, which between them make up most of the colour, is a purply mauve (between 67A and 72B) that pales towards the edges. The throat shows as a pale pink. When the flowers first open they are small and very much redder in colour, the white areas showing purple. The flowers are fringed and slightly reflexed, with the single petals just touching each other, occasionally with a slight gap between them. The flowers are up to 3.2 cm (1.25 in) across and are carried on 20 cm (8 in) stems. The blue-green foliage forms good neat mats. This is an old pink of unknown origin.

'PAINTED LADY'   It is impossible to say what the definitive 'Painted Lady' is like as there have been so many with this name. I suspect that over the centuries it has been applied to different pinks in different parts of the country. Most agree that they are singles.

(1) Moreton described one that he found in Monmouthshire, which had a white ground on the upper surface and 'painted' a delicate pink on the under surface. This he claims is the true form. Closely allied to this, with claims that it is the same plant, is a flower painted a delicate pink on both sides of the petals, with the reverse side being more of a silvery pink. This is fringed and is a late flowerer. Several authorities agree with Moreton, claiming that the 'Painted Lady' pink is painted on the underside of the petals while the 'Painted Lady Carnation' is painted on the upper surface.

(2) Another that is still in existence with this name has a very pale pink ground that only shows as a narrow margin round the edge of the petals and as two pale eyes in the middle of each petal. The central area is a reddish purple and the lacing a purple colour, between them they cover most of the petal. The lacing has a tendency to fade. The flowers are rather small being only 2–2.5 cm (0.75–1 in) in diameter. The margins are fringed and the flowers are fragrant.

(3) Prichard of Christchurch, Hampshire, introduced a semi-double in the late 1940s with this name. It has a white ground and carmine pencilling.

(4) Reginald Kaye also entered the lists but backed off, renaming his 'Painted Lady' 'Pink Damask' (*qv*).

'PAISLEY GEM'   There are various versions of this plant around, one of which is 'Dad's Favourite' masquerading under a false name. It is a semi-double, verging on double, with a white ground and a rich black-maroon (187A) central eye. It also has a similar coloured lacing that in some years can be perfect, but in others intermittent or even absent all together. It is more noticeable after a cold spring. The flowers are slightly fringed and are fragrant. They are about 3.8 cm (1.5 in) in diameter and are carried on 30 cm (12 in) stems. It was raised by John Macree, a muslin worker of Paisley, in about 1798. He is reputed to have presented a plant to George III. It was rediscovered in the Macree family garden by G.M. Taylor of Longniddry. Sue Farquhar's stock can be traced back to Macree through the Rev. C.O. Morton, who got it from the garden of Macree's great-grandson.

Although 'Dad's Favourite' is similar in appearance, 'Paisley Gem' has blacker lacing and the flower stem is longer and stronger. According to Moreton the flower is also more perfect; the lacing in his day, for example, was continuous, although modern stock that can be traced back through Moreton seems to be intermittent in some years. For some curious reason plants of 'Paisley Gem' were, for some time, labelled at Kew as 'Nancy Lindsay'.

'PAMELA'   An Allwood modern pink with double flowers with a pink ground, edged with white. It is fragrant and flowers over a long season, as with so many Allwoodii. It was introduced round about the Second World War, but seems to have now disappeared. There are also two border carnations with the same name.

'PAN'   (1) One of the Allwoodii alpinus group for the rock garden, most of which, including this, have unfortunately disappeared. This is a single with a blush pink ground and a noticeable green centre. The flowering stems were about 10 cm (4 in) high. It was introduced in about 1929 and sounds far too intriguing to have lost.

(2) There is also another single, this time raised by G. Winter. This has a bright red ground and a maroon centre. The flowers are fringed and very fragrant. They flower on 20 cm (8 in) stems over a long season. It was introduced in the late 1940s but does not seem to be still in cultivation.

'PATCHWORK'   A wonderful, fresh-looking dwarf pink. The flowers are single with a very pale pink, almost white ground striped purple (61A) from the central zone. This central area is spotted with the ground showing through. The edges of the petals turn up slightly, giving the flower a very squared-off look. The margins are slightly fringed. The flowers are about 3.8 cm (1.5 in) across and they are carried on 15 cm (6 in) stems. It was introduced by Fielden & Crouch, possibly in the 1930s. The plant is still in existence.

'PATIENCE'   (1) An Allwood modern pink with a white ground laced with magenta (71C) and zoned with ruby (59A). The flowers are 5 cm (2 in) across and are carried on 30 cm (12 in) stems. The petals are broad and slightly serrated. It is a bushy plant with an erect habit. It was introduced by Allwood in the 1950s and received a HC in 1953 and an AM in 1956, both as a border plant, from the RHS.

(2) There is also an undescribed pink introduced by A.J. Hull of Pensilva in 1949. One border carnation and one perpetual-flowering carnation have also been given this name.

'PATRICIA'S CHOICE'   A double self of a rich red (46A) colour, tinged with a blackish bloom. The colour pales towards the centre of the flower. The flowers are 5 cm (2 in) across and are borne of 36 cm (14 in) stems. They are slightly scented. The petals are cut. The plant was raised by J.W. Radcliffe of Romford. The RHS awarded it a C in 1978.

'PAUL'   An Allwood modern pink. This is a double with a shell pink (49A) ground striped and flecked with a salmon pink (47C). The flowers are quite large, being about 6.4 cm (2.5 in) across and are carried on 38 cm (15 in) stems. The edges of the petals are almost smooth. The flowers are slightly scented. The plant was introduced by Allwood in about 1970 and is still in cultivation. The RHS awarded it an HC in 1970 and an AM in 1977, both as a plant for the border. One parent of 'Saint Asaph'.

'PAUL HAYWARD'   A semi-double or flat double very similar in habit to 'Freckles', but a couple of tones darker. The ground is a dark rose pink and the stripes a deep red. The flowers are about 5 cm (2 in) across and are carried on 25 cm (10 in) stems. It was recently introduced by A.N. Hayward and is still in cultivation. The Paul Hayward in question is the son of the current owner of Haywards Carnations.

'PEACH'   (1) An imperial pink introduced by C.H. Fielder of Lindabruce Nurseries in about 1959. It is a double with, as its name implies, a peach pink ground and a scarlet centre. It has a long flowering season. Although introduced over 30 years ago, it is still in cultivation. There is also one perpetual-flowering carnation with the same name.

(2) See also 'Whatfield Peach'.

'PEGGY'S PRIDE'   A flat semi-double with large white petals with the slightest greenish tinge towards the centre in some flowers. The flowers are 5 cm (2 in) across and are borne on 45 cm (18 in) stems. The margins of the petals are only very slightly fringed; they appear almost smooth. It has a slight fragrance. The plant was introduced by Wilfred Price of Romford, Essex sometime in the late 1960s. It was awarded a C in 1969 and an AM

134 A–Z of Border Pinks

in 1970, both as a border plant, by the RHS. It is still in cultivation and is used in show work.

'PENELOPE' An Allwood modern pink. This double has a very pale rose pink ground with a central zone and lacing of a velvety chocolate crimson. As with most Allwoodiis, it has a long flowering season. The plant was introduced in 1957, but seems to have disappeared from cultivation. Seven border and two perpetual-flowering carnations share the same name.

'PENNY RED' A single pink with very attractive flowers that have a dry-looking red, almost crimson (53B) ground and a brown maroon (185A) central zone that fades as it goes down the throat. The ground has a velvety blush to it. The flowers are fringed. It is still in cultivation.

'PENTON PRIDE' A modern semi-double pink with a almost white ground touched with pink (65A). The central zone and lacing are a pinkish-purple (61C). The flowers are up to 5 cm (2 in) across and are carrried on 43 cm (17 in) stems. They are fragrant. The plant, which has a bushy habit, was raised and introduced by E.J. Jordan of Waltham Cross.The RHS awarded it a HC as a border plant in 1965.

'PETTICOAT LACE' A flat double with a dark rose-pink (62A) ground and a maroon (59A) central area and lacing. The latter follows the serrated margins, giving it a frilly appearance that fits the name well. The flowers are 3.8–4.5 cm (1.5–1.75 in) across. The flowers are very fragrant. The foliage is a grey-green, typical in habit of most modern pinks. It was introduced in the mid 1970s by A.N. Hayward of Hayward's Carnations and is still in cultivation.

'PHEASANT'S EYE' A distinctive double (verging on semi-double) flower that has a white ground and a central zone of velvety maroon (59A). There is also a paler, purple (72B) lacing on the very margins of the petals, paling as it ages. The white ground in the middle of each petal covers over half of the petal. The distinctive feature is that when the petals first open, the middle ones stand upright, forming a pheasant's ear above the maroon eye. The flowers are quite small, only 3.2–3.8 cm (1.25–1.5 in), and are carried on 30 cm (12 in) stems. The petals are quite deeply and finely fringed with the tips of the teeth being white. The flowers are fragrant. It is a very old cultivar of

unknown origin, but it is said to go back to the seventeenth century. The form described above is still in cultivation, as are others that lay claim to the same name. They are all similar to the above, except that some are single.

'PHILIP' This is one of the Allwood modern pinks. It has a large double flower with a purple ground with a somewhat paler edge. It is fragrant and free-flowering. It was introduced in about 1954, but has lapsed into obscurity.

'PHOEBE' (1) Another Allwood modern pink. This is also a double, this time a salmon-red self. The margins of the petals are serrated and the flower is very fragrant. The plant is very floriferous over a long season, as are most of the Allwoodiis. The flowers are carried on 30 cm (12 in) stems. It was introduced by Allwood in about 1923, but has since disappeared. It was sent for trial at Wisley in 1933, but seems to have failed to get an award.

(2) There is another pink introduced by E. Ladhams of Godalming in about 1940 with the same name. This is described as being a semi-double with a colour like mulberries and cream. I have not heard of it still being in existence, but if it is it will at least not be confused with the previous 'Phoebe'.

(3) There are also three border carnations and one perpetual-flowering carnation sharing this name.

'PICTURE' A flat double or semi-double of a clear pink (50D flushed slightly darker) that darkens towards the centre where the petals are still folded. The flowers are about 5 cm (2 in) across and have a slight fringing round the margins. They have a clove scent. It was introduced by the Lindabruce Nurseries of Lancing in about 1962 and is still in cultivation. The RHS awarded it an AM in 1962 as an exhibition flower. There are one border carnation and two perpetual-flowering carnations sharing the same name.

'PIKE'S PINK' This is a very popular pink for the rock garden or for the front of border. (Its popularity may be with the producers rather than the gardener.) It is a semi-double bordering on double with a pink (69A) ground and a darker pink or purple (74B) central band. It fades rather ungraciously to a washed-out lilac. The petals are fringed and the flowers fragrant. They are about 3.2 cm (1.25 in) across and are carried on 10 cm (4 in) stems. The plant forms good clumps of blue-green foliage. It was introduced by J. Pike of Acton in about 1965. The RHS has awarded it an AM in 1966 and a FCC in 1972 as a plant for the rock garden. Plants with single pink flowers have been offered as this plant and may still be in circulation.

'PINK ALICE'   A full petalled single flower of a lilac pink (a pinker 75B) that pales as it goes over. The petals are slightly fringed. The flowers are about 3.8 cm (1.5 in) across and carried on 30 cm (12 in) stems above a blue-green foliage that is not as coarse as on modern pinks. It is still in cultivation.

'PINK DAMASK'   A single-flowered pink with a white ground and a deep pink central zone. The flower ages to a uniform, very deep pink. It was introduced by Reginald Kaye of Waithman's Nurseries in about 1980 as a cross between 'Highland Fraser' and an unknown form. The plant is still in cultivation. It was originally called 'Painted Lady' and could be in circulation under that name.

'PINK JEWEL'   A semi-double with a rose-pink (67B) ground, paling towards the centre. The colour is not a pure one but is mottled with a paler one. The flowers are small, only 1.25 cm (0.5 in), and the plant is just 5–10 cm (2–4 in) tall when in flower, making it suitable only for the rock garden. The flowers are fringed and fragrant. Its origins are unknown, but it appeared in the early 1980s. In Europe it is known as 'Pink Juwel'.

'PINK MRS SINKINS'   Essentially, this is the same as 'Mrs Sinkins' except that it is a lilac (75C) pink with a slight touch of rose pink (74C) in a central band. It also shows green in the throat. The flowers are about 5 cm (2 in) across and have all the fragrance of its forebear. It flowers on 25–30 cm (10–12 in) stems. The calyx splits and the flowers have a deep fringing, which gives it a very blowsy appearance. It was introduced as a sport from 'Mrs Sinkins' by C. Turner of Slough at the turn of the century. There is controversy as to whether this plant is the same as 'Excelsior'. There seems to be several versions of 'Pink Mrs Sinkins' around and I am inclined to favour the above plant with the same-sized flowers as 'Mrs Sinkins' for this name. The very large 'cabbagy' versions, with or without the purple band, would seem to be 'Excelsior' (or in some cases even the 'Earl of Essex'). Another of the current versions has a salmon pink ground with no markings. With so many versions around it is unlikely that there will ever be a consensus and many will continue to use 'Excelsior' as a synonym for 'Pink Mrs Sinkins'.

'PINK MONICA WYATT'   A double pink with a light pink ground (38D) with an irregularly defined central zone of deep pink (51C) fading and becoming pale green towards the base of the petal. The flowers are slightly fringed and fragrant. It was raised by R. Bloomfield of Dawlish as a sport of 'Monica Wyatt' in about 1987. It is still in cultivation.

'PINK PEACH'   A modern pink from the Lindabruce Nurseries. This is a double with a pink (54D) ground and a salmon pink (48B) central zone. The flowers are up to 5 cm (2 in) wide and are carried on 30 cm (12 in) stems. They have a little fragrance. The broad petals are slightly fringed. The plant was raised in about 1960. The RHS awarded it an AM in 1961 as an exhibition plant, followed by a C in 1962, a HC in 1963 and an AM in 1973, all as a border plant.

'PINKIE'   One of the Allwoodii alpinus group of dwarf plants for the rock garden or front of border. This one is a single that is a silvery rose (73C) self. It is moderately fragrant and 3.8 cm (1.5 in) flowers appear over a long season on 10–12. 5 cm (4–6 in) stems. The broad petals are serrated. The plant was introduced in about 1935 and, like so many of this group, has now unfortunately disappeared. The RHS awarded it an AM as a border plant in 1954. There are also two perpetual-flowering carnations with the same name.

'PIXIE'   There are quite a number of plants with this name, although I doubt whether there are many in existence.

(1) A pink for rock gardens that is still in existence is one simply described as pink and flowering on 7.5 cm (3 in) stems, mainly in June. I have not seen it so can add little more.

(2) Allwood produced one of their alpinus pinks for the rock garden in about 1929. It was a single white self. This seems to have disappeared.

(3) More recently (1964) East Lodge Gardens of Enfield introduced a pink with a white ground, veined with pink.

(4) There are also two border carnations and two perpetual-flowering carnations with the same name.

'PLENUS ALBUS'   *see 'Albus Plenus'*

'PLOVER'   Another of the extinct pinks in the House of Douglas bird series. This is a double with a bright rose-pink ground and a crimson centre. It is fragrant. The plant was introduced in about 1955.

'PLUM DIADEM'   Although sold recently, I have very little information about this plant except that it had a carmine ground with a dark centre. It was possibly introduced by Pouncey of Three Legged Cross, Wimborne. It is still in cultivation.

'POLAMENS OLD PINK'   There were plants under this name at Kew in 1990, but they were in fact 'Allspice'. No other information can be found about it.

'POLLY ANNE'   *see 'Whatfield Polly Anne'*

'POM POM'   *see 'Whatfield Pom Pom'*

'POSY'   *see 'Whatfield Posy'*

'PRELUDE'   A modern double pink with a pale pink (65D) ground flushed with slightly darker pink (73D). The flowers are 3.8 cm (1.5 in) across and are carried on 36 cm (14 in) stems. They have a slight fragrance. The broad petals are fringed. The plant was raised by E.A. Tickle of Purley. The RHS awarded it a PC as an exhibition plant in 1973, and a C in 1976 and a HC in 1979, both as border plant.

'PRESTON PINK'   A pink that had been in a nurseryman's possession for so long that the real name, if any, had been forgotten. It is, in fact, 'Show Beauty' (*qv*) but has been sold under this name.

'PRETTY'   This is quite a small double flower with a pale pink ground and a crushed strawberry centre diffused around its edges into the ground. The margins of the petals are fringed and it appears to have no scent. It is about 3.2 cm (1.25 in) in diameter and is carried on 20 cm (8 in) stems. It was introduced in the mid-1980s and is still in cultivation.

'PRETTY LADY'   *see 'Whatfield Pretty Lady'*

'PRICHARD'S VARIETY'   A semi-double for the rock garden. It is a shell-pink self of compact habit, being carried on 15 cm (6 in) stems. It is a bit of a mystery as it is not listed in the *IDR*, and

yet it is an old variety from at least the 1920s as it was used by Alan Bloom (crossed with *D. pavonius*) to produce 'Dubarry' and 'Oakington'. More recently 'Nicola Jane' has been produced by the same cross. It is still in cultivation.

'PRIDE OF AYRSHIRE'   A famous, very old pink. It is a single with a pale pink ground showing mainly at the margins, and a velvety crimson (59A) central one and lacing that covers virtually the whole flower, except where pinholes show the ground through it. It has a silvery sheen caused by minute white hairs. The petals are spikely fringed. The flowers are quite small, being only 3.2 cm (1.25 in) across and are carried on 25 cm (10 in) stems, which tend to be a bit floppy. It was discovered at the Post Office in Maybole, Ayrshire. It is still in existence, but its age is showing as it is difficult to propagate.

'PRIDE OF CHARLOTTE'   An eighteenth century pink with large double cherry-red flowers. It was still in existence in the 1950s, but has since seemed to have disappeared.

'PRINCE CHARMING'   A dwarf pink suitable for the rock garden or a trough. It is a single with a pink (68A) ground that opens slightly darker, and pales into the throat. It has a somewhat washed-out appearance. The petals are slightly overlapping and upward curved at the edges. They are fringed. The flowers are only 2 cm (0.75 in) across. The plant forms quite a tight-spreading cushion only about 3.8 cm (1.5 in) high, with the flower stems reaching 7.5–10 cm (3–4 in) high. It was introduced sometime around 1950 and is still widely seen in cultivation.

'PRINCE OF CARRICK'   A single pink of Irish origin with a salmon pink (pinker 48C) ground, a pale scarlet zone and a ring of grey mottling towards the margins. The flowers are up to 5 cm (2 in) across and are deeply toothed. It can be traced to 1750, but Moreton feels that it goes back further, to Elizabethan times. It unfortunately does not now seem to be around. Margery Fish refers to it as 'Earl of Carrick' and it is also known as 'Daydawn'. Margery Fish also says that it is difficult to keep, which may account for its demise.

'PRINCE OF WALES'   Well, there had to be a pink of this name, and once I started looking they all began to fall out of the woodwork. There are at least 13 pinks, 29 border carnations, two perpetual-flowering carnations and one malmaison carnation, enough to write a book about. The only one that need detain us here was introduced by C.H. Herbert in 1927 as an offspring of his famous 'Bridesmaid'. This is a large double that is a salmon self. It has a long flowering season from June into September. The flowers are fringed, very fragrant and appear on 30 cm (12 in) stems. It is a pity that it is not still with us. All the other pinks are either eighteenth or nineteenth century and are not worth pursuing as none of them is extant, as far as I know.

'PRINCESS'   A single simply described as multicoloured. It has a dwarf habit (flowering stems only 23 cm (9 in) high) and is highly fragrant. It has a long season but tends to be biennial, requiring regular propagation. This may be the reason why it appears to have vanished. There is also a pink, introduced in about 1826 by Warner, described as laced red. There are also five border carnations and five perpetual-flowering carnations sharing the same name.

'PRINCESS CHARMING'   This rock garden plant is a form of *D. gratianopolitanus*. The single flowers are pinky purple (72D), viened with a deeper shade of purple. The flowers are 2.5 cm (1 in) across and are carried on 15 cm (6 in) stems. It was awarded an AM as a border plant in 1948. There was also one border carnation and a perpetual-flowering carnation with the same name.

'PRINCESS CHRISTIAN'   A double with smooth edged petals of a pinky mauve with a central zone of chocolate maroon. (Rather mysteriously Ingwersen describes the ground as pure white, but all other authorities agree that it is a mauvy pink). It has a long flowering season and the flowers appear on 30 cm (12 in) stems. It is an old pink that now seems to have disappeared. There is also a perpetual-flowering with the same name.

'PRINCESS ELIZABETH'   This is a double flower that is a cerise pink self. The flowers are medium-sized and very fragrant. They have a long season and appear on 30 cm (12 in) stems. It was introduced by C.H. Herbert of Acocks Green in about 1927 and named after the present Queen. As one would expect, there are also several others with the same name: two eighteenth century pinks (both simply described as 'laced'), five border carnations and one perpetual flowering carnation.

'PRIORY PINK'   An old cultivar with semi-double, verging on double, flowers of a bright mauve pink (73A), flushed with a much paler pink (about 73D), darker when it first opens. The size of the flower is 3.8–5 cm (1.5–2 in), bigger when the calyx splits, which it occasionally does. The flowers are fringed and fragrant. The foliage is a good blue-green and forms a good cushion from which the flowers spring on 30 cm (12 in) stems. It is still in cultivation.

'PRISCILLA'   An Allwood double modern pink. The flowers are pure white with deep crimson (59A) central zoning and lacing. The flowers are up to 4.5 cm (1.75 in) across and are carried on 36 cm (14 in) stems. The broad petals are slightly serrated. It is a bushy plant with a spreading habit. The RHS awarded it a C in 1954 and an AM in 1955, both as a border plant. There is also one border carnation with the same name.

'PRUDENCE'   (1) An Allwood modern pink that is a flat double with a very pale pink (65D) ground and a large central area, and a quite wide lacing of a rich, velvety crimson (59A), paling to a muddy purple as it goes over. As the flower ages the ground also turns to white. The flowers are 3.8 cm (1.5 in) across and are carried on stems up to 36 cm (14 in) high. It was introduced in the early 1950s and is still in cultivation. The RHS awarded it a HC in 1953, an AM in 1956 and a FCC in 1961, all as a worthy plant for the border.

(2) Allwood tended from time to time to use the same name twice, presumably when they thought the original plant had been superseded. This is a case in point as they had introduced their original 'Prudence' in 1929. This one was also a double, but this time it had a salmon pink ground and a central area and lacing of a deeper salmon. The flowers were well scented and appeared on 30 cm (12 in) stems. It was scented. The RHS awarded it an AM in 1929. This form has disappeared.

(3) There are also one border carnation and one perpetual-flowering carnation with the same name.

'PTARMIGAN'   Having decided on a theme for names, one has to stick to it, even when it produces the most unlikely names for a pink. The House of Douglas applied this name to a double that has a white ground and a central zone of velvety maroon. It is clove scented and flowers in June and July on 38 cm (15 in) stems. It was introduced in 1949. However unlikely a name this might be, there are also three border carnations that use it (two, however, are from Douglas, who obviously liked the name).

'PUCK'   One of the Allwoodii alpinus group of dwarf pinks for the rock garden, the passing of the majority of which I seriously lament. This single-flowered pink has a white ground and a maroon eye. The flowers are borne on 15 cm (6 in) stems. It was introduced by Allwood in about 1928 but has long since disappeared. There is one border carnation with the same name.

'PURLEY KING'   This is a white that is heavily centred and laced with maroon. The flowers are quite small. It was introduced by E.A. Tickle sometime around 1974. The RHS awarded it a PC as an exhibition flower in 1974. It is still in cultivation.

'PURPLE JENNY'   An Allwood modern pink with flat semi-double flowers of a bright mauve magenta (74A) with just a hint of a darker purple central zone. The flowers pale slightly as they age but go over quite well considering its strong colour. This bright colour, however, does make them difficult to place in the border. They are up to 5 cm (2 in) across and are quite coarsely serrated at the margins. It is a recent introduction and is still in cultivation.

'QUEEN MARY'   A large-flowered double pink with a rose-pink ground and a crimson central area. The petals are fringed and the flowers very fragrant. It has a long flowering season and has 30 cm (12 in) flower stems. It was introduced by C.H. Herbert in about 1926 but has disappeared. There are also two border carnations and one perpetual-flowering carnation with the same name.

'QUEEN OF HEARTS'   An annual F1 hybrid. See also 'Queen of Henri'.

'QUEEN OF HENRI'   This is a bit of an enigma. Several nurseries are offering it in differing parts of the country (and they are the same plant) but there seems to be no written record of the plant. This would not matter except that it has a remarkable resemblance to 'Waithman's Beauty'. To further add to the confusion, all entries for this plant in UK *The Plant Finder* have been put under 'Queen of Hearts', a name I cannot find elsewhere but which, incidentally, would be a very good name for this plant as the pink 'eyes' look like hearts against a velvety background. (Further confusion is added in *The Plant Finder* by the fact the 'Queen of Hearts' has a symbol denoting that

there is a synonym elsewhere but this synonym is missing.) The flowers are single with slightly reflexed petals. The main colour is given by the central area and lacing, which cover virtually the whole petal, and this is a reddish purple (a brighter 59A) redder towards the margins. The ground is pink (63D) that shows through as two irregular 'eyes' in the middle of each petal. The colour fades and becomes duller as the flower ages. The petals are covered with short red hairs that give it a velvety look when young. The flowers are slightly fringed and fragrant. They are about 3.2 cm (1.25 in) across and are carried on 20 cm (8 in) stems. The plant has the fine foliage of an old-fashioned pink. Most of the 'Waithman's Beauty' I have seen look identical, except I have a form that has a more pronounced fringing on the petals (which have a pink tinge to them) and is inclined to lose the eyes more readily as the flower ages. The foliage is a good crisp silver-blue green nearer to the modern pinks than the old-fashioned ones. A further confusion is that 'Queen of Henri' is very similar to 'Squeeks'.

'QUEEN OF SHEBA'   This is a very old form from the seventeenth century and, for once, everybody seems to be in agreement over it. The flowers are single with a white ground overlaid with a crushed raspberry (59C) central zone and lacing that covers nearly all the petal except for two 'eyes' in the middle of each petal, a narrow margin round the edge of the petals and inside the throat. The edges of the eyes are feathered and the edges of the petals are toothed which is emphasised by the white margins. The reverse of the petals is ivory white. The petals are slightly reflexed. The flowers are about 2.5 cm (1 in) across and are carried on 25 cm (10 in) stems. They are fragrant. The plants form a sprawling mat of blue-green, long and thin (grass-like) foliage. We are lucky that this plant is so well established in cultivation. In spite of its reputed age it is still easy to grow.

'RACHEL'   This is one of Allwood's modern pinks, but this time a single-flowered form. The flowers have a silvery rose-pink ground and pale pink in the centre. They are about 12.5 cm (5 in) across and are carried on 30 cm (12 in) stems. The petals are serrated and the flowers are very fragrant. The plant has a long flowering season. It was introduced by Allwood in about 1930, and was awarded an AM as a flower for cutting by the RHS in that year. The name is sometimes spelt as

'Rachael', as indeed it was when it was awarded the AM. This plant seems to have disappeared, but there is still in existence a dwarf form with single, soft pink, 1 cm (0.4 in) across flowers that bears the same name.

'RAEDEN PINK' A semi-double, verging on double, that is a mauve-pink (64D) self. It is a pretty pink helped in its appearance by the noticeable fringing to the petals. The flowers are 3.2 cm (1.25 in) across and fragrant. They appear above a good blue-green foliage. It is like a darker form of 'Rose de Mai'. It originated in Glasgow at the end of the nineteenth century and is still in cultivation. It is sometimes spelt 'Readen Pink'.

'RAMPARTS ANNABEL' A double pink introduced by Mrs Desmond Underwood of Ramparts Nursery. This has a deep pink (58C) ground that pales towards the edges, and a dark crimson (59A) central zone. The flowers are up to 6.4 cm (2.5 in) wide and appear on 30 cm (12 in) stems. They are fragrant. The broad petals are slightly serrated. The plant was raised by P.A. Fenn of Norwich in the early 1970s. The RHS awarded the plant an HC in 1972 as a border plant.

'RASPBERRY RIPPLE' A double flower with a pink ground flecked with a darker pink. It was introduced by Cecil Wyatt of Colehayes, Bovey Tracey and is still in cultivation.

'REBECCA' (1) An Allwood modern double pink. This one has a maroon pink ground and a chocolate maroon central zone. The flowers are very fragrant and are carried on 30 cm (12 in) stems. It was introduced by Allwood in 1924.

(2) Another pink with this name is a semi-double that is a deep cerise self. It is clove scented. It was introduced by E.A. Tickle of Purley in 1957.

(3) A third was introduced in 1849 by Brightmore. This has a white ground and was laced with red.

(4) There are also two border carnations and one perpetual-flowering carnation with the same name.

'RED DENIM' This is a lovely single with slightly reflexed petals. The ground is a dry but bright cerise (darker 66A), slightly flecked and thinly striped with a deeper reddish purple (a brighter 61B), giving the impression of very narrow stripes radiating from the centre. The throat is paler. The reverse of the petals is the same, but

more silky and flushed with a apricot buff colour when young. The petals are deeply fringed. The flowers are 4.5 cm (1.75 in) across and carried on 20 cm (8 in) stems. The foliage is fine and a pale green, making a reasonable clump, although it can look scraggy with age. Michael Williams, propagator at Ingwersens, discovered it amongst a batch of supposedly *D. alpinus* seedlings while on holiday in St Austell, Cornwall in 1984 and introduced it through Ingwersens. This is a worthy plant fortunately still in cultivation.

'RED EMPEROR' A floriferous pink with a large maroon double flower lightening to crimson at the centre. It is fragrant and flowers in June and July on 23 cm (9 in) stems. It was introduced sometime before 1952 but now seems lost to cultivation.

'RED PENNY' A lovely plant for the rock garden or front of border. It is a single with flowers of a good red (53A) ground with a broken central band of maroon (187A). The ground is slightly touched with a dusky crimson. The flowers are about 3.2 cm (1.25 in) across and are carried on 12 cm (5 in) stems. It has a good flat flower with a noticeably serrated edge. Unfortunately, it has a habit of flowering itself to death and is difficult to propagate. No matter how often the flower heads are sheared off, it throws up more, giving very little propagating material. There are several plants in cultivation with this kind of colour, but this is one of the best.

'RED RIDING HOOD *see 'Arthur'*

'RED VELVET' A very good plant for the rock garden or front of border position, with a very apt name. It is a single with overlapping petals. It is a beautiful rich velvet crimson (redder 59A) with a very narrow band of brighter crimson round the edge of the fringed petals. There is a slight hint of two 'eyes' of a slightly paler red in the centre of each petal. The flowers are about 2.5 cm (1 in) across and are carried on 5–15 cm (4–6 in) stems. They have a very good scent. The plant forms wide cushions with its fine blue-green leaves. This is one of the best rock garden plants and is fortunately still in cultivation.

'REDPOLL' Another of the House of Douglas pinks named after birds. This, as they all are, is a double. The flowers have a dark pink ground with a dark red central zone. They are fragrant and are carried on 38 cm (15 in) stems. The plants flower in June and July. It was introduced by Douglas in about 1950, but is no longer around. *IDR* (probably copying it from Genders) spells this 'Redpole', which must be incorrect.

'REDSHANK'   Yet another in the Douglas bird series. This is a double with a bright cherry red ground and a deep crimson central zone. The flowers are fragrant. It was introduced in about 1954 but, as with the others, has disappeared.

'REDSTART'   Also one of the House of Douglas pinks in their bird series. This double has a lavender rose ground and a maroon central zone. The flowers are fragrant and are carried on 38 cm (15 in) stems in June and July. It was introduced in about 1951.

'REGGIE'   Another Allwood modern pink. This one has large double flowers with a brownish maroon (183C) ground and a brighter red (53B) central zone. The flowers are fragrant. The flowers are 4.5 cm (1.75 in) in diameter, with broad, cut petals. It is a compact plant with stiff flowering stems. The plant was introduced by Allwood in about 1946. The RHS awarded it an AM as a border plant in 1946. There is also a border carnation with the same name.

'REUBEN THAIN'   A floriferous single with a blood red ground and an extremely dark maroon centre that is almost black. It is fringed and highly fragrant. The flowers are carried on 30 cm (12 in) stems over a long season. It was introduced by G. Winter of Wramplingham in about 1929 but, alas, now seems to have disappeared.

'REVÉ'   A mule pink with double flowers of a salmon pink with the slightest trace of a very narrow zone of darker pink. It has a slight fragrance. The leaves are a clear-looking grey-green and are quite wide. The plants are good and strong, but look as though they are best treated as annuals and propagated each year. They are still in cultivation.

'REVELS' LADY WHARNCLIFFE'   *see* '*Lady Wharncliffe*'

'RICHARD GIBBS'   An attractive plant for the rock garden. It is a full single or semi-double with seven or eight petals. Their colour is a light purplish pink, darker when they first open, with

a slight trace of a central zone caused by purple hairs in a beard. The throat is almost white. The flowers are about 2 cm (0.75 in) across and are carried on very thin stems up to 25 cm (10 in) high that give a very airy appearance. The flowers are fringed and slightly fragrant. The plant was introduced sometime before 1935, but is still in cultivation.

'RICHMOND COTTAGE'   A plant for the rock garden. This double flower is a very luminous cerise-purple self. The flowers are 2.5 cm (1 in) across and are carried on 10 cm (4 in) stems. The petals are fringed and the flowers very heavily fragrant. The blue-green foliage makes a very good mat with quite coarse leaves reminiscent of the mule pinks. It flowers over a long period making it difficult to get cutting material. The foliage and the shape of the flower indicates that this might be a short mule pink, but the discoverer has had the plant for many years, which is unusual for mules. The luminosity of the colour seems a 'modern' colour so perhaps it is a modern pink crossed with *D. barbatus*'.

'R. L. GIBSON'   *see* '*Donizetti*'

'ROBERT'   One of the Allwood modern pinks that is a single, although there seems to be two plants involved.

(1) The original plant was described as having a magenta-rose ground with a pale or light maroon central zone. It was highly scented and was raised in about 1914. It was awarded an AM in 1920 by the RHS.

(2) The current one is a single with overlapping petals of a light pink ground with a purply pink lightly striped through it.

(3) There are also two border carnations with the same name.

'ROBIN'   (1) A double Allwood modern pink with brilliant orange-scarlet petals. It was introduced by Allwood in about 1927 but seems to have vanished.

(2) This name also occurs in the Douglas bird series. This one is a double with an apple-blossom pink ground and crimson central zone and lacing. It is fragrant. It was introduced by the House of Douglas in about 1952, but has disappeared.

(3) There is also a carnation of this name.

'ROBINA'   An Allwood modern pink, this time a semi-double. The flowers are red (between 44B and 44C) ground flushed with a brighter red. They are up to 5 cm (2 in) wide and are borne on 30 cm (12 in) stems. The broad petals are serrated. The plant was raised and introduced by Allwood in the early 1950s. The RHS awarded it an AM in 1954 and a FCC in 1956, both as a border plant.

'RODNEY' Another Allwood modern pink, this time a semi-double. The flowers are red (between 44B and 44C) paling slightly towards the outer edges of the petals. They are up to 6.4 cm (2.5 in) across and appear on 30 cm (12 in) stems. There is a slight fragrance. The broad petals are slightly fringed. The RHS awarded the plant a HC as a border plant in 1961. There are also four border carnations with the same name.

'ROGER' (1) An Allwood modern pink with double flowers of a pale scarlet (43B) colour. The flowers are up to 5.8 cm (2.25 in) across and carried on 30 cm (12 in) stems. The broad petals are serrated. The flowers are strongly clove scented. The calyx occasionally splits. They have a bushy habit. It was introduced in the mid-1950s. The RHS awarded it an AM in 1958 as a border plant.

(2) The above is the second plant introduced by Allwood with this name. The first was introduced in the early 1930s. It is a double with a pale rose ground and a deep crimson central zone. It was awarded a HC as a border plant in 1933.

'ROODKAPJE' An introduction from Holland, this semi-double has a mauvy-pink self, consisting of a pale lilac pink (70D) flushed over by a purple (70A). The flowers are about 3.8 cm (1.5 in) across and are quite deeply fringed. The flower stems are about 25 cm (10 in) high.

'ROSALIE' An Allwood modern semi-double pink that is a deep pink (48C) self. The flowers are up to 5.8 cm (2.25 in) across and are carried on 30 cm (12 in) stems. They are fragrant. It was introduced by Allwood in the late 1950s. The RHS awarded it a C in 1960, a HC 1963 and an AM in 1965. See also 'Rosealie'.

'ROSE' *see 'Whatfield Rose'*

'ROSE DE MAI' This is a wonderful pink and one of the first to flower. The double flowers are a mauvy pink (70D) self, stronger in colour towards the centre in some years forming a purple-pink eye. They do suffer from having paler or white spotting, especially in wet weather, which gives

them a washed-out appearance. The flowers are 4.5 cm (1.75 in) across (wider when it splits its calyx) and are borne on 30 cm (12 in) stems. They are fringed and fragrant. The flowering period is from May into July. The later flowers can appear completely out of character and would be hard to identify as 'Rose de Mai'. The plant forms straggly mats of grey-green foliage that can look forlorn in winter but which revives in the spring. It was introduced by Duchamp of Vienna at about the turn of the century and is still very much in cultivation. I have come across plants of this being sold mistakenly as 'Lilian' that are bound to still be in cultivation under this name. Margery Fish refers to the plant as having no trace of mauve, calling it a good pink. Certainly all the plants that I have seen under this name are what I would call a mauvy pink, so either we are talking about different plants or we see colours differently.

'ROSE JOY' This is a double that is a purple-pink (61C) self, paling slightly towards the centre as it goes over. The flowers are 5 cm (2 in) across and have a slight, but wide, fringing. They are fragrant. The calyx splits occasionally. The plant has a long flowering season. It has the typical blue-green, coarse foliage of a modern pink. It was introduced by T.A. Percival of Spalding in about 1983 as a sport of 'Joy'. It is still in cultivation.

'ROSEALIE' A double that is a bright rose-pink self. The flowers are strongly scented. The compact plant was produced by the Lindabruce Nurseries of Lancing and is still in cultivation. See also 'Rosalie'.

'ROYALTY' A double that is a purple-red self. It was introduced by the Lindabruce Nurseries of Lancing in about 1965 and is still in cultivation. It was awarded a PC in 1968 by the RHS. There are two border carnations and three perpetual-flowering carnations with the same name.

'ROYSII' This is a dwarf pink for the rock garden or front of border. Originally it must have been a single clone, a deep rose pink with a buff reverse (probably indicating that it has *D. pavonius* blood in it and, indeed, it was at one time considered to be a variety of that plant, but now considered a hybrid). However, many plants of this name are now grown from seed and there is quite a variety of different coloured pinks and the foliage varies in its finesse and colour (all indicating that it is a hybrid rather than a variety). It is doubtful whether the plants from the original 1920s plant could now be identified. In other words, this name now covers a strain rather than a single clone. Seed is widely available through seed exchanges and I have grown plants from it with many dissimilar plants resulting. The original plant was easy to grow and long-lived and, certainly, these qualities have come through to the strain.

'RUBY'   In addition to being a synonym for 'Houndspool Ruby', there are many other pinks with the same name that should be recorded.

(1) Allwood introduced one of their dwarf alpinus group with this name in 1938 when they exhibited the plant at the RHS. It was a semi-double, ruby-claret self. It seems to have disappeared from cultivation.

(2) They also introduced the name as one of the modern pinks as early as 1917. This was a double with a red maroon ground and a chocolate central zone which has long disappeared.

(3) Bakers Nurseries of Codsall introduced a single in 1929 that was a ruby red self. There is no evidence of its survival today.

(4) Not to miss out on the act, C.H. Herbert of Acocks Green also introduced one with this name: a double ruby red self that has also vanished.

(5) There were two from the nineteenth century that are not worth recording.

(6) There are six border and six perpetual-flowering carnations all sharing the same name.

(7) See also 'Whatfield Ruby'.

'RUBY DORIS'   In spite of this being a synonym for 'Houndspool Ruby' (which was a sport of 'Doris') it is a name in its own right for a plant introduced by Allwood in about 1981. It is a floriferous double with a deep rose (58C) ground and a brownish-maroon (185A) central zone. White flecks appear on the flower as it ages, giving it a washed-out appearance. The flowers are 5–6.4 cm (2–2.5 in) across and are carried on 30–38 cm (12–15 in) stems. The flowers are quite broadly fringed and fragrant. The plant is still in cultivation.

'RUFFLING ROBIN'   *see 'Solomon'*

'RUFUS'   (1) There are two pinks with this name. The first is a very early Allwood modern pink. This is a double with a deep pink ground

'Ruby Doris'

and a maroon central zone. The flowers are sweetly fragrant and have a long season. They are borne on 30 cm (12 in) stems. Introduced by Allwood in 1916, it has now disappeared from cultivation.

(2) The other is a semi-double from C.H. Herbert of Acocks Green. This is a rosy-red self and was introduced in about 1923.

(3) There are also one border carnation and one perpetual-flowering carnation with the same name.

'RUPERT'   This is another double Allwood modern pink, this time from the mid-1930s. The flowers are a brilliant orange scarlet. They are fragrant and are borne on 30 cm (12 in) stems. The plants have a long flowering season. It does not appear to still be in cultivation.

'RUSSELL'S SEEDLING'   This is a plant mentioned by Genders, but there seems to be no other reference. It has a single with a crimson red ground and a pink central zone. I have not heard of it still being in cultivation.

'RUSSLING ROBIN'   *see 'Fair Maid of Kent'*

'RUTH'   (1) A semi-double, verging on double from Allwood. It is brick red and has a maroon central zone. The large flowers are 5.8 cm (2.25 in) across. They are deeply fringed and very fragrant. They have a long flowering season, from June into the autumn. The flowers are borne on 30 cm (12 in) stems. It was introduced in the early 1930s but seems to have now disappeared. The RHS awarded it an AM in 1933 as a plant for the border and cutting.

(2) The plant under this name still in cultivation is dwarf double. It has purplish-pink flowers. It comes from unknown parents and was introduced by Ingwersens and named after a member of staff.

'RUTH FISCHER'   A compact plant with small, very white, double flowers that emerge from dark buds. They are sweetly scented and on 23–30 cm (9–12 in) stems. The plant is early into flower, but only has a short season, from May into July. It has very good foliage. It was introduced in 1923 and, although around after the Second World War, seems to have now disappeared.

'RUY BLAS'   A single with a carmine ground and a crimson central zone. It has a long flowering season. The flowers appear from June into the autumn on 30 cm (12 in) stems over silver-grey foliage. It was introduced by M. Prichard of Riv-

erslea Nurseries, Christchurch in about 1921, in which year the RHS awarded it an AM.

'SAINT ASAPH'   This is a double pink with a white ground with a purple (61B) central zone. The margins are noticeably toothed. The flowers are not fragrant and are carried on long 48 cm (19 in) stems. The plant was raised by J. Gould of Aldridge, Walsall in about 1987 as a cross between 'Alice' and 'Paul'.

'SAINT AUDREY'   A double with a very pale mauvy-pink (73C), suffused with purple from the lacing, giving it a pale purple appearance. There is a central zone of purple (72C) and slightly paler lacing. The flowers are about 3.8 cm (1.5 in) across. It was introduced by J. Gould of Aldridge, Walsall in about 1982. It is still in cultivation.

'SAINT BERTRAM'   A double pink with a pale pink (65C) flecked with dark purple (67A). The colours darken as the flower ages. They are slightly fringed and appear to have no scent. The flowers are carried on 45 cm (18 in) stems. The plant was introduced by J. Gould of Aldridge, Walsall in the mid-1980s as a cross between 'May Jones' and 'Houndspool Ruby'. It is still in cultivation.

'SAINT BOTOLPH'   Another pink in the same series, this time a semi-double that is a red (53C). The flowers are toothed around the margins. It is unscented. The flowers appear on 30 cm (12 in) stems. The plant was raised by J. Gould of Aldridge, Walsall in 1985 as a cross between 'May Jones' and 'Houndspool Ruby'. It is still in cultivation.

'SAINT CHAD'   A double with a rose pink (68B) ground and a darker (57B) central zone. The plant was raised and introduced by J. Gould of Aldridge, Walsall in 1983.

'SAINT CUTHBERT'   A flattish double that is a pure white self. The flowers are 5 cm (2 in) across and are noticeably fringed. They are slightly scented with a clove fragrance. The plant was raised and introduced by J. Gould of Aldridge, Walsall in 1985 and is still in cultivation.

'SAINT EATA'   A semi-double, verging on double, with a purple (59D) ground, and a much deeper and redder (59B) eye. The flowers are fringed and slightly fragrant. They are carried on 28 cm (11 in) stems. The plant was raised and introduced by J. Gould of Aldridge, Walsall in the mid-1980s as a cross between 'May Jones' and 'Houndspool Ruby'. It is still in cultivation.

'SAINT EDITH'   A semi-double with narrow petals with a bright pink (68B) ground, a dark maroon (187A) central zone and a lighter (59B) lacing. The central zone is spotted with the ground showing through. The flowers are very slightly fringed. They are 3.8 cm (1.5 in) across and are borne on tall, 45 cm (18 in) stems. They have a strong clove scent. The plant was raised and introduced by J. Gould of Aldridge, Walsall and is still in cultivation. The RHS awarded it an AM as a plant for the garden and exhibition in 1984 and, after trials, a C as a border plant in 1986. It is one of the parents of 'Saint Neot' and 'Saint Petroc'.

'SAINT EDMUND'   A semi-double with a white ground, a raspberry red central zone and lacing of a pale purple. The central zone is a bit spotty with the ground showing through. The lacing looks a bit washed out and not consistent in colouring. The petals are very slightly fringed but it hardly notices. It is still in cultivation.

'SAINT GEORGE'S'   A dwarf, single plant for the rock garden with a white ground and a narrow pink central band. It is heavily fringed. The flowers are borne on 15 cm (6 in) stems. It is an old variety that was still in existence in the early 1970s, but I have not seen it recently; doubtless there are still plants in somebody's garden.

'SAINT GUTHLAC'   This is a fancy semi-double, verging on double, with very pale pink (almost white) with purplish-red (60B) stripes and flecks, which give it its main colour. The flowers are 3.8 cm (1.5 in) across and are just noticeably fringed. I have not detected a scent but other reports state that it is very slightly fragrant. They are carried on 36 cm (14 in) stems. The plant was raised and introduced by J. Gould of Aldridge, Walsall in about 1983 and is still in cultivation. The RHS awarded it a PC in 1985, and a HC in 1986 and an AM in 1987, the last two as a border plant.

'SAINT HILDA'   A semi-double pink with a pure white ground, a deep purple (deeper 61A) central zone that pales with age and, occasionally, traces of similarly coloured lacing. The plant was introduced by J. Gould of Aldridge, Walsall in about 1985.

'SAINT KENELM'   Another double in the same series. This one has a deep red (53A) ground fading slightly (53B) towards the centre of the flower. The flowers are slightly scented and have a broad fringing. They are carried on 30 cm (12 in) stems. The plant was introduced by J. Gould of Aldridge, Walsall in the mid-1980s as a cross between 'May Jones' and 'Houndspool Ruby'.

'SAINT MODWEN'   A double that is a rose madder self. The flowers are fragrant. The plant was introduced by J. Gould of Aldridge, Walsall in about 1983.

'SAINT NEOT'   This one in the series has double flowers with a dark pink (63B), a crimson (59A) central zone and purple (59C) lacing. The ground pales on the margins, which are slightly indented. The flowers are not fragrant and appear on long 51 cm (20 in) stems. The plant was raised by J. Gould of Aldridge, Walsall in about 1985 from a cross between 'Alice' and 'Saint Edith'.

'SAINT NICHOLAS'   A small button of a double pink with a ground of a deep purply red (60B to 60C) and a deep crimson (59A) zone that is hardly noticeable. The flowers are fragrant and moderately fringed. They are 2.5–3.2 cm (1–1.25 in) across and carried on 20 cm (8 in) stems above a blue-green foliage that is quite wide when compared with the flower size. The calyx has a habit of splitting, although this does not make the flower appear blousy. As the flowers age they are covered with small but distinctive yellow spots. There is great debate as to whether 'Lawley's Red' (*qv*) is the same as 'Saint Nicholas'. It also seems likely that at least some of the plants currently named 'Mr Neville' are also the same plant. This is an old cultivar and is still in cultivation.

'SAINT NINSAP'   A semi-double with a pale pink ground flushed with the cerise red of the stripes and flecks. Some of the stripes are quite broad. The flowers are up to 5 cm (2 in) across. It is still in cultivation.

'SAINT OSWALD'   A double pink with a white ground and a purply crimson (61A) central zone. The flowers are up to 5 cm (2 in) across and are carried on 45 cm (18 in) stems. The flowers are coarsely toothed and have a very heavy clove scent. It was raised in the mid-1980s by J. Gould of Aldridge, Walsall from a cross between 'Alice' and an unknown plant. It is still in cultivation.

'SAINT OSYTH'   A semi-double in the series, this one having a dark rose-pink (68B) ground with a raspberry red (60A) central zone and lacing that have spotted edges bleeding into the ground. The lacing also touches the margins of the petals, which are noticeably fringed. The lacing fades and breaks up as the flowers age. The flowers are 3.8 cm (1.5 in) across and are carried on 38 cm (15 in) high stems. They are fragrant. The plant was introduced by J. Gould of Aldridge, Walsall in 1983. The RHS awarded it a HC as a border plant in 1987.

'SAINT PETROC'   Another semi-double with a purplish pink (63B) ground and a purple (61B) central zone and lacing. The margins of the flowers are noticeably toothed and the jagged edge to the lacing follows this outline. The flowers do not appear to have any scent. The flowering stems are up to 30 cm (12 in) high. The plant was raised by J. Gould of Aldridge, Walsall in about 1987 as a cross between 'Saint Edith' and 'Dad's Favourite'. It is still in cultivation.

'SAINT PHOCAS NOSEGAY'   A plant known to Margery Fish, this has a light crimson ground and purple markings. There is no evidence that it is still in existence.

'SAINT TEILO'   A double with a deep candy pink (58C) ground and a purple (58A) central zone and lacing. The petals are slightly indented. The flowers are not scented. The flowering stems are up to 40 cm (16 in) high. The plant was raised by J. Gould of Aldridge, Walsall in 1987 as a cross between 'Saint Audrey' and 'Camelford'.

'SAINT WILFRID'   A modern double pink with a deep purplish pink (64C to 64D) ground. It is clove scented. The plant was introduced by J. Gould of Aldridge, Walsall in about 1984.

'SAINT WINIFRED'   This is a very fresh-looking flower. It is a double that is a dark rose-pink (64C) self. The flowers are only very slightly indented and appear almost smooth. They are also fragrant. They are about 3.8 cm (1.5 in) across but can be larger as the calyx splits. The flower stems are about 30 cm (12 in) high. It is still in cultivation.

'SAINT WYSTAN'   A double with a pinkish red (55B) ground and a dark rose-pink (57A) central zone. The plant was introduced by J. Gould of Aldridge, Walsall in 1983.

'SALLY'   A single Allwood modern pink. This one has a flesh pink ground and a darker central zone. It is very fragrant. The flowers have a long season and appear on 30 cm (12 in) stems. It was introduced by Allwood in about 1933 and was selected for trial at Wisley in 1939, but is no longer about.

'SALLY'S MAUVE'   A double with white, finely fringed petals, a narrow band of mauve (80A) towards the centre, and a green throat. The flowers are 4.5 cm (1.75 in) in diameter, more when the calyx splits, as it usually does. The split calyx and fringing give the flower a very frilly appearance. The flowering stems are 20–25 cm (8–10 in) high. The flowering period is in June and July. It is very similar to both 'Bridal Veil' and 'Madonna'. It is still in cultivation.

'SALMON LEAP'   A double, pink self from Cecil Wyatt of Colehayes, Bovey Tracey.

'SALMON QUEEN'   (1) An imperial pink from C.H. Fielder of the Lindabruce Nurseries. This one is a very large double, salmon pink itself. It has a long flowering season from June until the end of autumn. It was introduced sometime around 1947, but has since vanished. The RHS awarded it an AM in 1950 as a border plant.

(2) The House of Douglas also introduced a plant with the same description as the above in about 1951. They could both be the same plant, but it is now impossible to say as neither seems to be in cultivation.

(3) There are three border carnations and a perpetual-flowering carnation with the same name.

'SAM BARLOW'   A much-loved, old-fashioned pink. The flowers are fully double with a white ground and a very dark maroon, almost black (187A) central zone. It has a medium fringing and the globular calyx splits, giving it a very blousy, frilly look. The flowers are very fragrant. They are about 5 cm (2 in) across and appear on 20 cm (8 in) stems. It has the short flowering season of most old-fashioned pinks, namely June and July. The plant forms a good mat of blue-green foliage, although it does suffer from some dieback in the centre. Its origin is obscure, but it is reputed to have been raised in the nineteenth century and is, fortunately. still in cultivation. The RHS have awarded it an AM in 1933 and another in 1946, both as border plants. It should not be confused with 'Samuel Barlow', which is a border carnation.

'SAMUEL DOBIE'   A modern double that is a camellia pink (68B) flushed darker towards the centre when the petals are still bunched. The flowers are 5.8 cm (2.25 in) across and appear on 36 cm (14 in) stems. They are slightly fringed and are fragrant. It occasionally splits its calyx. It is a recent introduction that is still in cultivation.

'SANDERLING'   Another of the obscure House of Douglas series named after birds. This is a double (as they all are) with a crushed strawberry pink ground and a maroon central zone. It was introduced in about 1958 but has since vanished.

'SANDRA'   An Allwood modern pink. This is a double that is a sugar pink self. The flowers are very strongly scented and have a long flowering season. The foliage is a good silver green. It was introduced by Allwood in about 1965 and is still in cultivation. There are also one border carnation and two perpetual-flowering carnations with the same name. It produced the sport 'Betty Webber'.

'SARAMANDA'   A large single with over-lapping petals that have a light purple (68B) ground, with the slightest trace of a darker zone, paling as it goes into the throat. The white styles make a pleasant contrast in the centre of the flower. The flowers are quite luminous in an evening light and could easily be mistaken at a distance as a large *Lychnis flos-jovis*. The petals have a slight fringing, occasionally cut quite deep, and are slightly curled up at the margins. The flowers are 4.5–5 cm (1.75–2 in) in diameter and carried on 25 cm (10 in) stems. The flowers are slightly fragrant. The plant was introduced by R.P. Tolley of Worcester Park in the late 1980s from unknown parentage. It is still in cultivation. The RHS awarded it a PC in 1989 as an exhibition flower.

'SATAN'   Not exactly a name one would expect for a pink, but there it is. It is a double with a velvety red (53A). The flowers are up to 5.8 cm (2.25 in) across and are carried on 36 cm (14 in) stems. It has strong clove scent. The plant was raised by P.A. Fenn of Norwich. The RHS awarded the plant a C in 1967 as a border plant.

'SCHUMANN'   A large single pink with a red ground and a deeper crimson eye. It flowers over a long season on stems that rise 23–30 cm (9–12 in) high. It was possibly raised in the 1930s, but is no longer in cultivation.

'SEAMEW'   Another of Douglas' odd bird names. This double has a pale pink ground with a deep crimson central zone and lacing. The flowers are fragrant. It was introduced in about 1960, but has since disappeared.

'SEASHELL'   Another House of Douglas plant, but this time a descriptive name rather than one of their bird series. Descriptive as the double has a shell-pink ground and a rosy purple central area. The flowers are fragrant and appear on 38 cm (15 in) stems. It was introduced in about 1948, but has now vanished.

'SELINA'   A modern double pink with a pink ground that fades at the edges and, occasionally, on the body of the petals, and a central zone of red (45D). The flowers are up to 4.5 cm (1.75 in) across and are carried on 28 cm (11 in) stems. They are fragrant. The broad petals are slightly serrated. The plant was raised by P.A. Fenn of Norwich.

'SERIN'   Yet another of the disappeared bird-name series from the House of Douglas. This double has a purple ground and a very deep crimson central zone. It has a short season, flowering in June and July from 38 cm (15 in) stems. Douglas introduced it in 1949.

'SHOW ACHIEVEMENT'   The first of what is going to be a long series of plants suitable for showing, but also good for the border. This is a double with a soft salmon-rose ground that deepens towards the centre of the flower. The flowers are 5.8 cm (2.25 in) in diameter and carried on 38 cm (15 in) stems. The broad, flat petals are serrated and evenly arranged. It was introduced by Allwood in about 1945 and was thought by Genders to be one of the best of all pinks. Unfortunately I have not seen it about lately. The RHS awarded it an AM in 1951 and a HC as a border plant in 1954.

'SHOW ARISTOCRAT'   A semi-double, verging on double, with a pale pink (39B) ground with a slight trace of a darker pink (49C) in the centre. Some flowers have a purple (64B) flecks and stripes in them. The flowers can be up to 6.4 cm (2.5 in) across and carried on 38 cm (15 in) stems. The petals are only slightly indented and the flowers are fragrant. This is a vigorous plant with a bushy habit. It was introduced by Allwood around World War II and is still in cultivation. The RHS awarded it an AM in 1951 and a FCC in 1952, both as a worthy plant for the border.

'SHOW BEAUTY' A flat semi-double with a very open centre to the flower (appearing like a rather full-petalled single). The flower has a very fresh appearance with a dark rose (64C) ground and a dark, but bright, red (redder 59A) centre. The flowers are about 5 cm (2 in) across (occasionally even larger, the award plant being 7.5 cm (3 in)) and are carried on 38 cm (15 in) stems. They are fragrant. The margins of the petals are broadly, but not deeply, fringed. The flower has a noticeably long and narrow calyx. This pink is later flowering than most other pinks. The foliage is quite narrow but long, and blue-green in colour. The plant was introduced by Allwood in about 1939. It was awarded an AM as a border plant by the RHS in 1948. This plant has also been distributed under the name 'Preston Pink'.

'SHOW BOUNTIFUL' A dark pink self introduced by Allwood in about 1958 but not around now.

'SHOW BRIDE' A semi-double with a pink (39D) ground and a pale red (44D) central zone. The flowers are about 5 cm (2 in) across and are carried on 51 cm (20 in) stems. The broad petals are serrated. The plant has a bushy, erect habit. It was introduced by Allwood in about 1953. The RHS awarded it an AM in 1955 and an HC in 1964, both as border plants. It is still in cultivation.

'SHOW CAMEO' This one has a light pink ground and a contrasting, dark maroon eye. It was introduced by Allwood in about 1955, but unless some show enthusiast has got it tucked away, it has disappeared from circulation.

'SHOW CELEBRITY' A double with a reddish purple ground and a darker central zone. It is clove scented. The plant was introduced by Allwood in about 1970, but has since vanished. The RHS awarded it a HC as a border plant in 1970.

'SHOW CHARMING' A semi-double with a light pink (36D) ground, but with a very wide (up to 2.5 cm (1 in) wide) coral (45C) central zone. The flowers are up to 5.8 cm (2.25 in) across and are carried on 45 cm (18 in) stems. The petals are waved. The flowers are clove scented. It was introduced by Allwood in 1955 and is still in cultivation. The RHS awarded it an AM as an exhibition plant in 1959, and a C in 1960, a HC in 1964 and an AM in 1968, all as a border plant.

'SHOW CLOVE' A semi-double, verging on double with a deep rose ground and a maroon central zone. It has a smaller flower than most of the show pinks. The flowers are fragrant and are carried on 30 cm (12 in) high stems. The flowering season is a long one, from June well into autumn. Allwood introduced the plant in about 1952, but it seems to have languished.

'SHOW CRIMSON' Another small-flowered, flat double. This one is rose red (57A), darkening towards the centre and with a golden sheen. The flowers are about 3.8 cm (1.5 in) across and are carried on 30 cm (12 in) stems. It is strongly scented. The flowering season is a long one, from June into autumn. It was introduced by Allwood in about 1940 but now seems to have vanished. The RHS awarded it an AM in 1946 as an exhibition variety, and an HC as a border plant in 1951.

'SHOW DAINTINESS' A double with a pink (50C) ground, a slight trace of a salmony eye, and a touch of green at the base of the petals. The flowers are up to 5.8 cm (2.25 in) across and are borne on 30 cm (12 in) stems. They are fragrant. The petals are slightly fringed. Allwood introduced it in about 1956, but it no longer seems to be in general cultivation. The plant was awarded a HC in 1961 and an AM in 1963 by the RHS, both as border plants.

'SHOW DISCOVERY' A large-flowered double with a violet cerise (57D) ground and a maroon, almost velvet black (187A) central zone. The flowers are very fragrant and have a long season, well into the autumn. The 6.4 cm (2.5 in) flowers appear on 38 cm (15 in) stems above a silvery foliage. The plant was introduced by Allwood in about 1946, but is not to be seen today. The RHS awarded it an AM as an exhibition plant in 1950 and an AM as a border plant in 1952.

'SHOW DISTINCTION' Another large double show pink. This time it has cerise crimson flowers, tinged with fuchsia pink. They are fragrant. Allwood introduced it in about 1953 and it is still in cultivation.

'SHOW EMBLEM' A semi-double, verging on a flat double, that gives the overall impression of being a soft shell pink (50D), although it is really a very pale pink overlaid with a slightly darker one. The flowers, which pale with age, have a slight fringing and are fragrant. They are about

4.5 cm (1.75 in) across. The plant was introduced by Allwood in about 1966 and this one is still in cultivation. The RHS awarded it an AM as an exhibition plant in 1966 and a HC as a border plant in 1967.

'SHOW ENCHANTRESS'   A double that is a salmon-pink (44D) flushed scarlet (43B) self. The 5.8 cm (2.25 in) flowers have a long season from June into autumn and are carried on very strong 30 cm (12 in) stems. The broad petals have serrated margins. It was introduced by Allwood in about 1946 and is still in cultivation. The RHS awarded it an AM as an exhibition plant in 1949, and an AM in 1950 and a FCC in 1952, both as a border plant. It is also known as 'Show Gem'. It was one of the parents of 'Fair Carl' and 'Fair Jessica'.

'SHOW EXCELLENCE'   A double with a delicate fuchsia pink (65D) ground and a deeper pink (57B) central zone. The flowers are 5 cm (2 in) in diameter and are carried on 36 cm (14 in) stems. The petals are very broad and are slightly cut. It was introduced by Allwood in about 1949 but has since disappeared. The RHS awarded it a HC in 1953 and an AM in 1954, both as a border plant. It was also awarded a PC in 1956 as an exhibition plant.

'SHOW EXQUISITE'   This one is a double with a soft pink (55D) ground and just the trace of a deeper (52D) eye. The flowers are large, up to 6.4–7.5 cm (2.5–3 in) across. It does not seem to still be in cultivation. The RHS awarded it an AM in 1949 and another in 1952, both as a plant for exhibition, and both under the name 'Exquisite', which is now considered a synonym.

'SHOW FORTUNE'   A double that is a simple rose-cerise self. It is very fragrant and has a long flowering season, appearing on 30–38 cm (12–15 in) stems. It was introduced by Allwood in about 1946, but has since disappeared.

'SHOW GEM'   *see 'Show Enchantress'*

'SHOW GLORY'   A flat double or semi-double with a deep rose (50A) colour that fades towards the centre of the flower. The flowers are large, being 6.4 cm (2.5 in) across, and are carried on 30–38 cm (12–15 in) stems. The broad petals are flat and slightly fringed. The plant was introduced by Allwood in about 1948 and is still in cultivation. The RHS awarded it a C in 1950 and an AM in

1951, both as a worthy border plant. It is one of the parents of 'Fair Carl' and 'Fair Jessica'.

'SHOW GRACEFUL'   This is a semi-double with tufts of petals at the centre. Their colour is a pale pink (36C) ground, fading into a greenish amber eye at the extreme centre of the flower. The flowers are serrated at the margins and are very fragrant. They are 5.8 cm (2.25 in) in diameter and appear on 45 cm (18 in) stems. It flowers over a long season, from June well into autumn. The plant was introduced in about 1947 by Allwood, but now seems to have disappeared. The RHS awarded the plant an AM in 1951 and a FCC in 1952, both as a border plant. It produced the sport 'Show Harlequin'.

'SHOW GRANDEUR'   Allwood at this time must have employed a person full time just in making up names for this series. This one is a dark pink self. It was introduced in about 1958, but has since vanished.

'SHOW HARLEQUIN'   A double with a pink ground and wide cerise stripes and a pale greenish central eye. The flower is clove scented. Allwood introduced it in about 1952 as a sport from 'Show Graceful', but it has since disappeared.

'SHOW IDEAL'   This one is still in existence. It is a double with a creamy white, flushed with pink (39D) and with a narrow carmine (52B) central zone. The flowers are very fragrant. They are 5 cm (2 in) in diameter and carried on (12–15 in) stems over a long season. The plant was introduced by Allwood in about 1945. The RHS awarded it an AM as an exhibition flower in 1948, and a HC as a border plant in 1952.

'SHOW LADY'   A large semi-double or flat double with a salmon pink (52D) ground and an amber central zone. The large (7 cm (2.75 in) tall) flowers are fragrant and appear on stems up to 36 cm (15 in) long over a long season. It was introduced by Allwood in about 1940, but does not seem to now be around. The RHS awarded it an AM as an exhibition plant in 1946, and an HC as a border plant in 1948.

'SHOW MAGNIFICENCE'   Another double, this time of an apple blossom pink (39D) veined and overlaid with deep pink (52C). The flowers are up to 5.8 cm (2.25 in) across and are carried on 36 cm (14 in) stems. It was introduced by Allwood in about 1969 and is still in cultivation. It was awarded a HC in 1969 and an AM in 1970, both as a border plant.

'SHOW PAGEANT' A double that is a crimson self. It was introduced by Allwood in about 1949, but seems to have vanished.

'SHOW PARAGON' A double that is a light pink self. It is clove scented. The plant was introduced by Allwood in about 1954, but now seems to have disappeared, although, like most of these show plants, some may be still be lovingly tended somewhere. The RHS awarded it a HC in 1960 as a border plant.

'SHOW PEARL' A semi-double or flat double with a pure white flower, although there is a tinge of green at the base of the petals when the flower first opens. The petals are rounded and the flower opens flat. There is a very slight indentation on the petals. The flowers are about 5 cm (2 in) across and are carried on 25–30 cm (10–12 in) stems. They are fragrant. The plant was introduced by Allwood in about 1948 and is still in cultivation. The RHS awarded it an AM as an exhibition plant in 1950, and an AM in 1950 and a FCC in 1951, both as a plant for the border.

'SHOW PEERLESS' A double with a white ground and a pink (48C) central zone. The flowers are up to 5 cm (2 in) across and are carried on 30 cm (12 in) stems. The broad petals have serrated margins. The plant is vigorous and has a bushy habit. It was introduced by Allwood in about 1946, but has since vanished. The plant was awarded an HC in 1952 by the RHS.

'SHOW PERFECTION' A large, flat semi-double with tufts of petals in the centre. The flowers have a soft rose-pink (67D) ground and a deep maroon (185B) central zone. They are very fragrant. The 5.8 cm (2.5 in) flowers appear on 30 cm (12 in) stems over a long period. The plant was introduced by Allwood in about 1947, but has since disappeared. The RHS awarded it a AM as an exhibition plant in 1949, and a HC in 1950 and an AM in 1951, both as a border plant.

'SHOW PORTRAIT' A double that is a dark red (46A) with a touch of purple in it. The flowers are up to 5 cm (2 in) in diameter and are carried on 36 cm (14 in) stems. The margins of the broad petals are finely serrated. I have not been able to

detect a fragrance though it is claimed to be clove-scented. Allwood introduced it in about 1950 and it is still in cultivation. The RHS have awarded it an AM in 1952 and a FCC in 1953, both as a border plant.

'SHOW SALMON' This is a self that is a deep salmon pink that pales towards the margins. It was introduced by Allwood in about 1946, but has since vanished from cultivation.

'SHOW SATIN' Another self, this time a shell pink double. It is clove scented. It was introduced by Allwood in about 1960 and is still in cultivation. The RHS awarded it a HC as a border plant in 1970.

'SHOW SPLENDOUR' Yet another self, this time a salmon-red one. It was introduced by Allwood in about 1951, but seems to have gone the way of many in this series.

'SHOW SUPREME' A double with a ruby rose ground, touched with cerise and with a darker central zone. The flowers are very fragrant and appear on 30–38 cm (12–15 in) stems over a long period, from June into autumn. Allwood introduced the plant in about 1948, but it has since vanished.

'SHOW TRIUMPH' Allwood obviously ran out of names towards the end of the alphabet and this is the last in the series. It is a dark red self and was introduced in about 1961. It no longer seems to be around.

'SIMPLICITY' This is a double-flowered pink, with flowers of a cherry-red ground and a darker red central zone. It is a vigorous plant introduced by C.H. Herbert of Acocks Green in about 1926. It has since vanished.

'SIR CEDRIC MORRIS' *see 'Cedric's Oldest'*

'SIR DAVID SCOTT' A delightful semi-double with a velvety maroon (187B) main colour with just a hint of pink (68B) on the fringing to the petals and in the throat. The flower is quite small, only 3.2 cm (1.25 in) in diameter. They are carried on 25–30 cm (10–12 in) stems. The flowers are fringed at the margins and are fragrant. They occasionally split their calyces but still remain relatively neat. The foliage is very narrow. It is not a very strong plant, but it is not too difficult to propagate. It is thought to have originated in the seventeenth century (the ease of propagation, however, makes one wonder) but was found more recently by Valerie Finnis in Northamptonshire and she named it after her husband. It is still in cultivation.

'SISKIN'   One of the House of Douglas' bird name series. This is a double with a shell pink ground and a deep red centre. It is fragrant and was introduced in about 1955. As with most of this series, it is no longer in existence.

'SKYLARK'   Another in the series named after birds. This one is a double with a bright pink ground and a crimson central zone. It was introduced by the House of Douglas in about 1957, but has since vanished.

'SNOW QUEEN'   An imperial pink from C.H. Fielder's Lindabruce Nurseries. This is a large double that is a glistening white self. It has a strong fragrance and a long flowering period, from June into October. It was introduced in about 1947. There are also an annual pink (D. chinensis), two border carnations and two perpetual-flowering carnations with the same name.

'SNOWFINCH'   A pure white double with a purple central zone. The flowers are fragrant, as are all in the series named after birds. It was introduced by the House of Douglas in about 1954, but has since vanished from cultivation.

'SOLOMON'   A single with a velvet, crushed raspberry (a richer 61A) main colour and mauvish-pink (75B) tips to the fringing of the petals and odd spots showing through the red. The flowers are about 2.5 cm (1 in) across and are deeply fringed. It is an old variety and its age is beginning to show as it is not an easy plant. It is also known as 'Ruffling Robin'.

'SOPS-IN-WINE'   A name that is very old, but whether the plants that now go with it are as old, is another matter. It is a name that was used of carnations and pinks either because they are reminiscent of sops (pieces of bread) floating in wine or because the pinks themselves were used in wine to act as a cheap substitute for cloves. Either way, some of the earliest references to pinks (and carnations) are as sops-in-wine and it seems likely that it was used as a generic name covering a type of pink rather than one particular kind. It

therefore seems equally likely that there were many different plants represented by this name in different parts of the country and over several centuries. The main type that has come down to us is a fringed, frilly double with an almost black, maroon (187A) central zone. Some current plants bearing this title have a paler more purple (61A) zone. The flowers are quite blousy and large, up to 5 cm (2 in) or more across. Claims to have the 'true' sops-in-wine should be treated with caution, particularly if it is borne in mind how easy all the current contenders can be propagated. A plant that could only be increased vegetatively would be likely, after many centuries, to be extremely difficult to cope with. Other contenders for the title are red singles with white 'eyes' in the middle of each petal (the sops floating in the wine), but these always seem to turn out to be 'Waithman's Beauty' or other recognisable modern cultivar. Yet other authorities claim that 'Sops-in-Wine' was a crimson self like 'Crimson Clove', but smaller. What ever you have got, enjoy it and its name, and do not be too down-hearted that you have only got a nineteenth or twentieth century imitation as I doubt whether knights or peasants enjoying one in their wine were particularly worried as to what its true cultivar name was.

'SOUTHMEAD'   A dwarf pink self for the rock garden. Raised by Colonel Mooney of Weald in about 1966 and named after his house. It is still in cultivation.

'SPARK'   A wonderful but rather difficult pink. It is a single of a fabulous rich, deep red (bright 60A) with a velvety texture, and a darker (187B) central eye. The reverse is an uneven deep purple pink. The flowers are about 3.8 cm (1.5 in) across and are borne on stems about 15 cm (6 in) long. The petals are fringed and the flowers have a slight fragrance. It could be a mule as the foliage is inclined towards D. barbatus in appearance, although it is not as strong or vigorous as some of the others and has a more sprawling habit. The flowering season is a long one. It will flower itself to death and is only short lived, so cuttings should be taken regularly. Indeed, it may be necessary to keep one plant sheered of flowers to produce cutting material. To prolong its existence, it has been suggested that a lime-free soil helps, but I have not found this of any noticeable benefit. Ingwersen suggests a rich gritty soil and I think this is more likely to help as long as the soil is not too wet. It is an old cultivar of unknown provenance and is

'Spark'

still in cultivation, but needs hard work to keep it so. One problem clouds the horizon: in the 1940s there were two forms, one more robust than the other, but paying for this by having not such good flowers. I am not certain which form we have inherited; perhaps both.

'SPARROW'   Yet another of the House of Douglas' bird name series. Sparrows are not particularly beautiful birds, but once committed to a series of names I suppose you must stick to it. This is a double with a pale pink ground, and a crimson central area and lacing (does that sound like a sparrow?). The flowers are fragrant. It was introduced in about 1958, but has since disappeared.

'SPENCER BICKHAM'   The plants I know of this name are delightful singles with a light purple ground (77B), a crimson (71A) central eye and the beginning of lacing, which together form a letter 'w' at the base of the petals. The purple ground is in fact pink, but is flushed with the crimson giving it a purple effect. The flowers are about 2.5 cm

(1 in) across and are borne on 10 cm (4 in) stems. The petals are slightly fringed. It has a short flowering season, from June into July. The plant was introduced by R. Veitch at the turn of the century, possibly using *Dianthus gratianopolitanus* as one of the parents (at the time *D. deltoides* was suggested as the other parent). A black-and-white photograph of the plant in the Veitch nursery at the turn of the century show a ground flushed with a deeper colour and just the trace of a narrow central band. Dark calyces are also in evidence and the petals appear deeply fringed. This, we must conclude, is the true plant and it may still be in cultivation as plants of this name are still widely grown. The RHS awarded it an AM in 1906.

'SQUARE EYES'   *see 'Old Square Eyes'*

'SQUEEKS'   This is a single flower that is a bright pink (68B) that is almost obscured with deep crimson (59B) except for two 'eyes' in the middle of each petal. The flowers are about 2.5 cm (1 in) across and are carried on 30 cm (12 in) stems. They have a slight scent. This plant was introduced by A.G. Weeks of Limpsfield in about 1965. Plants of this name are still in existence, although some of them have turned out to be the ubiquitous 'Queen of Henri'. The RHS awarded it a HC in 1965 and an AM in 1966, both for the rock garden.

'STARTLER'   This is a very flat semi-double that is an orange-pink self. It was raised by P.A. Fenn of Norwich in about 1974 and is still in cultivation.

'STELLA'   An Allwood modern double that is a white self, although the centre appears a creamy white where the petals are still bunched. The flowers are up to 5 cm (2 in) wide and are carried on 30 cm (12 in) stems. They have a slight fragrance. The RHS awarded it a HC in 1969 as a border plant.

'STERIKER'   This is a pink for the rock garden. It is a single with a cerise (57A) ground and a crimson or paler cerise (59A) central band inside. The flowers are about 2.5 cm (1 in) across and are carried on 23 cm (9 in) stems. They appear to have no scent. The plant has a spreading habit. The RHS awarded it a C for the rock garden in 1966.

'STONECHAT'   (1) A double in the bird series for the House of Douglas. This is a clear pink self. The flowers are fringed and fragrant, and are carried on 38 cm (15 in) stems. The plant has a short flowering season, from June into July. It was introduced in 1949 but has disappeared.
(2) Douglas issued another pink with the same name in 1959. This had a deep pink ground and a crimson central eye. This has also vanished.

'STRAWBERRIES AND CREAM'   This is a large double with a pale pink (49D) ground and salmon pink (51B) flecks. The centre is flushed a slight yellowish buff. The petals are very slightly fringed but appear almost smooth. The flowers are fragrant and are about 5 cm (2 in) in diameter and are carried on 30 cm (12 in) stems. The plant was introduced by Cecil Wyatt of Colehayes, Bovey Tracey in about 1981 and it is still in cultivation. It is one of the parents of 'Strawberry Fair'. The RHS awarded it a HC as an exhibition plant in 1984 and a C as a border plant in 1985.

'STRAWBERRY FAIR'   A double pink self. It was introduced by Cecil Wyatt of Colehayes, Bovey Tracey from 'Strawberries and Cream'.

'SUFFOLK CHORISTER'   Another double, this time with a white ground and a purple-red central zone that is diffused into the ground and sometimes gives rise to a trace of lacing. The flowers are 5 cm (2 in) across. It is still in cultivation.

'SUFFOLK PINK'   A double with a dark rose-pink ground and a touch of red in the central eye. The petals are slightly fringed. The flowers are about 4.5 cm (1.75 in) in diameter. There seems to be no noticeable fragrance. The name is an invalid one, but there seem to be a number of plants around bearing it, so it is recorded here as such.

'SUFFOLK PRIDE'   This is a flat semi-double with rounded petals and virtually no indentations so they appear smooth. It is a bright purple-pink with a slight trace of a red central eye. It is paler towards the edges as it goes over. The flowers are up to 5 cm (2 in) across. It is still in cultivation.

'SUFFOLK SILK'   Another flat semi-double, this one pink flushed with a salmon pink that gives it its dominant colour. It is brighter towards the centre. It is about 3.8 cm (1.5 in) across and noticeably fringed. It is still in cultivation.

'SUFFOLK SUMMER'   A double with a pale pink (49C) ground flushed with a darker pink (52C) that is particularly noticeable towards the centre and when the flowers first open. The flowers are about 5 cm (2 in) across and are coarsely fringed. They are borne on 30 cm (12 in) stems that tend to flop. The foliage is strong and a good blue-green. It was raised by G.D. Kiddy of Wissett and is still in cultivation. The RHS awarded it a PC in 1990 and a C in 1991 as a border plant.

'SUPERB'   (1) A large double with a lavender pink ground and a dark crimson central zone. The flowers are fringed and very fragrant. They are borne on 30 cm (12 in) stems over a long season from June into the autumn. The plant was introduced by C.H. Fielder of the Lindabruce Nurseries in about 1946, but seems to have now vanished.
(2) This is a popular name and there are another nine pinks bearing it, but they are all from the eighteenth or nineteenth centuries and with rather vague descriptions that make it highly unlikely that they will resurface. There are also 13 border carnations and two perpetual-flowering carnations with the same name.

'SUSAN' (1) A semi-double, verging on a flat double, with a light pink (62C) ground flushed with a deeper pink moving out from the rich crimson (59A) central eye. Although it has not occurred on any flowers I have seen (nor was it stated in the report of the 1949 award), Allwood's latest catalogues states that there is also lacing. The flowers are about 3.8 cm (1.5 in) across (sometimes larger) and slightly serrated on the margins. They are scented. Introduced by Allwood in about 1917 and it is still in cultivation. The RHS awarded it an AM in 1927, and a HC in 1949 and a FCC in 1960, the last two as a border plant.

(2) Another 'Susan' also seems to be in circulation. This is a single with a few extra petals, thus verging on a semi-double. It has a white ground and a narrow crimson (59A) band in the centre of the flower. The ground turns to a blush pink (65B to 65C) as it ages. The flowers are 3.2–3.8 cm (1.25–1.5 in) across and are deeply fringed. They are fragrant. The flowering stems are about 28 cm (11 in) long. Whether this is a plant that has been given this name, whether it has been mislabelled at some stage, or whether it is simply a seedling mistakenly given this name, I do not know. It is not listed in the *IDR*.

(3) The *IDR* does, however, list another pink with this name. This is a double with a crimson ground and is flecked. It is recorded as pre-1951.

(4) There are also two perpetual-flowering carnations with the same name.

'SUSANNAH' (1) Another Allwood modern pink, this time a double with a pure white ground and a splash of rich, velvety crimson (59A) in the centre, and a white throat. The flowers are 3.8 cm (1.5 in) across and are carried on 10 cm (4 in) stems. The petals are slightly toothed and the flowers are slightly fragrant. It was recently introduced by Allwood as a sport from 'Susan'. It is still in cultivation. It is a good fresh-looking plant that goes over well.

(2) There was a pink introduced in about 1846 by Meade with the same name. It has a white ground and rosy-purple lacing.

(3) There are also two perpetual-flowering carnations with the same name.

'SUTTON PINK' A mule pink with clusters of semi-double flowers of a mauvish rose pink. The flowers are fragrant and appear in June and July. As with all mules, it is essential to take cuttings each year. This is reputedly an old cultivar found in a Lincolnshire garden.

'SUTTON'S FREEDOM' A mule pink from a chance cross between a sweet william (*D. barbatus*) 'Sutton' and *D. superbus*. The flowers are bright rose-pink and are borne in large heads, each flower being 6.4 cm (2.5 in) across. The flowers are sweetly fragrant and the petals deeply fringed, more so than the sweet william's. The plant is about 76 cm (30 in) tall and, although the general appearance is that of a sweet william, the leaves are narrower and the stems more slender. It flowers in June and July. It was introduced by Suttons of Reading. The RHS awarded it an AM in 1933 as a plant for the border and for cutting. It no longer seems to be in cultivation.

'SWANLAKE' One of C.H. Fielder's imperial pinks. This flat double is a pure white self, although it has a green throat. The flowers are 5 cm (2 in) in diameter. The petals are waved and the edges are only slightly fringed, giving the flower a good 'solid' look. They have a good fragrance. The rigid stems are up to 36 cm (14 in) tall. It has a long flowering season, from June into the autumn. The plant was introduced in about 1957 and is still in cultivation. It has a good track record both as a border plant and as an exhibition plant as the RHS have awarded it a HC in 1958, AM in 1959 and FCC in 1969 as the former, and an AM in 1957 and a FCC in 1961 as the latter. In the 1957 award report the name was spelt as two words 'Swan Lake' but subsequent awards gave it as one word, which seems to be the correct spelling.

'SWANSDOWN' Listed in the 1991 UK *Plant Finder* as being sold by one nursery, but that nursery denies any knowledge of it, so it remains a mystery.

'SWAY BELLE' A double with a mauvish pink (pale 62D) ground with mauve (68A) stripes and flecks. The large flowers are up to 6.4 cm (2.5 in) across, making it look more like a carnation than a pink. They are fragrant. The plant has a long flowering season. It was introduced in about 1991 by Steven Bailey of Sway, who retains Breeder's Rights on the plant. The colours make it difficult to place in a border and it is probably best treated as a cut flower.

'SWAY BREEZE' A double that is a deep rose pink. It has a long flowering period. It was introduced in about 1991 by Steven Bailey of Sway, who retains Breeder's Rights on it.

'SWAY CANDY'   A fancy double with a pale pink (56D) ground and a luminous mauve pink (68D) stripes and flecks. The large flowers are up to 6.4 cm (2.5 in). The margins of the petals are only slightly indented and appear almost smooth. There is no or only a slight fragrance. It has a long season from June into autumn. The plant was introduced in about 1990 by Steven Bailey of Sway, who retains Breeder's Rights on it. The RHS awarded a PC to it in 1990 under the name 'Candy', subject to it being renamed.

'SWAY GEM'   A floppy double with bright red (46A) flowers. They are slightly fragrant and occasionally split their calyx. The flowers are large, up to 6.4 cm (2.5 in) across. They have a long flowering period. The plant was introduced in about 1991 by Steven Bailey of Sway, who retains Breeder's Rights on it.

'SWAY MIST'   A double with a camellia pink (68A) ground, darker towards the centre where the petals are bunched. Hidden in the centre is a crushed raspberry-coloured (redder 57A) central eye. The flowers are about 5 cm (2 in) across and are very slightly indented. They have a slight fragrance. The plant was introduced in about 1991 by Steven Bailey, who retains Breeder's Rights.

'SWEET ALICE'   A modern semi-double pink with a white ground tinged with pink (65B) and a purple (between 71A and 71B) central zone. The flowers are up to 4.5 cm (1.75 in) wide and are carried on 45 cm (18 in) stems. They are fragrant. The plant was raised by C.C.G. King of Orpington in the early 1960s. The RHS awarded it a C in 1964.

'SWEET WIVELSFIELD'   A strain of annual pinks raised by Allwood by crossing Allwoodii modern pinks with D. barbatus (sweet william).

'SWEETHEART ABBEY'   This is an old variety that is still very popular. It is a flat double with the main colour being a crushed raspberry (60A) that fades towards the edges, which are white tinged with pink (67A). Fine silvery hairs give the red area a sheen. The red is slightly stippled with the pink showing through. The petals are deeply fringed, which is accentuated by the feathering of the edge of the main red colour as it enters the pale margin. The flowers are about 3.8 cm (1.5 in) across and are carried on 25 cm (10 in) long stems. They are fragrant. The foliage is narrow. The plant is an old variety of unknown date. It comes from

Sweetheart Abbey the naming of which, according to legend, is because the founder, Devorguila, the daughter of the last king of Galloway, had her husband's heart buried with her in front of the high altar. 'Sweetheart Abbey' can get confused with 'Hope', especially when the latter is going over (becoming more spotty and diffuse) but the former has more deeply fringed petals and the colour is not as 'solid' when the flowers first open.

'SWEETNESS'   A strain of annual pinks raised by Allwood by crossing 'Sweet Wivelsfield' and 'Loveliness'.

'SYSTON BEAUTY'   A double, white self. The petals are fringed and the flower is fragrant. It is still in existence.

'TAFFETA'   A double with a dark pink ground very heavily flecked and striped with crimson (53C). The flecking is so heavy that it is impossible to say precisely what colour the ground is. The flowers are about 5.8 cm (2.25 in) across. They are coarsely toothed and slightly fragrant. They have a tendency to split their calyces. The plant is a recent introduction and is still in cultivation.

'TANIA'   An Allwood semi-double modern pink. The fragrant flowers are white flushed with a deep pink, and have a red (47A) central zone. They are about 5 cm (2 in) across and are borne on 23 cm (9 in) stems. The plant has a spreading habit. The RHS awarded it a HC as a border plant in 1967, but it has since disappeared.

'TARIF'   A single pink with a purple (64B) ground and a deeper purple-red central zone. The margins of the flowers are toothed. They are not fragrant. The flowering stems are 15 cm (6 in) long. It was raised as a chance seedling by T.J. Wood of Southcombe Gardens, Devon in about 1985.

'TERRY SUTCLIFFE'   A very good new pink. It is a single with a rich velvety crimson ground (brighter 59A) with a central pink (64D), tinged with the crimson, eye on each petal that expands as the flower ages until, in some cases, it covers virtually the whole petal except the basal blotch. The flowers are about 3.8 cm (1.5 in) across and are carried on 20 cm (8 in) stems. The petals are slightly fringed and the flower is fragrant. The plant was introduced in the mid-1980s. Terry Sutcliffe is a gardener from Somerset. It is still in cultivation.

'THELMA' An Allwood modern pink. The flowers are a heavily veiled crimson on a paler ground. It was introduced in the early 1970s. There are also two border carnations and one perpetual-flowering carnation with the same name.

'THERESA' An Allwood double modern pink with a deep pink (55B) ground flushed with purple (74C) stripes. The large flowers are about 5.8 cm (2.25 in) across and are carried on 36 cm (14 in) stems. They have a strong clove fragrance. The broad petals are slightly serrated. The RHS awarded it an AM in 1961 as a border plant.

'THETIS' A single with a pale pink ground and a light red centre. The flowers are heavily fringed and very fragrant. They are carried on 30 cm (12 in) stems over a long season, from June into autumn. It was introduced by G. Winter soon after the Second World War. There is also one border carnation with the same name.

'THOMAS' A popular Allwood modern pink. It is a double with a deep, dusky red (185B) ground with a maroon (187C) central band. The flowers are quite large, up to 5.8 cm (2.25 in) across, and are carried on 25–28 cm (10–11 in) stems. It is slightly fringed. It has better foliage than many of the other modern pinks, still coarse but more compact. It was introduced by Allwood in about 1931 and is still widely in cultivation. The plant was sent for trial at Wisley in 1933, but seems to have failed to get an award. It has, nonetheless, stood the test of time.

'THOMAS LEE' A border carnation, mistakenly given in the UK *Plant Finder* as a pink.

'THOR' An Allwood pink for the rock garden. The double flowers are a deep red (46A). They are about 4.5 cm (1.75 in) across and are carried on 15 cm (6 in) stems. They have a strong clove fragrance. The plant is compact and vigorous, and was introduced in the 1950s. The RHS awarded it a HC in 1959 and an AM in 1962, both for the rock garden. It does not now seem to be around.

'TIMOTHY' An Allwood double modern pink with a white or silvery pink ground flecked and striped with cerise (67C). The flowers are 5.8 cm (2.25 in) across and carried on 45 cm (18 in) stems. The margins of the broad petals are finely serrated. The plant was introduced by Allwood in about 1956 and is still in cultivation. 'Andrew' is a sport

from this plant. The RHS have awarded it a HC in 1956, an AM in 1959 and a FCC in 1961, all as a border plant. There is also one border carnation with this name.

'TINKERBELL' An Allwoodii alpinus for the rock garden or front of border. This is a single with a pale pink ground and a bright tan central zone. The flowers are fragrant and carried on 15 cm (6 in) stems. They have a long flowering season, from June into the autumn. The plant was introduced by Allwood in about 1935 but, unfortunately, has disappeared from cultivation. There are also one border carnation and one perpetual-flowering carnation with the same name.

'TINY RUBIES' This is a double pink that is a rose-red self. It is a cultivar of *D. gratianopolitanus*. It is still in cultivation.

'TITANIA' Another Allwood alpinus for the rock garden. This is a single with a maroon ground with a central zone that is even darker, almost black. The flowers have a slight fragrance and are carried on 15 cm (6 in) stems from June into autumn. It was introduced by Allwood in about 1932 but is no longer in cultivation. There are also two border carnations that share this name.

'TIVERTON' *see 'Musgrave's Pink'*

'TOLEDO' A popular show pink that can also be grown for the border. It is a flat double or semi-double with a purply red (paler 61A) ground, a maroon (187A) central zone and a slightly lighter and browner lacing. The flowers are up to 3.8 cm (1.5 in) across and are carried on 30 cm (12 in) stems. They are very slightly fringed, almost unnoticeably so. The plant was introduced by R.P. Tolley of Worcester Park in about 1972 and is still in cultivation. The plant was awarded a HC as an exhibition plant by the RHS in 1982.

'TOLLACE' A single modern pink with a white ground tinged with very pale pink (62D), a crimson (59A) central zone paling to white as it disappears down the throat, and light maroon (186B) lacing. The flowers are about 3.8 cm (1.5 in) across and are carried on 30 cm (12 in) stems. The broad petals are slightly fringed. The flower has a slight fragrance. It was introduced by R.P. Tolley of Worcester Park in 1973. The RHS awarded it an AM as a plant for exhibition in 1981 and a HC as a border plant in 1982.

'TREASURE'   A double that is a salmon-pink (between 52C and 52D) self. The flowers are about 5 cm (2 in) across and are carried on 45 cm (18 in) stems. They are clove scented. The broad petals are almost smooth on their margins. It was introduced by the Lindabruce Nurseries of Lancing in about 1971 and it is still in cultivation. The RHS awarded it a PC as an exhibition plant in 1971, and a HC in 1972, an AM in 1964 and a FCC in 1979, all as a border plant.

'TREE PIPIT'   A double with a shell-pink ground, a maroon central zone and rose lacing. The flowers are fragrant and are carried on 38 cm (15 in) stems during June and July. It was introduced by the House of Douglas as part of their bird series in about 1949. It has now disappeared from cultivation.

'TREVOR'   An Allwood modern pink. The flowers are double, blood-red selfs with a velvety bloom. They are up to 5.8 cm (2.25 in) across and carried on 30 cm (12 in) stems. They are clove scented. It was introduced by Allwood in about 1968 and is still in cultivation. The RHS awarded it an AM as an exhibition plant in 1968 and an AM as a border plant in 1969.

'TRIBIGILD'   A single with a velvet magenta-purple ground with paler flecks and edges. It is not fragrant and the edges are smooth. The flowers are carried on 15 cm (6 in) stems. It was raised as a chance seedling by T.J. Woods of Southcombe Gardens in 1985.

'TRIUMPH'   (1) A double with a rose red ground and a maroon central zone. The flowers are very fragrant and appear over a long season, from June into the autumn, on 30 cm (12 in) stems. It was introduced by C.H. Herbert of Acocks Green in about 1930, but has since vanished from cultivation.

(2) There was another pink introduced in about the middle of the last century by Church. The only description of it is 'dark', so it is unlikely to reappear.

(3) There are also three border carnations and two perpetual-flowering carnations sharing the same name.

'TWINKLE'   This is an imperial pink. It is a large double with a bright rose ground and a red central zone. The flowers are fragrant and have a long season, from June until the end of autumn. It

was introduced by C.H. Fielding of Lindabruce Nurseries, Lancing, but does not now appear to be in cultivation.

'TWITE'   A double with a soft salmon-pink ground and a maroon central zone and lacing. The flowers are fragrant and carried on 38 cm (15 in) stems in June and July. It was introduced by the House of Douglas as part of their bird name series in 1949 but, as with all this series, it is no longer in cultivation.

'TYRIAN ROSE'   A modern semi-double pink with a pink (55B) ground flushed with a deeper pink (55A) and a central zone of deep red (53A). The flowers are up to 4.5 cm (1.75 in) across and are carried on 25 cm (10 in) stems. They are fragrant. The broad petals are slightly serrated. The plant was raised by C.C.G. King of Orpington in the early 1970s, but does not now seem to be in cultivation. The RHS awarded it a HC in 1975 as a border plant.

'UNIQUE'   (1) A beautiful pink reputed to have come down to us from the seventeenth century. It is now difficult to propagate, which indicates that the plants we have are probably quite old. The single flower has a raspberry red (59D) ground with an irregular central zone and lacing of a very dark crimson (187A), almost black. As it goes over, the lacing becomes browner and two 'eyes' tend to be formed in the centre of each petal. The flowers are about 3.8 cm (1.5 in) across and are carried on 25–30 cm (10 – 12 in) stems in June and July. The petals are noticeably coarsely fringed. They do not seem to be fragrant. A wonderful plant of unknown origin, fortunately still in cultivation. Moreton had what he considered to be the original plant, but lost it and feared that 'Unique' itself had disappeared, although he still had several crosses that he had made from it. It is difficult to know whether the existing plant is one of these crosses or has descended by a different path from the original plant (or, indeed, is a new plant with a great resemblance to the original),

(2) There are also another four pinks bearing this name, only one is from the twentieth century. This is a dwarf variety with a dark maroon ground, blotched with red. It was introduced by Messrs M. Prichard in about 1949, but does not seem to still be in cultivation. There are also 13 border carnations and four perpetual-flowering carnations with this name.

'URSULA LE GROVE' A curious but beautiful single pink. The flower has a pure white ground with a narrow, crushed raspberry (brighter 59A) central zone and irregular, but same width, lacing. The white also shows in the throat. The flowers are about 3.8 cm (1.5 in) across. It was originally introduced by C.O. Moreton and named after his daughter. It is still in cultivation. It sometimes goes under the name 'Old Feathered'. See page 166.

'VALDA WYATT' A very popular, flattish double with a clear purple pink (63D) flushed darker towards the centre and with redder (68A) markings in the central zone. The flowers are 5 cm (2 in) across and are carried on 30 cm (12 in) stems. They are slightly indented, looking almost smooth, and are fragrant. The plant was introduced by Cecil Wyatt of Colehayes, Bovey Tracey, and named after his wife. It is still widely available. The RHS awarded it a PC in 1980, an AM as an exhibition plant in 1981, an AM as a border plant in 1982, and a FCC as the same in 1983.

'VALERIE' A single flower with overlapping petals. The ground is pink (65B). It has a wonderful wine-red (redder 59A) central zone and lacing that seems to cover nearly all the petal, except around the margins and in the throat where the pink ground shows. Two irregular 'eyes' appear in the centre of the petal as the flower ages. The flowers are about 3.8 cm (1.5 in) across and are carried on 25 cm (10 in) stems. They are fragrant. The above plant is the one that I know in cultivation under this name, but the one that was given the award, which we must assume was the original, was recorded somewhat differently. This was white with a velvety crimson (59A) central zone and lacing that was more purple (61A). The flowers are given as being 4.5–5 cm (1.75–2 in) across and borne on 33 cm (13 in) stems. The plant was introduced by E.A. Tickle of Purley in the 1960s. The RHS awarded it a HC as a border plant in 1967 and an AM as an exhibition bloom in 1971.

'VALERIE FINNIS' There are no written records and the only plants I have seen under this name appear to be the same as 'Valerie' (*qv*).

'VANDA' An Allwood modern pink. It is semi-double with a deep lilac ground, paling towards the edge, and a darker central zone. It is highly scented. The plant was introduced by Allwood in about 1980 and is still in cultivation.

'VANESSA' An Allwood double modern pink with a deep rose pink (63B) ground streaked and spotted with crimson (60B). The flowers are up to 5.8 cm (2.25 in) across and are carried on 28 cm (11 in) stems. They have a strong scent. The RHS awarded the plant a HC in 1967 and an AM in 1968, both as a border plant. It does not appear to be in cultivation. There are one border carnation and one perpetual-flowering carnation with the same name.

'VANITY' Moreton describes a large single pink of this name with a scarlet ground and a darker eye. The petals are fringed. He suggests that it was introduced in about 1830. The plant was still in existence in the 1950s, but has since slipped into oblivion.

'VERA' (1) An early Allwood modern pink. This is a single with a dark salmon (43C) ground fading towards the edge, and a coral (45C) central zone. The flowers are 5 cm (2 in) across and are carried on 23 cm (9 in) stems. The broad petals are serrated. The flowers are fragrant. The plant has a spreading habit. It was introduced by Allwood in about 1952, but has since disappeared from cultivation. The RHS awarded the plant an AM as an exhibition flower in 1952 and a HC as a border plant in 1953.

(2) Allwood also introduced a plant with this name in 1920. This was a pale pink self. As far as I know it is not still in cultivation.

(3) There are also two border carnations and three perpetual-flowering carnations with the same name.

'VICTOR' A double modern pink with a cerise (57B) ground shading to a rose pink. The flowers are up to 5.8 cm (2.25 in) across and are borne on 36 cm (14 in) stems. It is very fragrant and flowers from June well into autumn. It was introduced by Allwood in about 1946, but is now lost to cultivation. The RHS awarded it an AM in 1948 and a FCC in 1949, both as a border plant. There are two border carnations and three perpetual-flowering carnations bearing the same name.

'VICTORIA' A double pink for the rock garden. The flowers are a mid-pink with a deeper central zone. It is still in cultivation. There are also umpteen other pinks and carnations with this name.

'VICTORIAN'   A very large double with a white ground and a maroon, almost black, central zone and lacing. The latter are very even. The flowers are fragrant and appear June into autumn on 30 cm (12 in) stems. It is an old cultivar of unknown origin that was still in existence after the Second World War, but I have not heard of it lately. There is also one border carnation with the same name.

'VICTORY'   A small double pink that is a deep ruby self. The flowers are fragrant and appear on 30 cm (12 in) stems from June into the autumn. It was introduced by C.H. Herbert of Acocks Green in about 1923, but has since disappeared. There are seven other pinks, mainly from the eighteenth and nineteenth centuries, 13 border carnations and four perpetual-flowering carnations, all with this same name.

'VIDA'   A winter single with a salmon pink ground and a crimson central zone. The flowers are very fragrant and carried on 30 cm (12 in) stems from June into the autumn. It was introduced by G. Winter of Wramplingham in the 1940s.

'VIRGINIA'   An Allwood modern pink. This one is a double white self. The flowers are up to 5 cm (2 in) across and are carried on 18 cm (7 in) stems. They have a slight scent. The RHS awarded it an HC in 1965. It no longer seems to be in cultivation. There are two border carnations and one perpetual-flowering carnation with the same name.

'W.A. MUSGRAVE'   *see 'Musgrave's Pink'*

'WAGTAIL'   Yet another in the inexhaustible series of pinks named after birds by the House of Douglas. This is a double with a pale rose pink ground and a small deep rose central zone. The flowers are fragrant and are carried on 38 cm (15 in) stems during June and into July. It was introduced in 1950 but has since disappeared from cultivation.

'WAITHMAN'S BEAUTY'   This is a single with a deep raspberry red (brighter 187C) ground with two irregular white 'eyes' in the centre of each petal. The throat is also white. The petals are fringed and the flowers are fragrant. They are about 3.2 cm (1.25 in) across and are carried on 20 cm (8 in) stems. This delightful plant was introduced by Reginald Kaye of Waithman Nurseries sometime around 1951. It is often confused with

'Queen of Henri', which is very similar except that it has pink (63D) 'eyes'. There is a form being sold by one nursery with this name that is very attractive but it certainly is not 'Waithman's Beauty'. It is a single red with irregular dark pink blotches covering large areas of the petals (a bit in the manner of 'Unique' but not such good colouring). *IDR* incorrectly spells the Kaye plant 'Waithman Beauty'.

'WAITHMAN'S JUBILEE'   A single with a velvety crimson (59A) ground (deeper than 'Waithman's Beauty') and two deep pink (63B) 'eyes' in the centre of each petal into which the crimson flushes. The pink also appears in the throat and there is just a hint of it on the margins of the petals as it bleeds over from the reverse. The flowers are similar to 'Queen of Henri' except that the pink is deeper in colour. They are about 3.2 cm (1.25 in) across and are carried on 20 cm (8 in) stems. It was introduced by Reginald Kaye, who thought it an improvement on 'Waithman's Beauty'.

'WANDA'   An Allwoodii alpinus for the rock garden. This is a single with a white ground and a distinct maroon central zone. The flowers appear over a long season on 10–12 cm (4–5 in) stems. It was introduced by Allwood but seems to have disappeared from cultivation.

'WARDEN HYBRID'   A semi-double pink for the rock garden. The flowers are magenta. They are carried on 15 cm (6 in) stems above a bright blue foliage. The plant was introduced in about 1974 and is still in cultivation. It is also known as 'Welwyn Hybrid'.

'WASHFIELD'   *see 'MUSGRAVE'S PINK'*

'WAXWING'   Another of the House of Douglas' bird series. This is a double with an apple-blossom pink ground and a maroon central zone. The flowers are very large and are carried on 38 cm (15 in) stems in June and July. It was introduced in 1949 but has since disappeared.

'WEETWOOD DOUBLE'   A semi-double pink for the rock garden with a pale pink ground and a darker eye. The petals are toothed. It has a strong fragrance. The flowers are carried on 10 cm (4 in) stems. The plant was raised from unknown parents by Harold Bawden in about 1983 and named after his garden in Devon. It is still in cultivation.

'WEETWOOD WHITE'   A pink for the rock garden with white flowers. It was introduced by Harold Bawden and named after his garden in Devon. It is still in cultivation.

'WELCOME'   An imperial pink with large double flowers of deep rose red (57A). The flowers are about 5 cm (2 in) across and are carried on long, rigid stems. The broad petals are waved and slightly serrated. The flowers are fragrant and have a long flowering season, from June into the autumn. It was introduced by C.H. Fielding of the Lindabruce Nurseries in about 1958, but unfortunately no longer seems to be in cultivation. The RHS awarded it an AM as an exhibition flower in 1958.

'WELLAND'   A carmine pink self introduced by Reginald Kaye of Waithman Nurseries in the mid-1960s. It is still in cultivation.

'WELWYN HYBRID'   *see Warden Hybrid'*

'WEMBDON LOUISE'   A double with a light purplish pink (73C) ground and a dark red (59A) central zone and lacing. It is not fragrant. It was introduced by F.C. Jarman of Wembdon, Bridgwater in about 1981.

'WEMBDON SARA'   A semi-double, verging on double, with a pink (62C) ground, a red (59A) central band that covers half the petal, and jagged-edged lacing some way in from the margins of the petals. These margins are fringed and the petals wavy, giving the flower quite a frilly appearance. The ground shows inside the central band. The lacing bleeds into the ground giving it a flushed look. The flower is fragrant. It was introduced by F.C. Jarman of Wembdon, Bridgwater in 1981 and is still in cultivation. The RHS awarded it a HC as a border plant in 1991.

'WENDY'   One of the Allwoodii alpinus group. This is a single with a magenta-pink colouration. The flowers have a long season from June into the autumn. It ws introduced by Allwood in about 1929. There are also one border carnation and one perpetual-flowering carnation with this name.

'WHATFIELD ANONA'   The first of a series of dwarf pinks for the rock garden. This one is a semi-double with a purple-pink (72D) ground with a crimson (59A) central zone. The flowers are about 2.5 cm (1 in) across and the petal margins are noticeably serrated. They are just slightly fragrant.

The flower stems are about 1.25 cm (5 in) high. The flowering season is in May and June. It was raised by Mrs J. Scholfield of Whatfield near Ipswich in about 1980. It is still in cultivation.

'WHATFIELD BEAUTY'   A good clump-making, floriferous plant with double flowers of a bright rose pink and a slight hint of a red band near the centre of the flower. The flowers are about 3.2 cm (1.25 in) across and are coarsely fringed. They flower over a long season on 15 cm (6 in) stems. It was raised by Mrs J. Scholfield of Whatfield near Ipswich and is still in cultivation.

'WHATFIELD BLOODSTONE'   A single dwarf pink with a bright purple-pink flower with a deep maroon central zone that fades to pink as it goes down the throat. The petals are fringed. The flowers are about 2.5 cm (1 in) across and are carried on 12.5 cm (5 in) stems. It was raised by Mrs J. Scholfield of Whatfield near Ipswich. It is still in cultivation.

'WHATFIELD BLUE BIRD'   A small pink for the rock garden or front of border. It is a double with a bright pink-purple (68A) colour. This pales towards the margins and the centre shows green when the calyx splits. The margins of the petals are coarsely fringed. The flowers are about 2 cm (1 in) across but can be up to 5 cm (2 in) when the fat calyx splits. It is rather an untidy flower. The flowering stems are about 15 cm (6 in) high. It is currently in cultivation.

'WHATFIELD BRILLIANT'   According to Mrs J. Scholfield this is not a Whatfield name and she has no knowledge of such a plant, but the one in circulation with this name closely resembles 'Whatfield Gem', indeed it is probably that plant. The plants being sold through nurseries have double flowers that are a rich raspberry red (bright 60A) with darker, maroon (187A) blotches and a fine pink (65D) line round the edge of the petals, looking a bit like a smaller version of 'Indian'. The reverse of the petals are pale pink with darker pink showing through. The petals are fringed, quite narrow and curled, giving the flower a frilly look. The flowers are 3.2 cm (1.25 in) across and are carried on short 5–7.5 cm (2 – 3 in) stems.

'WHATFIELD CHERRY BRANDY'   A lax plant with single flowers of a wonderful velvety red (redder 187A) with a pale pink on the very edge, coming over from the reverse. The throat pales to a white, and the white of the styles and stamen make a nice contrast. The petals are slightly hairy, which add to the velvety texture. They are also fringed. The flowers are about 3.2 cm (1.25 in) across and are borne on rather floppy 15 cm (6 in) stems. It was raised by Mrs J. Scholfield of Whatfield near Ipswich. It is still in cultivation.

'WHATFIELD CRUSHED STRAWBERRY' A single pink for the rock garden. The petals are a pale pink flushed with a deep rose pink (64D) and have a narrow maroon (53A) zone near the centre of the flower. This zone fades to white as it passes into the throat. The name of the plant is a reasonable description of the overall effect of the colour. The plant produces a good strong flush of flowers in May and June, and then throws up the occasional flower until the frosts. It was raised by Mrs J. Scholfield of Whatfield near Ipswich in about 1980. It is still in cultivation.

'WHATFIELD CYCLOPS' A dwarf pink with tight mats of foliage. The flowers are semi-double, with a bright pink (65B) ground and a maroon (59A) eye. They tend to pale with age. The reverse is the same colour. They are fragrant, measure about 2.5–3 cm (1–1.25 in) in diameter and are carried on 10–15 cm (4–6 in) stems. The petals are fringed. It was introduced by Mrs J. Scholfield of Whatfield near Ipswich in about 1986. There are three other plants that bear the name 'Cyclops'.

'WHATFIELD DAWN' A dwarf pink with small semi-double flowers. The ground is a pale pink flushed with a deeper pink (overall effect of 65A) and the central zone is maroon (59A) paling as it disappears down the throat. This zone is wide taking up about half the petal. The flowers are about 2 cm (0.75 in) across and carried on 7.5 cm (3 in) stems. It was raised by Mrs J. Scholfield of Whatfield near Ipswich and it is still in cultivation.

'WHATFIELD DOROTHY MANN' This is an attractive double with a very pale pink ground and a slight, spotted, purple (61B) central eye that flushes the ground at the inner ends of the petals. Some flowers appear almost white, especially the older ones. The flowers are up to about 3.2 cm (1.25 in) across and the margins of the petals are serrated giving the flower quite a frilly look. They are fragrant. The flowering stems are up to 15 cm (6 in) high making it suitable for the rock garden. The plant is named after the wife of Donald Mann, the well-known propagator, who has introduced

many of this series into the nursery trade. It was raised by Mrs J. Scholfield of Whatfield near Ipswich in about 1987. It is still in cultivation.

'WHATFIELD ELIZABETHAN HART' This dwarf pink has large single flowers. It is distinctively deeply fringed and has a deep crimson ground (60B) and a darker (59A) central band. The flowers are 3.8 cm (1.5 in) across and are carried on 10 cm (4 in) stems. Elizabethan Hart is wife of Lewis Hart of Hadleigh. The plant was raised by Mrs J. Scholfield of Whatfield near Ipswich. It is still in cultivation.

'WHATFIELD FUCHSIA' A double-flowered pink for the rock garden. This one has a light purple pink (73A) ground, flushed with a paler colour. It darkens towards the centre, and the occasional splash of a darker pink. The backs of the petals are the same colour. The flowers are up to 3.2 cm (1.25 in) across, sometimes wider as they occasionally split their calyx. The petals are fringed. The flowers appear on 15 cm (6 in) stems above a good mat of blue-green foliage. It was raised by Mrs J. Scholfield of Whatfield near Ipswich. It is still in cultivation.

'WHATFIELD GEM' This is a rock garden plant in the 'Whatfield' series. It has a double flower with a crimson ground with a pale pink edge and occasionally blotches of the same colour, particularly as the flower gets older. The calyx often splits showing the pale green throat in a rather untidy manner. It looks very similar to a stalkless 'Indian' at only 2.5–5 cm (1–2 in) high. The reverse of the petal is white with pink showing through. It only has a short season in May and June. The plant was raised by Mrs J. Scholfield of Whatfield near Ipswich. It is still in cultivation.

'WHATFIELD HART'S DELIGHT' A single pink with a crimson (60B) ground and a maroon, almost brown, (187A) central band. The petals are noticeably fringed. The white stamens make a conspicuous contrast. The flowers are up to 3.2 cm (1.25 in) across and are carried on 12 cm (5 in) stems. It has a long flowering season. It was named after Lewis Hart, a well-known plantsman from Hadleigh. Mrs J. Scholfield of Whatfield, near Ipswich raised the plant and it is still in cultivation.

'WHATFIELD JOHN TURK' A single with a salmon pink ground and maroon streaks and blotches. They are 3.2 cm (1.25 in) across. The main flush of flowers is in June and July but a few odd flowers continue to appear. John Turk is a professor of pathology and is a friend of Mrs J. Scholfield of Whatfield near Ipswich. The plant was introduced by her and is still in cultivation.

'WHATFIELD JOY'   This is a rock plant with a single flower of a lilac pink ground with a darker centre. The petals have smooth margins. The plants form good clumps and are very floriferous in a short season from May into June. It was raised by Mrs J. Scholfield of Whatfield near Ipswich in about 1967. It is still in cultivation.

'WHATFIELD MAGENTA'   This is one of the best pinks in the series and, along with 'Inshriach Dazzler', one of the best of the rock garden pinks currently available. The flowers are single, with overlapping petals, and are a luminous magenta (74A) that is beautifully set off by a deep blue foliage. There is a slight trace of a crimson (59A) central zone merging into a paler pink throat. The petals are fringed (not smooth as listed in the *IDR*). The flowers are fragrant. They are about 3.2 cm (1.25 in) across and are carried on 7.5 cm (3 in) stems. The flowering season is in May and June.

It was raised by Mrs J. Scholfield of Whatfield near Ipswich in about 1984 as a seedling from 'Blue Hills'. It is still in cultivation.

'WHATFIELD MINI'   A single pink, with overlapping petals, for the rock garden. It is white (or very pale pink) flushed with a pale pink. It is darker when it first opens, and pales when it goes over. It has the occasional trace of a thin purple eye. The petals have serrated margins and the whole flower is fragrant. The flowers are about 2.5 cm (1 in) across and are carried on 7.5 cm (3 in) stems above a good mat of blue-green foliage. It flowers in late May and into June. It was raised by Mrs J. Scholfield of Whatfield near Ipswich in about 1976 and is still in cultivation.

'WHATFIELD MISS'   This is a single for the rock garden with a pale lavender-pink (75B) with a fine purple-pink (74D) spots flushed onto it. The flower fades as it goes over. The petals are coarsely toothed. The flowers are fragrant. They are up to 2.5 cm (1 in) across and are carried on stems that are up to 15 cm (6 in) high above strong grey-green foliage. It was raised by Mrs J. Scholfield of Whatfield near Ipswich. It is still in cultivation.

'Whatfield Magenta'

'WHATFIELD MISTY MORN'   This is one of Mrs Scholfield's own favourites. It is a semi-double, or occasionally a flat double, with a ground of mauve-pink (76D), flushed with a rose pink (73A) giving an overall impression of a lilac pink (75A) with pale stripes and streaks. The darker colour is more noticeable at the margins. The calyces are a very dark red, which is an added attraction. The flowers are 3.2 cm (1.25 in) across and are carried on 20 cm (8 in) stems. Its name derives from the curious misty appearance the plant has when it is in full flush. It was raised by Mrs J. Scholfield of Whatfield near Ipswich. It is still in cultivation.

'WHATFIELD NINE STAR'   An attractive dwarf pink for the rock garden or front of a border. This double flowers a luminous cerise pink (67A), appearing stronger in the centre when the petals are still bunched up. When examined closely it can be seen that it is a pink overlaid with cerise. The flowers are about 3.2 cm (1.25 in) across and are carried on 12 cm (5 in) stems. The petals are fringed. It was raised by Mrs J. Scholfield of Whatfield near Ipswich. It is still in cultivation.

'WHATFIELD PEACH'   Another in the rock garden pink series from Whatfield. This one is a single with overlapping petals of a rose pink (64C) ground, finely dotted with a darker colour (63B) giving them a dry look. It has a slight beard. The petals are rather floppy and reflexed, but the colour makes it an attractive plant. The flower margins are coarsely fringed. The flowers are up to 3.2 cm (1.25 in) across and are carried on 15 cm (6 in) stems above a blue-green, fine-leaved foliage. It was raised by Mrs J. Scholfield of Whatfield near Ipswich. It is still in cultivation.

'WHATFIELD POLLY ANNE'   This can be considered either a flat double or a semi-double. It has a white ground with a dotted central zone of mauve-purple (74A), covering more of the petal when the flower is young, retreating and fading as it ages. The petals are quite heavily fringed, giving it a pretty look. The flowers are about 2.5 cm (1 in) across and are carried on 15 cm (6 in) stems. The name is sometimes misspelt as 'Poly'. It was raised by Mrs J. Scholfield of Whatfield near Ipswich and is still in cultivation.

'WHATFIELD POM POM'   A dwarf pink with very double flowers. These are a deep pink self with fringed margins. They are fragrant. There is a mass of fine, blue-green, grasslike foliage, but the plant does not flower very well. The flowers are about 2.5 cm (1 in) across and supported on 12.5 cm (5 in) stems. It was raised by Mrs J. Scholfield of Whatfield near Ipswich in about 1967. It is still in cultivation.

'WHATFIELD POSY'   A dwarf pink with good silver foliage with quite wide leaves. The flowers are a flat semi-double with a deep rose ground with slight traces of red stripes coming out from the centre. The flowers are about 2.5 cm (1 in) across. The plant was raised by Mrs J. Scholfield of Whatfield near Ipswich. It is still in cultivation.

'WHATFIELD PRETTY LADY'   Another pink for the rock garden, or front of border if you wish. This one is a full semi-double that is almost double. The flowers are a lilac pink (75C) darkening towards the centre. The colour varies considerably with the age of the flower. As they go over they fade to almost white, but are flushed with mauve (68A). The flowers are about 3.2 cm (1.25 in) across and are carried on 15 cm (6 in) stems above a blue-green foliage. The petals are coarsely toothed giving the flower a pretty look. They are fragrant. It was raised by Mrs J. Scholfield of Whatfield near Ipswich in about 1971 and is still in cultivation.

'WHATFIELD ROSE'   A fragrant single-flowered pink with a deep rose pink (67A) ground and a large, maroon (59A) central eye. The petals are coarsely serrated and the flower is up to 3.2 cm (1.25 in) across. It is eminently suitable for the rock garden and grows no taller than 12.5 cm (5 in) high. The foliage is blue-green with a hint of purply red in it. The main flowering season is in May and June, but it carries on with occasional flowers until the frosts. It is a long-lived plant, the original one being still in existence after 15 years. It was raised by Mrs J. Scholfield of Whatfield near Ipswich in about 1976 and is still in cultivation.

'WHATFIELD RUBY'   A single with overlapping petals. The ground is a deep rose pink (61B) and there is a maroon (59A) central zone that turns browner as the flower ages. The ground is not a pure colour but has slight spotting and flushing of a darker red, which gives it a characteristic texture. The central band is not a very thick band and is more or less an irregular line. The white styles make a nice contrast. The calyces are a rich brown and add to the overall effect. The petals are coarsely serrated. The flowers are about

'Whatfield Ruby'

2.5 cm (1 in) across and are carried on 10 cm (4 in) stems above a good mat of fine, blue-green foliage. The flowers are fragrant. The plant has a long flowering season with intermittent flowers appearing until late in the autumn. It was raised by Mrs J. Scholfield of Whatfield near Ipswich in about 1985 and is still in cultivation.

'WHATFIELD SEEDLING'   Not such an inspired name as most of the other plants in the series. This is a dwarf, single pink with a pink ground streaked maroon. The petals are fringed. The flowers are scented and are borne on 10 cm (4 in) stems. It has a long flowering season, in May and June, with the occasional flowers appearing well into the autumn. It was raised by Mrs J. Scholfield of Whatfield near Ipswich in the early 1980s. It is still in cultivation.

'WHATFIELD WHITE'   A single with petals that are pure white except for a faint trace of purple flecking round the centre. This band disappears as the flower ages, but the flower takes on a purple tinge. The petals are fringed, but this is not noticeable as they tend to curl up giving them a triangular appearance, typical of many of the rock garden pinks. The flowers are up to 2.5 cm (1 in)

across and are carried on 10 cm (4 in) stems above a good mat of fine, blue-green leaves. They do not appear to be fragrant. In severe winters the plant is cut back to bare stems and appears to be dead, but it normally revives in the spring. The flowering season is a long one, odd flowers appearing until the frosts come. It was raised by Mrs J. Scholfield of Whatfield near Ipswich in about 1983 and is still in cultivation.

'WHATFIELD WISP'   The last in the current series of rock plants. This is a very good plant with attractive colouring and fragrance, and a reasonable foliage. The flowers are single and of a lilac pink fading to almost white in the centre. The petals overlap slightly giving a good undulating effect (as long as the weather has not wrecked them). The petals are fringed. The flowers are up to 2.5 cm (1 in) across and the flowering stems are up to 10 cm (4 in) high. It has a long flowering season, with a few flowers appearing after the main flush in May and June. It was raised by Mrs J. Scholfield of Whatfield near Ipswich in about 1974 and is still in cultivation.

'WHEATEAR'   A double in the House of Douglas' bird series. This has a bright rose ground with a crimson central zone. The flowers are fragrant and are carried on 38 cm (15 in) stems during June and July. It was introduced in about 1949 but has since vanished.

'WHITE AND CRIMSON'   A double with a pure white ground and a purple (71A) central eye, fading to white in the throat. The flowers are about 4.5 cm (1.75 in) across. The petals are very slightly fringed, but this is hardly noticeable. They are slightly fragrant. It is a recent introduction that is still in cultivation.

'WHITE BARN'   A selected form from the 'Highland Hybrids'. It is a floriferous single with rose-pink flowers. It forms good cushions of blue-grey foliage. The flowers appear on 12.5 cm (5 in) stems. It was introduced by Beth Chatto and named after her house.

'WHITE DORIS'   *see 'Haytor White'*

'WHITE INCHMERY'   A flat semi-double pink with a pure white flower. These are up to 5 cm (2 in) wide and carried on 28 cm (11 in) stems. The broad petals are slightly fringed. The plant is bushy and erect in habit. It was raised by T.T. Burnett of Petersfield in the 1950s, but seems to have now vanished. The RHS awarded it a C in 1954 and an AM in 1955, both as a border plant. It is also incorrectly known as 'Inchmery White'.

'WHITE LADIES'   An old cultivar that seems to have several versions in cultivation. It is a double with pure white flowers that are slightly creamy towards the centre. Most contemporary forms about 5 cm (2 in) across, although some versions are much smaller, only 2.5 cm (1 in) across; all are larger when the calyx splits (showing the green claws of the petals). The petals are serrated, but not so finely cut as 'Mrs Sinkins'. In some versions the petals are smooth. They all have a sweet fragrance. I suspect this is another of those old cultivars that has existed in different forms right from the start.

'WHITE QUEEN'   (1) A double white from the House of Douglas. It is fringed and very fragrant. It flowers in June and July on 38 cm (15 in) stems. It was introduced in the early 1920s but has since disappeared.

(2) There was another white self with this name introduced in about 1907.

(3) There are also an annual pink, a border carnation, a perpetual-flowering carnation and a malmaison carnation, all sharing this name.

'WHITE SHOCK'   A double white self with very deeply fringed petals. It is very fragrant. This pink was grown in the second half of the seventeenth century, and is possibly still around under the name of 'Old Fringed' but if it is the same or just a similar plant we will never know.

'WHITEHILLS'   A small pink for the rock garden. It is a single with a pink ground and a crimson central zone. It grows on tight cushions and is less than 7.5 cm (3 in) high. It is quite an old form and is still in cultivation.

'WIDECOMBE FAIR'   A fully double modern pink with a pale pink (49D) ground with a touch of cream in it. It varies in intensity with darker flushes and streaks, particularly towards the centre. The flowers are large, being up to 6.4 cm (2.5 in) across and carried on 38 cm (15 in) stems. The petals are fringed, which is particularly noticeable when the flowers first open. It has no or slight fragrance. It was introduced by C. Wyatt of Colehayes, Bovey Tracey in about 1971 and is still in cultivation. The RHS awarded it a PC in 1981, and a C in 1982 and a HC in 1987, both as a border plant.

'WILLIAM BROWNHILL'   An old-fashioned pink that is semi-double, verging on double, with a white ground and a maroon (187A) central zone covering half the petal. The white ground can also be seen in the throat. The flowers are about 3.8 cm (1.5 in) across and are carried on 25 cm (10 in), somewhat drooping, stems. They are widely cut but almost smooth. Unlike many of the other doubles of the period, it does not readily burst its calyx. It has supposedly typical foliage of an old-fashioned pink that can get a bit straggly. It was introduced by William Brownhill in the late eighteenth century and is, fortunately, safely in cultivation. But perhaps this is wishful thinking as Moreton (1955), although acknowledging its eighteenth century origins, claims that it had recently been discovered, and Ruth Duthie has pointed out that the petals are too smooth for a plant of this period. Another point is that Margery Fish claimed that it was difficult to propagate, but there now seems to be no problems, so perhaps the plant now in cultivation is of recent origin. The RHS awarded it an AM as an exhibition bloom in 1950 and a C as a border plant in 1951.

'WILLIAM OF ESSEX' An old-sounding name but in fact a relatively new cultivar. It is a semi-double, verging on double, with a red (53A) ground, darker towards the margins, and touched with darker crimson bloom, usually in stripes. The flowers are 3.8–5 cm (1.5–2 in) across and are carried on 20–23 cm (8–9 in) stems. They are very fragrant. The petals are fringed on their margins. The plant has very good silver foliage, making compact mats. It was raised by Jack Gingell of Ramparts as a sport from 'Freckles' in the early 1980s. He wanted to call it Prince William in honour of the prince's birth, but was prevented from doing so as there were already pinks with that name, so he added the honour of his county to the name. The RHS awarded it a C in 1987 as a plant for the border.

'WINDWARD ROSE' An odd name, but then pinks seem to attract odd names as all the obvious ones have already been used up on long-defunct plants. This is a dwarf single pink for the rock garden. It is a deep rose pink self. It has a long flowering period, carried on 15 cm (6 in) stems. Its introduction and reason for the name remains unknown, and will probably do so as it no longer seems to be in cultivation.

'WINK' One of the Allwoodii alpinus group. This is a single usually described as having a white ground, a purple or deep magenta (74B) central zone and a cream throat. A couple of sources refer to the central band being rayed. There has been a plant in circulation for the last 15 years or so under this name that is white which only has a couple of plum-coloured flecks where a central band would normally be. Is this what is meant by rayed or is this plant a seedling or another of the Allwoodii alpinus? (I have seen similar plants labelled 'Dewdrop'.) The description of the award plant is that given first above. It also includes the fact that the flower stems are rigid and 10–12.5 cm (4–5 in) long, with the single flower being 3.2 cm (1.25 in) across. These details of size accord with the one in cultivation. The original was introduced in 1932 by Allwood and I would be grateful if anyone who can remember the original plant can let me know what it looked like and whether the plant in circulation is the correct one. The RHS awarded it a C in 1950, HC in 1952 and an AM in 1953, all as a border plant, although it would have to be the front of a border as all the sources and the present plant agree that it is only 10–15 cm (4–6 in) high.

'WINNIE LAMBERT' A semi-double bordering on double that is a bright cerise self, growing on 23 cm (9 in) stems. It was introduced by M. Prichard & Sons of Riverslea in about 1933. It no longer appears to be in cultivation.

'WINSOME' A imperial pink from C.H. Fielder. It is a large flat double or semi-double with small tufts of petals at the centre. The flowers have a pure rose-pink (66B) ground and a crimson (59C) central zone. They are 6.4 cm (2.5 in) in diameter and appear on 38 cm (15 in) stems over quite a long period from June until the beginning of autumn. It is heavily fragrant. It is a vigorous and yet compact plant. The plant was raised and introduced by Fielder at his Lindabruce Nurseries in about 1947. It has a good track record both on the show bench and in the border as the RHS has awarded it an AM in 1949 and a FCC in 1954, both as an exhibition flower, and a HC in 1950, an AM in 1951 and a FCC in 1952 as a border plant. This is a good plant, fortunately, still in cultivation.

'WINSTON' The last in the sequence of Allwood modern pinks with personal names. This is a double with bright crimson (46A) flowers flushed with a brighter, paler red (45A). The petals are deeply cut and the flowers are very fragrant. The flowers are 4.5 cm (1.75 in) across and are carried on 23 cm (9 in) stems. Like most Allwoodiis, this flowers over a long period, from June into September. The plant has a somewhat spreading habit. It was introduced by Allwood in about 1936, but has since vanished from cultivation. It was awarded an AM as a garden plant in 1949.

'WISP' (1) One of the Allwoodii alpinus group. This is a single with a white ground and a velvety crimson eye. The flowers are very fragrant and borne on 15 cm (6 in) stems over a longer period, from June into late autumn. The plant was introduced by Allwood in about 1941. They sent it for trial at Wisley in 1947, but it does not seem to have been given an award. It has since, regretfully, disappeared.

(2) See also 'Whatfield Wisp'.

'WOODLARK' A double with a white ground and a crimson central zone and lacing (which sounds horribly like the description of nearly all of the plants in this bird series, how much they vary we will probably never know as they have all disappeared from cultivation). As with all the series, this was fragrant and flowered in June and July. It was introduced by the House of Douglas in about 1949.

'WOODPECKER'   Another in the Douglas bird series. This is a double with a light pink ground and a maroon central zone. It is fragrant and flowered in June and July on 38 cm (15 in) stems. The plant was introduced by the House of Douglas in about 1949.

'WOOLEY DOD'   A single pink named after the famous botanist. It has large flowers of a deep rose red. The petals are deeply fringed and the flowers are very fragrant. They are carried on tall stems, up to 45 cm (18 in) long. The flowering period is a long one, from June until September. Its origin is unknown but it was probably pre-Second World War. However, it is now not in cultivation.

'WRYNECK'   The last of the House of Douglas pinks with bird's names. This is a double with a bright pink ground and a bright crimson central zone. The flowers are fragrant and they appear in June and July, carried on 38 cm (15 in) stems.

'YELLOW HAMMER'   This is a blind, and not another Douglas pink, but an Allwood one. The name derives from its unusual colour: yellow. It has the dubious distinction of being the first yellow pink to be produced by the introduction of *D. knappii* blood into the Allwood strain. The flowers are double but small, and borne in trusses (both the influence of the *D. knappii*). They are slightly fragrant. Allwood introduced the plant in about 1938, but it was not a very robust plant and has disappeared. The RHS awarded it a HC as a border plant in 1950. There are also two border carnations laying claim to the same name.

'ZEUS'   A single with a pale scarlet ground and a chocolate maroon central eye. The flowers are very fragrant and are fringed. They flower over a long season on 30 cm (12 in) stems. It was introduced sometime around the Second World War but has since vanished.

Bibliography

Allwood, Montagu C. *Carnations and all dianthus*. Allwood Bros., 1926.

Cook, E.T. *Carnations, picotees and the wild and garden pinks*. Country Life, 1905.

Duthie, Ruth. *Florists' flowers and societies*. Shire Publications, 1988.

The Plant Finder. Moorlands Publishing Co. Ltd, annual publication.

Fish, Margery. *Cottage garden flowers*. Collingridge, 1961.

Genders, Roy. *The cottage garden and the old-fashioned flowers*. Pelham Books, 1969.

Genders, Roy. *Garden pinks*. Garden Book Club, 1962.

Ingwersen, Will. *The dianthus*. Collins, 1949.

The International dianthus register. 2nd edition plus annual supplements. Royal Horticultural Society, 1983 +.

Köhlhein, Fritz. *Nelken*. Ulmer, 1990.

McQuown, F.R. *Pinks, selection and cultivation*. MacGibbon and Kee, 1955.

Mansfield, T.C. *Carnations in colour and cultivation*. Collins, 1951. (Includes pinks)

Moreton, C. Oscar. *Old carnations and pinks*. George Rainbird, Collins, 1955.

Taylor, George M. *Old fashioned flowers*. John Gifford, 1946.

Societies

The following societies may be worth joining as a way of contacting other gardeners with a similar interest in pinks and as sources of information, seed and plants.

Alpine Garden Society, AGS Centre, Avon Bank, Pershore, Worcestershire, WR10 3JP.

American Rock Garden Club, 15 Fairmead Road, Darien, Connecticut 06820 USA.

British National Carnation Society, 3 Canberra Close, Hornchurch, Essex RM12 5TR.

Hardy Plant Society, Bank Cottage, Great Comberton, Pershore, Worcestershire, WR10 3DP.

Index of Illustrations

General Index